Journey Through Transformation

A guide to mystical awakening, kundalini, emotional clearing and spiritual emergence

Kaia Nightingale, MA

Copyright © Kaia Nightingale 2007
All rights reserved
No text or graphics in this book may be reproduced or transmitted without permission in writing from the author. Research information and tables may be used in presentations and publications if the author is clearly attributed to the work.

Cover design, illustrations and graphs by Kaia Nightingale.

ISBN : 1-897357-64-8

> This book provides information from a spiritual perspective. For health issues, please consult a qualified health care professional.

Experiences during spiritual transformation are unique to each person. For individual help, counselling and support, Kaia Nightingale can be contacted through her website:
www.kaia.ca.

Contents

Introduction ix
    How this book came to be xiii
    Acknowledgments xxi

1 Anatomy of Transformation 1
    In essence, spiritual transformation has three main facets: 1
    1 Shifting Consciousness 1
    How did we lose touch with so much of ourselves? 6
    How do these states of consciousness feel? 7
    Energy anatomy 8
    The seven main chakras: 9
    Spectrum of love 9
    2. Clearing limiting mental and emotional patterns 10
    3. Aligning our day-to-day life with our new awareness 12

2 Journey's Terrain 15
    A short précis of the basic process. 15
    Why do we start transforming more quickly? 16
    Why the discomfort? 21

3 Mystical Experiences 23
    What are these experiences? 25
    Mystical Experience of 110 adults 25
    Paranormal perceptions: 26
    Kundalini 28
    Energy pouring in the crown – 'sahasraric' energy 30
    Out of body experiences 30
    Seeing lights, hearing sounds 31
    Hearing Sounds 32
    Past lives 33
    Near Death Experience (NDE) 33
    Alien encounters and UFO sightings 34
    Negative states 35
    Revelations 35

    Awakening, Unity Consciousness 37
    Changing your spiritual practice 38
  Frequently asked questions 40

4 Our Reactions 47
  Responses to the mystical experience and altered states ... 47
  Responding to energy 50
  I always knew I was special – I'm the Messiah! 51
  Wow – something great has unfolded! 51
  I am present with what is. 52
  This is OK…I think… 52
  I don't trust this, it's weird 52
  I hate what is happening – it should go away 52
  Reacting to the purification processes 53
  Ideally 53
  What is transformation about? 54
  Why bother transforming? 55
  Contradictions 55
  Blaming God for changing your life 57
  The multi-layer approach 58
  Others' reactions to us 59
  Loving, light, open and free 59
  Fearful, depressed or anxious 60

5 Handling Sensitivity 61
  How grounding can help us handle our sensitivity 62
  What can we do to become more grounded? 64
  Managing sensitivity 65
  How to create a shield 66
  Protective crystals 68
  Cloth wraps 68
  Fitting in 68
  Cellular sensitivity – often called allergy 69
  How to handle sensitivity: 70
  Trial and error 70
  Kinesiology – muscle testing 70

6 Weird Sensations 73
  Pain that eludes traditional medical diagnosis 73
  Headaches 76

- Energy blocks 77
- Kriyas 77
- Crawling sensations on the skin 78
- Weird energy 79
- Kundalini fire 79
- Explanations: 80
- Causes of the fire 81
- Dealing with kundalini fire 81
- Energy swings 83
- Left-right side imbalance 83
- Energy pouring in the crown 84
- Electric currents 84
- Distortions in time 86

7 Internal Clearing 87
- Resistance to the process 88
- What spiritual books often don't tell you: 88
- Other things that spiritual books rarely tell you: 91
- Emotional Clearing 92
- What emerges from Pandora's Box? 93
- If you want to avoid dealing with your emotions 93
- What is truly transformative? 95
- Working with deep trauma 99
- Professional help 99
- E.M.D.R. – clearing past trauma 99
- Intent 100
- Creative expression 100
- Cathart 102
- Bach Remedies 102
- Which remedies? 102
- How to use Bach remedies: short term use (1-2 days): 103
- Visualization 103
- Crystals 103
- Dealing with Fear 104
- Don't worry, no one's watching 105
- Ways we avoid clearing emotion: 105
- Make your transformational process a priority 106

8 Working With Your Mind 107
- When our minds tumble with thoughts 107

What is happening?...107
What do you do with this busy mind?..............................108
Quieting the mind 109
Aligning your mind with your inner being 109
Transforming conditions 110
Counterproductive mental habits 110
Re-writing the script 111
Putting your life in perspective 111
Prayer 111
Affirmations..111
Bach Flower Remedies for the mind 112
Byron Katie's method of freeing the mind 112
To clear memories through focused contemplation 113
Energy Psychology Emotional Clearing Techniques 113
Other techniques to clear the energy fields 115
Physical illness 116
Roots of disease 116
Physical purification and clearing 117

9 Sleep, sex, food & changing moods 119
Changing sleeping patterns 119
Blocks to sexuality: 123
Changes in eating patterns..123
Not needing to eat 123
Eating huge amounts without putting on weight.............123
Eating large amounts and getting fat 124
Feeling spaced out..124
Lack of mental clarity 124
Despondency..125
Depression..126
Dark night of the soul 127
Archetypal dreams and images 127
Falling from openness 128
Nothing means much 129
Adapting to a more internal focus..................................130
The ego struggles 131
Transformational ingredients 132
FAQ. 133

10 Spiritual Emergency...137
Who is good to talk to? 141

    Where do you go for help?...142
    Energy workers..144
    Spiritual Counseling 146
    Psychics 146
    Entities..147
    Are you crazy? 148
    Medical help 152
    What the labels mean: 154
    Medication 155
    Institutions 157
  What helped me most? 159
    Self Help 160
    Who helped? 162

11 Standing on our Tails..163
    What most enables transformation? 164
    What resists transformation, and why? 164
    We want to change, but:...164
    Fear of being abnormal 167
    Fear of insanity 168
    What, if anything, needs to transform, and why?.............169
    Contradictions with religious or spiritual beliefs...............169
    Internal contradictions 171
    Honest self-observation 171
    Where are we going? 173

12 Re-aligning our Lives..175
    How aligned are we? 177
    Changes in diet or eating patterns 178
    Switching to a vegetarian diet..179
    Switching back to meat eating 179
    Friendships 180
    Hurdles: 180
    Not fitting in – with friends 180
    Not fitting in – with your family 181
    Not fitting in socially...181
    Not fitting in with your spiritual group............................182
    Feeling alone 184
    How to meet like-minded people.....................................185
    The work ethic – live to work (rather than work to live)...185

- Health and well-being 187
- Changing your work direction 187
- If you have not yet clarified an alternative life direction ... 188
- Redefining our work 189
- Taking the plunge 189
- Today's Religions 189
- Science... 190
- Money 191
- Remaining true to yourself 192
- Criticizing life 192
- Your ideal.. 192

13 Reaping the Fruits 193
- The kinds of gifts that may come our way: 193
- Why are you have these new perceptual skills? 196
- Great possibilities! 196
- Integrity and good judgment...................................... 196
- FAQ 197
- Learning to work with intuitive gifts 198
  - Healing.. 198
- Other benefits of spiritual transformation 201
- Four fundamental stages for complete transformation..... 202

14 Visions and Resources 207
- Resources 209
  - England www.SpiritualCrisisNetwork.org.uk 209
- Supportive resources.. 211
  - We are better off seeing through our spiritual illusions: ... 211
  - For caretakers of those in spiritual crisis: 212
  - Personal narrations: 212
  - When misdiagnosed by health professionals: 213
  - Distinguishing spirituality and madness 213
  - Near Death Experience... 213
  - Academic and scientific perspectives: 214
- Index... 215

Introduction

Personal transformation works somewhat like home renovation. Tired of colour schemes and furniture we used to like, we empty the room, strip it down, reorganize, throw stuff out, repaint, and buy new things. The room is disorganized and messy for a while, the contents of room all out in the open, but when finished, we have a lovely, harmonious room that suits us.

Spiritual transformation has some similar elements, although the internal renovation is not always consciously chosen. As our awareness expands, memories stuffed in the cupboards of our subconscious demand sorting through and clearing. Our life furniture, our concepts, lifestyles, leisure activities, career and friendships need redesigning to match our current awareness.

We'd like to wave a magic wand and instantly step into the perfectly refurbished, loving, wise person of our highest envisioning, without the time, effort, energy or interim mess. Ah, what a lovely thought! In real life, our spiritual refurbishment takes time, energy, and much intention.

Spiritual transformation is the evolution we go through inside as we become more attuned with our spirit essence. Part of this transformation involves expanding our consciousness, becoming aware of increasingly subtle existence. These subtle states of consciousness are always present, but our awareness has become confined to a narrow range in the spectrum. Another part of transformation is to harmonise our thinking, actions and day-to-day life with newly expanded awareness.

While some people experience fairly gentle, incremental change, others may journey through a variety of terrains during their transformation, from cosmic experiences of love and oneness to the dark night of the soul. The highs feel wonderful, but the lows can feel pretty grim. In ignorance of the bigger picture, during our low times we may end up complaining, resisting, and wishing the process would just stop and leave us alone. We end up resisting our own aspirations!

Numerous scriptures and books have been written on the many spiritual practices that expand consciousness, such as meditation techniques, prayer and energy healing, but there is very little written about what may happen after consciousness does open and we become aware of our expanded, loving essence, or our fear of this openness.

Profound insights change us deeply. Afterwards we often need to physically, mentally and emotionally 'catch up,' we need to align our way of living with this new awareness.

It is not always smooth. Energy sensations, mystical experiences, increased sensitivity, or agonizing old memories arising for clearing are common. The process may require fundamental changes in relationships or career direction. When our daily life hasn't been in resonance with our inner being, the process may turn our lives upside down until there is better fit. This side of spiritual life hasn't received much airtime!

We think we'd be happier living our highest potential, but we are so very attached to our 'normal' lives that when our boat gets swept upstream by a higher current, we wonder "Why me?" "Why now?" As we look back over our shoulder afterwards and see all the gifts that have come, we are grateful for the growth opportunity, but at the time, oh do we get confused, plaintive, fearful about what is going on inside us, and worried that we don't feel the way we used to. Our reflex is often to try to scramble back to the way we were, rather than move forward.

Our resistance and confusion is all the more when we shift into a deeper state of consciousness without any philosophical or spiritual understanding to give our experiences a context. Can major spiritual transformation happen to people who aren't remotely interested in it? Absolutely! Major shifts happen to ordinary folk who are simply going about their lives. Possibly the people who have the most difficulty accepting and managing their internal change are those who were not spiritually interested and hadn't consciously chosen to 'move ahead.' They often have absolutely no idea at all what is going on inside, no idea that the internal turmoil is part of a spiritually transformative process. They easily conclude that because they are not feeling 'ordinary' they must somehow be 'crazy' or 'ill' (by default, since we only have the two categories: normal and ill). Some people are unnecessarily medicated and humiliated by their diagnostic labels. What a shame! If they only knew!

When faced with the power and intensity of profound transformation, feelings of bewilderment or fear are also experienced by spiritual practitioners engaged in yoga, praying, chanting, and study of spiritual philosophy. Teachers, discourses and scriptures invariably say stunningly little about how these experiences feel, how to prepare for them, and what to do if spiritual practices actually work and we go through radical internal transformation.

You'd think that clergy, spiritual leaders or yoga teachers would offer understanding and good advice. Some do. Few have personally experienced radical transformation, and virtually no one has spiritual emergence training. Some spiritual teachers actually gloss over anything out of the ordinary, preferring to portray an idealistic picture of their path, and some imply that your transformation process happened because you were not practicing right or you have somehow gone astray. Their standard advice may well be to do more practice or have more faith, which may or may not be what is needed.

Medical professionals tend to make anything out of the ordinary into a disease with a dreadful sounding diagnostic label. Perhaps this labelling is as good for the business of medicine as glossing over internal challenge is for spiritual business, but neither approach is particularly helpful.

Right now, millions of people around the world are experiencing profound transformation, either due to spiritual awakening, work stress or unusual life situations. The seers of our time say that humanity's vibratory frequency is increasing so we will likely see more and more people going through intense and rapid spiritual unfoldment and personal clearing. If you find yourself in a time of profound internal change, be assured that you are not alone.

At this remarkable time when consciousness is opening up for so many people, it is a waste of this potential for us to be floundering in confusion because we don't have the understanding, information and tools we need to move ahead.

One of the reasons we feel alone or confused is simply because we so rarely know about each other's inner life changes. It's not something we talk about; for some reason internal transformation is a topic that is off the social menu. Our work colleague or best friend may be having similar experiences to us, but we'd never know. In the same way, these people have little idea what is happening inside us. We conceal this side of ourselves.

Part of the reason we say little is because we still haven't found words for all our internal realities. One objective of this book is to verbalise at least some unusual experiences. We are still finding words, and the words we currently have aren't used consistently by everyone, which can be confusing. One person may name a state of consciousness as 'the astral plane,' another person may call it the desire world or the higher emotional field. There are a zillion words for our inner Being/ source/ true nature/ Tao / Atman / God / divinity.

The English language is short of many spiritual words, so we have borrowed from other languages. Many words from Sanskrit are now in common use, such as the word 'kundalini,' referring to a powerful energy that moves up the spine. In the absence of other terms, we have broadened out the meaning of 'kundalini' to cover most of the non-ordinary energy movements that happen in the body during spiritual transformation. We could do with having more terms, so that we can be more specific. While words can never really convey the experience itself, they can approximate the experience in a way that other people can recognize.

It's validating, and sometimes a great relief to know that our experiences have happened to others, that we're not the only 'weird ones' being opened up and turned inside out. When we get a sense of the bigger picture, we see that whole chunks of our lives, both comfortable and uncomfortable, are part of an incredible journey towards our becoming our highest potential.

Having figured out the bigger picture, we may also need to know what to do about what is happening within us. How do we handle the powerful new energies that sometimes pour in when we open up? How do we manage the extra sensitivity? How do we integrate our new perceptions and spiritual gifts, while living in social contexts that largely pretend such things don't even exist?

This book takes a practical look at what we go through when our bodies, minds and lifestyles start catching up with our inner awareness. We peruse circumstances that touch on why these internal changes happen. We'll explore the different kinds of experiences people have and how they feel. We'll look at how we get out of balance, physically, mentally, emotionally and spiritually, and how to get back in balance, and some likely places to find help if you need it.

This book is a self-help resource. It covers experiences that most commonly occur, from the highs to the lows. The information here is drawn from my scientific research and others', my spiritual counselling sessions with clients, interviews of caretakers and health professionals who have helped people through awakening and deep transformation, and discussions with psychiatrists, physicians, emotional therapists, energy workers, and spiritual teachers. I have also included the results of my research examining the experiences, triggers, challenges and help sought by 110 people who felt they'd had a transformative spiritual experience. Annotating the effects of shifts in consciousness on our minds, bodies and nervous systems is a work in process; there are still pieces of the picture to figure out and put together.

Chapters 1 and 2 explore the transformation process itself. Chapter 3 looks at spiritual awakening and mystical experiences. Chapters 4-9 explore the adjustments and challenges on the path. Chapter 10 overviews spiritual emergency what resources are available in crisis? Chapter 11 looks at the ways we resist transformation and get in our own way, and Chapter 12 looks at how we can create day-to-day life that is congruent with the awareness we have opened to. Chapter 13 elucidates the fruits offered by the process. The final chapter offers new visions and resources.

There is no replacement for your intuitive knowing but the information here will hopefully enhance your inner awareness and help guide you on your journey as you grow into your most open, beautiful, loving and wise self.

How this book came to be

Thousands of Westerners have headed east, in the quest for enlightenment. We flocked to the gurus and Rimpoches, sat straight backed, did our pranayama, studied scriptures, dressed in white, orange or whatever colour the group wore, and attempted celibacy. After graduating with a BSc in psychology program at Bristol, England, I too headed out on a one-way ticket east.

November 1982, I was the new girl on the block at an ashram in the Himalayan foothills of northern India, having first visited this hermitage a year earlier. A 'keener' who sat in the front row, I attempted to diligently follow every word from my guru.

After two months of focused practice, an energy shot up my spine one day. It was exhilarating but a bit scary at the top – at the last moment I held back rather than going right up through the crown. Otherwise I didn't think too much of it. I had heard the energy was called 'kundalini.' OK.

Shortly after, I was sitting on a cliff edge overlooking a mountain river, going over notes I had taken at the morning's discourse. Realizing that the words wouldn't take me to the place they spoke about, I sat back, and watched a large bird glide down the valley. Some quantum shift in consciousness happened – I've no idea how – and I saw that the 'I' of the bird, and the 'I' that I essentially was, were exactly the same being. I was in all beings – equally. My pen and notebook still in hand, I found myself writing, "Then why am I this body rather than being the bird or ant?" "Because this is the body that is moving the pen," the pen wrote. Intuitively, this made total sense, even though it didn't make rational sense.

Awed, I returned to the ashram. Everyone at the ashram had studied a lot and talked about oneness, so I'd heard the words, and knew what this beautiful open experience was. I didn't know what to say about it – I just looked around wide-eyed.

The thinking of those around me was transparent to me, as were their energy fields, and all kinds of things I wasn't used to seeing or knowing. I found the mismatch between where in their consciousness people spoke from, and the philosophical ideas they were expressing, rather confusing.

For years following this experience, my body and energy fields went through periods of feeling 'stuffed,' overloaded, like they had energetic indigestion. At these times, my head felt hot, my crown burned, and I felt a painful pressure about 12" above my head (try telling that to a doctor!). I had frequent intense headaches. I was physically so hot that I lived through two Himalayan winters without owning a sweater, socks, or shoes, and frequently had to take cold showers or even pile snow on my head to remain cool enough. Something was out of balance, but I didn't know what, or why.

At first my guru insisted that I just needed more meditation, more practice. Doing more meditation at those times felt pretty intense – I was already feeling too open, too much energy. As I became more troubled and complaining, my guru gave me verses to learn by heart. Bhagavad-Gita chapter 6 verse 7 – "the yogi is indifferent to pain and pleasure, heat and cold, he is forever established and unwavering." When I commented that meditation and learning verses made the fire more intense, my guru was incensed, claiming I wasn't worth teaching if I couldn't follow his instructions. He started 'working on my conditions' – publicly ridiculing me for my ignorance, ostracizing me, ignoring me, but then being sweet when I started packing my bags. He then told the other disciples there that I was making it all up.

Why anyone would walk around in winter in a short-sleeved summer dress just to make up a story I don't know. The guru himself had lots of this fire – was he making it up? Perhaps he said this to assure people who were becoming afraid that it could happen to them.

I became more confused, and in increasing pain. I could no longer go out while the sun was up (it was way too intense), couldn't eat any food made with spices or ginger (more fire!), and couldn't handle anyone carrying high energy – all impossible things to avoid while living in this group in India. I looked bedraggled because I walked around with wet hair to keep my head cool. My disciple-peers told me I must be blocked, must have bad karma, or I must be practicing wrongly for such intense energy to happen. Some said I was purifying, the process of clearing the body, clearing karma, old memories, or mental patterns, but it was always coloured with, 'you must have so much to purify to go through this, (unlike-lofty-me)'. Their main advice was to drink a lot of water. It seemed something was wrong, something was out of balance, but what?

I constantly planned to leave, but my guru found endless ways of encouraging me to stay at the ashram, so I trusted that he had a bigger vision; that perhaps the treatment he was issuing me would someday work and I'd come out the other side.

The day before I did finally leave in 1985, the guru's wrath landed on me big time – I was verbally ripped apart, shredded. With all the kundalini energy and 'over-openness,' I wasn't steady enough for this. I arrived back in England, in February 1985, emotionally reeling. I couldn't get anything together. I was in shock, in enormous pain. Perhaps if I'd had more support, I could have made it through. As it was, a non-supportive incident with my family put me over the edge. Something deep inside snapped, cracked, and broke down.

Years of meditation had cultivated a powerful internal witness who was rock solid, and impartially aware that mentally and emotionally I had just had a nervous breakdown. I think even now, my family will be shocked to read this. They could see that I wasn't the bright, outgoing, confident person I used to be, but they couldn't see me as I was, or comprehend my condition. It didn't seem to occur to them to help.

I am grateful to my ashram friend Jean for rescuing me from this situation, marrying me, bringing me to Canada and financially supporting me for those first months while I found my feet. At the time, my main wish was, 'Oh please, can I just get back to being normal!' I didn't easily accept my condition. I was used to being resilient and pretty sharp intellectually. I had been unconditionally offered a place as a PhD student at Bristol University, tuition paid plus a salary, to continue my undergraduate research work. I went to India instead, and ended up in this over-sensitive, rather unstable state. What was wrong with me? How could I get better?

Did I resent life/God/ my guru/ this kundalini energy? You bet! I just had too little understanding of what was going on inside me to value the profundity of the transformation that was occurring. I wish I had known then what I know now.

By the early 90s my energy and emotions had settled down quite a bit. I started a master's degree in psychology, specializing in the internal states of meditation, and graduated four semesters later. The bouts of fire continued somewhat, as did my feeling fragile and oversensitive. I could hardly bear to be in the university setting or around most people. Past memories (going back lifetimes) came up relentlessly for clearing, one after the other. I shuttled from India to Canada and back between semesters, teaching yoga, meditation, chanting and philosophy as I went, dealing as best I could with endless inner 'processing.'

In Montreal, 1993, Jean introduced me to a healer, called Dawn. She talked about grounding, and gave me a massage every month. Before long I was spending half of every month barefoot on her land: enjoying sweat lodges, women's groups, gardening, picking and preparing herbs, and hanging out with her four home-schooled children. Grounding! Aha! – this was the key! This word did not exist in our vocabulary in India!

Having discovered grounding and energy healing, I went exploring. I received other energy work from various therapists which brought back my over-extended aura, cleared trauma, and helped me to deal with emotions related to past trauma. Other therapists helped me clear emotional 'stuff' from childhood, which I now understand was likely one of the fundamental causes of the energy imbalance. Coming from a (typically!) dysfunctional family, I suppose I had dealt with the pain of neglect and divorce by not being fully in my body, thus avoiding the emotional plane. I was strong, athletic, a gymnast, but this isn't the same as being energetically integrated. I learned that I had to clear this pain so that I could fully integrate. Without the spiritual openings, I might have gotten away with not being totally integrated, but after such deep openings we cannot hide – every imbalance is mega-amplified by the energy we open to.

T'ai Chi and qigong provided additional stability. Acupuncture was helping. I discovered that a Shiatsu treatment would clear the fire in the head quickly. I became increasingly comfortable and balanced.

During this time, I took a two-hour bus trip from Ottawa to Montreal. A woman who happened to be sitting beside me started talking, telling me how she was about to finish her PhD in clinical psychology when she had a spiritual opening. She was dropped from the program because she began to use her intuition (not considered scientific). Her spiritual group also didn't understand her. She went through so much that she hid in an attic for two years. Every so often she would say, "I'm so sorry, I don't know why I'm telling you all this, I don't usually speak about it", then went on, her story tumbling out.

I knew why she was telling me, and her consciousness realized she could safely speak with me. I decided right then that if I were ever to study anything else, I would research this area. Thank you, I think Susan was your name, for sharing your story. You sowed the original seed for this book. I think about you sometimes. I hope you came through OK.

Having become considerably more balanced and settled, with the loving support of warm and intelligent Harold, I returned to India for some years to continue my study of advanced yogic science and philosophy, and to finish sorting myself out.

A few penny-drop moments happened when a visitor to our community became 'overly-open.' It is easier to see events impartially when it's not about oneself. Listening to the doctors and nurses involved discussing whether she should have been made to take the drugs she refused, whether she should have been treated this way or that, I realized that we didn't, after so many spiritual openings in our community, really know what best to do. To 'help with her mind,' she was taught a pranayama (breathing exercise that opens consciousness further), given Reiki sessions (that poured in more energy), was taken walking high in the mountains (again, opens consciousness more). She was brought to lots of social events (way too much stimulation). A psychiatric nurse there thought our visitor should refrain from meditation and not attend more discourses, but no one implemented the recommendation. This young woman was not handling the consciousness she had opened to, yet no one had a clear direction for her. With all the caring around (and it was considerable!), the advice she was receiving wasn't working. An eye-opening moment for me was, oh, so it's not that I, alone, am unable to be helped by this yogic community – the so-called advice given, while well-meaning, is not necessarily appropriate or useful.

I saw the cover-ups – the attempt of the ashram to pretend that openings and 'strange' things didn't happen there. It brought back memories of earlier years when what was happening to me was dismissed, veiled over, though, luckily, tolerated. Other overly open people had been drugged and shipped back to the West. Why? Why couldn't we deal with the fact that sometimes consciousness opens up too far, and offer the grounding, energy work and emotional release work that would help people through?

Moved by the visitor's experience, I started to interview key caretakers during previous kundalini awakenings, several general practitioners and psychiatrists, and a few therapists. We'd had some colourful incidents over the years. One fellow had popped open after extensive hours of pranayama. Stripping naked, he ran across the mountainside. He took down the photos of the guru and sat on the guru seat himself. We had also witnessed a nurse, who, so we heard afterwards, had been partying and taking recreational drugs in the Caribbean for two weeks prior to coming to India, so we surmised she did not have the energy balance and centeredness needed to do deep spiritual practice. She will go down in ashram history not only for the tremendous power of her kundalini opening but also for biting the guru's arm! At another time, we took 2-hour shifts night and day to watch over a Tai Kwon Do black belt ashram member who was both overly open and in a fearful frame of mind. What wisdom could the caretakers offer in hindsight? I jotted notes as I listened to the colourful tales.

Meanwhile friends around the world surfed the Net (we didn't have Internet in our Himalayan town at that time) and sent me books and piles of printed matter. I read in awe – "Wow! So it's not just me, it's not just people doing hours of spiritual practice in the Himalayas that this happens to – spiritual openings and major transformation happens to people all over the world! Childbirth! Menopause! Stress!"

Reading web printouts posted to me; there was another penny-drop moment when I read that kundalini had an inherent intelligence, and that people's troubles come from resisting the energy, not sufficiently trusting it.

Deeply moved by these words, I lay on a large Tibetan carpet for while, attempting to clear out all the negative messages I'd picked up over the last years, reorienting myself to trust this energy, to flow with it, to dedicate myself to it. When I finally got up off the rug, I found myself starting up my laptop and writing, almost in a trance. Afterwards I turned off the laptop and, still in a haze, fell into a deep sleep. This writing-sleep cycle happened for days.

I didn't always feel like writing, but when the words started coming through, it felt like a choice between going with the flow, or feeling uncomfortable. So I wrote, and slept. When I awoke, I remembered nothing of what I'd just written.

In a short time, I had a manual written for caretakers of people in spiritual emergency. I gave copies to medical doctors, nurses and therapists at the ashram, accompanied by a red pen and the instruction, "Anything you find that isn't right, write on this manuscript. Please use this pen!" Many manuscripts came back with only minor comments, but I smile to remember the emergency room doctor who responded to my passages on the shortcomings of pharmaceutical drugs with a diagonal red line corner to corner across the page. "You have to be realistic here..." he argued. We haggled over this page for hours. Finally I came to a more moderate position.

Two psychiatrists from Germany who worked with spiritual emergence cases in hospitals, read a later version, and said it was the book that they would have written themselves. How promising!

I presented the completed manual to the ashram. I received a curt thank you, but they wouldn't need it since no more openings were going to happen. (Really?) One of the psychiatrists approached me hotly and said, "We don't need this here! Publish this in the West, but we don't want it here!" I can only suppose that even the presence of the manual implied,... what? -- that spiritual openings and major transformation happened in a place where people meditated for hours to gain enlightenment?

Despite the official ashram rejection, the good had already been done. Most of the key health providers in the community had already read the text during its editing process. When the next person went through a deep spiritual process, the professionals were ready. They worked together, forming a supportive group around the woman (one of the people who had many years earlier been drugged and shipped home), and she came through OK. The manual had helped its first person.

The manual also reached England where it passed from a friend's mother to a woman who'd been hospitalized due to her opening. Her husband read the manual, realized what was happening, got her out of hospital, and found the right help for her. I was later contacted to ask if I would mind if Findhorn, a spiritual community in Scotland, could use the writing as a training manual. Yes, of course.

Settling in Ottawa in 2001, I was surprised by how often the people I met were going, or had gone, through powerful spiritual transformation. At one yoga retreat, seven of the nine participants had been through intense transformation. Seven in one group! It was amazing watching them bond together. Where does one ever get the chance to talk about this unusual aspect of our inner lives?

During spiritual counselling sessions, clients who had mystical experiences or kundalini awakenings told me stories of their clueless kundalini yoga teachers and freaked out group leaders who didn't know what to do and were afraid of being sued. They told me about times spent in hospital because they didn't understand what was going on inside, and didn't know where else to go for help.

I started running weekend workshops to give basic care-taking information to healers, health professionals and therapists. The people who came shared their stories openly. A male workshop participant told of a major spiritual opening on a street corner on the way to work one morning. Good heavens!

I founded a spiritual emergence network of medical doctors and therapists in my hometown. It was supposed to be a referral and support network for those in distress. We didn't figure out how to reach these people (there is no system available to use, hardly even terminology that an awakened person who didn't know the spiritual words would recognize), but since we enjoyed meeting with each other, we continue to meet, meditate and share together.

I gave talks. I interviewed people. I created a documentary on DVD, ("*Spiritual Emergency*"), validating unusual experiences during spiritual emergence and alerting health professionals to the signs. I presented my data at a conference. My explorations continue. Every single client and workshop teaches me something.

Clients have often said, "I wish there was a book about this." In response, this book came about as an extended version of the original manual, extended and reformulated as a self-help book for people in profound transformation. If even one person is helped, the many hours it took to write will be worthwhile.

Acknowledgments

Thank you Donna Burry for your great editing and intelligent and perceptive suggestions. This book wouldn't be where it is today without your support, responsiveness and good will.

I have great appreciation for my partner Louis Radakir for being at my side, and giving me the space to pursue large projects, ready to help with technical support and proof reading when needed.

Deep thanks to Jean Bouchart D'Orval and Harold Breck for your love, support and belief in me. Your reassurance, constancy and the strength of your meditation practice helped me through.

Warm thanks to Tania Dolley and Lee Hunter who posted out to India the books and information on spiritual emergence that initiated this research.

My thanks to the many medical doctors, psychiatrists, therapists, healers and kundalini care-takers who shared their experiences and views on various aspects of spiritual emergency. Thanks to my guru and all teachers and friends who have supported my transformation journey, offering inspiration, companionship and the light of their awareness. Thank you Andrea Jutras for introducing me to your energy work and many excellent professionals.

I thank the 110 participants of the Profound Spiritual Experience research for not only filling in the four-page questionnaire but also annotating with such interesting comments, many of which are included later in this book.

Thanks to every client and workshop participant; I learned from all of you, and the learning continues.

1

Anatomy of Transformation

If we want to get optimum performance out of our car, we need to know how the engine and its many components work. With this knowledge, when there is a problem with the engine we can figure out what it is and fix it. We can also use this knowledge to get the very best performance from our engine. We can tweak the engine timing and carburettor, clean the spark plugs, add a little oil, and hey presto, we have a more fuel efficient, fast, reliable and vibrant car.

In the same way, once we understand our makeup, we can optimise our own possibilities.

In essence, spiritual transformation has three main facets:
1 Shifting or expanding consciousness / increased frequency
2 Clearing the mental and emotional patterns that limit us
3 Aligning our day-to-day life with our new awareness

1 Shifting Consciousness
States of consciousness are like modes of operation. For example, we are aware that every day we spend time in three states of consciousness: waking, dreaming and in deep sleep. We have a whole range of different states of consciousness which we switch between during the day – mentally alert, intuitive, physical, day-dreamy, peaceful, and emotional.

We are not solidly in one state of consciousness all day, we fluctuate depending on our energy levels, comfort, and where our attention is. What we think of as normal consciousness is the range of consciousness

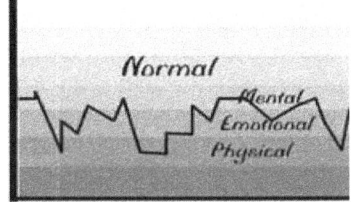

we have become accustomed to. For many people, this is a fluctuation between the physical, mental and emotional. Sometimes we are more expanded, sometimes more contracted. We are familiar with our own modes of consciousness and the modes of others around us – these modes are part of what differentiates our character.

We exist as a spectrum of states of consciousness. Each state resonates within a certain range of wave-length-frequency.

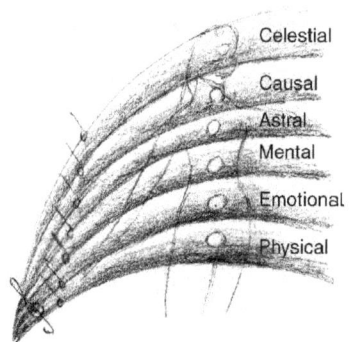

In the same way musical notes and colours are arranged in octaves or rainbows of frequencies, seven notes to an octave, seven colours in a rainbow, we find consciousness similarly arranged, with seven states of consciousness in this octave of our experience. Each layer of consciousness resonates at a different frequency. The slowest vibrational frequency creates the densest part of us, which we call the physical body. Successive layers of consciousness resonate at increasingly fine vibrational rates.

Our physical world works the same way. When H_2O molecules vibrate slowly, we call them ice. At a faster speed they are water, and when the molecules vibrate still faster, we have steam. Faster than that, those same water molecules will become light, then pure energy.

When we shift in consciousness, it is like awareness moving from ice to water, or water to steam.

At each vibratory rate, the water molecule has specific properties. We can walk on ice, but not water. We can drink water, but not steam. We can power an old locomotive train with steam, but not ice. Yet throughout, it's the same fundamental H_2O material.

Consciousness works the same way. Each state of consciousness has a specific level of density. The densest consciousness is our physical body, then the energy field, our emotions, the mind, the astral field, the causal plane, increasingly subtle layers of consciousness, and, finally the most subtle, our universal essence.

We have been more or less schooled and socialised to operate in, and validate, the physical and mental aspects of us, with lip service paid to the emotional. Mainstream ('normal') awareness focuses on what we have, what we do, and what we think and feel about it. After a large shift in consciousness we are like light or energy. We have added other levels of consciousness to our awareness.

Each layer has its own nature and truths. The way we see life depends on the vibrational rate of the state of consciousness our attention rests in at the moment of perceiving. We are generally unaccustomed to reflecting, 'oh, this is my emotional perspective on this, it differs from my intellectual position and my intuitive sense.'

Part of our transformation involves shifts in awareness or vibrational resonance. What are these shifts?

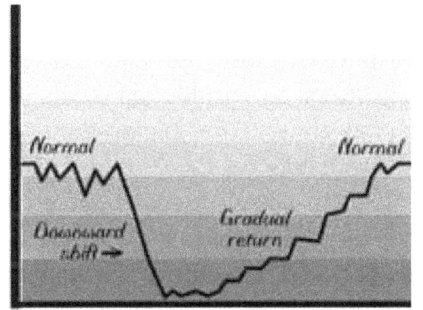

We're all familiar with downward shifts. They can happen when we eat a load of junk food, drink too much, watch hours of aimless TV or converse too long with a person who drains our energy. At the end of the day we are literally vibrating at a lower frequency of consciousness. We feel more sluggish, uninspired, dense, limited, and have very little available energy. Usually we return gradually to what we call 'normal' afterwards. We are internally wired to gravitate towards what we are familiar with, so after a shift in consciousness we tend to gradually shift back the modes of consciousness we are familiar with.

An 'upward shift' is the opposite of this. Upward shifts raise our vibrational frequency. If we are not afraid of the openness, these upward shifts leave us feeling exuberant, inspired, joyful or even virtually enlightened

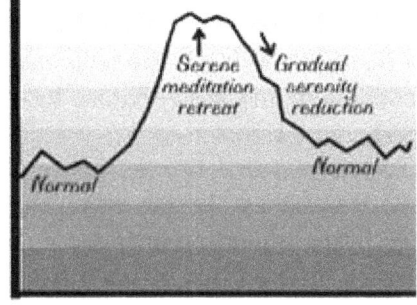

(albeit generally temporarily so). These shifts may happen through meditation, change of diet, yoga, qigong, workshops or retreats, or may happen through not eating or sleeping enough, childbirth, therapy, and life shocks like death or illness. Shifts can also happen for no discernable reason whatsoever – our awareness simply opens up.

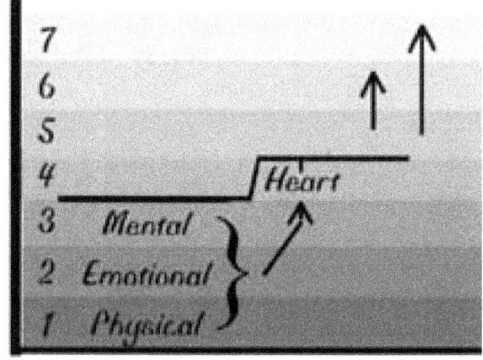

Taking a global look, we see humanity has evolved from a simple survival focus, to focussing on education, money and intellectual achievement. We are now attempting to shift from the intellectual focus to a heart focus where love, compassion and sharing become predominant values. We also see some people pushing the boundaries of consciousness to include all kinds of intuitive, spiritual and universal perspectives. The explorations of these people open the door for others to follow.

Our state of consciousness changes the way we feel and perceive. A large downward shift may leave us feeling blocked, limited or depressed. An upward shift may feel peaceful, blissful, or like walking out of the shadowy valley and arriving at the mountain peak. Naturally our perspectives change.

> ***Our greatest potential is reached when all levels of consciousness are open***

We can divide the spectral continuum into any number of levels, and call each section by a name we choose, but essentially the same reality underlies it. The table overleaf shows one way of dividing the continuum and giving names to the planes of consciousness and the way we view ourselves.

Paranormal experiences occur when our awareness opens to include the planes like the astral realm. When we perceive seeing energy fields around people, see coloured light, are aware of spirit guides, or have an out of body experience, it is often because our awareness is including information available in the astral plane.

State	How our life looks when viewed from each plane of consciousness
Oneness	The eternal Now, the unchanging. Nothing has ever become anything. Everything is of one consciousness.
Celestial	There is only love and light; nothing has intrinsic meaning, a play so consciousness can experience itself.
Cosmic	The essence of who we are is the same one essence of all beings. All life, all matter, arises from this one essential source. We are the source, the source is us.
Subtle	Who we essentially are is beyond time and causality. Time is an illusion created by our linear minds. We actually live all our lives simultaneously and can heal across time.
Causal	Our soul is a template carrying the seeds of our karma. We are a line of consciousness that manifests again and again throughout time until lessons are learned.
Love-compassion	We are one interconnected being of love. Whether we are physically with our loved ones or not, our hearts are forever united. Love transcends time and space. Our soul lives on after the body dies.
Astral	We are thought forms that aren't limited to the physical body. We can fantasize, get others to believe our thoughts, draw energy to us. We are not bound – we are infinitely creative.
Mental	We are what we think, what we think lays the basis of our decisions, our actions, and our way of interpreting the world. The information we have learned are assets, we may fight others to maintain our rightness.
Emotional	Life is about feeling. Birth is an expression of our desire for experience. When this body passes away, we hanker for another body to continue our experiences.
Life-force	We are the breath that brings life to the physical cells. We flow in and around all objects. We are an energy from which the physical body is formed and is fuelled.
Physical	Life begins when we emerge from the womb, and ends when we die. Life is about survival. There is nothing after this life. We are the body.

There are also increasingly subtle planes of consciousness that go beyond time which here are simply listed as 'ethereal' and 'celestial' because we don't yet have the words for them. Finally, what we call oneness is where all is merged as one universal essence. When we are open we include more states of consciousness in our awareness and so have more possibilities of perception and wisdom.

How did we lose touch with so much of ourselves?

As babies, our consciousness was expanded and included many subtle states of consciousness. Modelling on our parents, we sensed what they validated. We wanted to please our parents, and so were eager to experience the way they did to get the reward of their acceptance and praise.

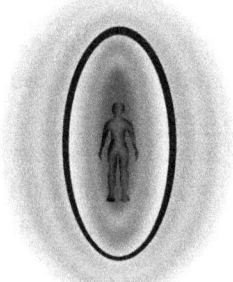

We grow a veil to screen out non-validated perceptions

Gradually we harmonized with their way of seeing. We learned what they considered 'real, and what was 'unreal.' 'Unreal' perceptions, such as mystical states of consciousness, were not validated, so gradually we figured it was best to screen them out, especially when these perceptions were considered 'bad', demonic, illusory, 'airy-fairy,' 'psychotic,' or 'weird.' In time, we learned to not let our attention leave this validated physical-mental world, often by creating a conceptual veil separating off the subtle world since it wasn't supposed to exist. This subtle wall or veil was great for keeping us attentive to the physical, emotional and mental, but it didn't allow us much access to deeper states of consciousness, and our attention gradually narrowed. In today's scientific world, being confined to the first few levels of consciousness is considered 'normal.'

We are encased in the body-mind

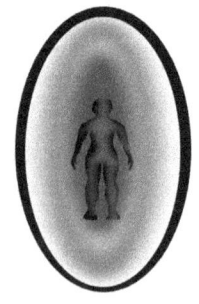

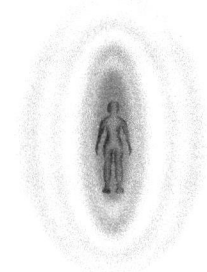
Another way of thinking about our range of awareness is by using the analogy of a radio. We are all radio receivers, but many radios have been limited to only pick up 3 or 4 channels – physical to mental wavelengths. Our spiritual practice may gradually widen the spectrum of wavelengths we can receive to infinite possibilities.

We realize that if one reason our awareness is limited is because at an early age we had learned to screen out our intuition and subtle perceptions, we can now send a new message to our mind – "Hey mind, it's OK now – you can relax and perceive much more!" Our adult minds are easily capable of receiving a wide range of consciousness while being able to operate seamlessly in the socially agreed reality when needed, and able to discriminate who we can share our deeper perceptions with.

How do these states of consciousness feel?
Most of the day we are too pre-occupied with our actions and thinking to notice what mode of consciousness we are in. In meditation, we are more watchful. Meditation is a time spent just being, watching, and allowing our awareness to tune in to subtler parts of ourselves.

During meditation, we can often sense when our attention shifts predominantly from one level to another. It is especially noticeable when we shift out of the mental realm into the blissful place that lies immediately beyond it.

During meditation, we can often sense when our attention shifts predominantly from level to another. It is especially noticeable when we shift out of the mental realm into the blissful place that lies immediately beyond it.

When we first sit down to meditate, our awareness is more as depicted at the bottom of the table. As we meditate, we become aware of an increasing number of chart levels.

Plane of consciousness	How our meditation feels when in each plane of consciousness
Oneness	We merge as one.
Celestial	We experience ourselves as undifferentiated light-love
Cosmic	The 'I' that I am is the same 'I' that you are
Subtle	Time stands still. Wisdom and revelations.
Causal	We are aware of the effect of each thought and action
Love-compassion	Love extends from our heart with a wish of peace, healing and goodness to all beings.
Astral	We shift out of the mind into the intuitive. Peace. Our higher awareness or spirit guides may offer directions.
Mental	We plan, learn, remember, solve problems, chat to ourselves, we think…. endlessly
Emotional	We feel waves of sadness, anger or elation
Life-force	We feel energy; we feel it flowing through chakras, meridians, and feel warmth in the palm of our hands.
Physical	We are a body, aware of breath, contact with the floor, pains, stiff joints, heat/cold, tension, hunger and thirst

Energy anatomy

We learned basic physical anatomy in school. Our life force and energy fields also have anatomical structure.

Our life force especially flows through a central channel running from the crown of your head to the base of the spine. When we are conceived, this central energy channel is the first thing that forms. Along the spine are seven main energy centres, called chakras. Chakra is Sanskrit for wheel – referring to the spinning energy in these centres.

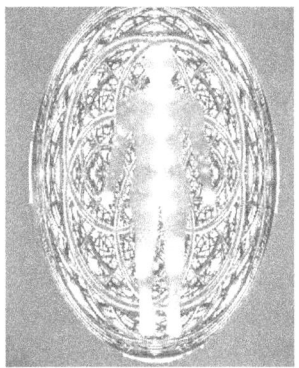

Chakras are centres of spinning energy that transmute energy from one vibratory level to another. Each plane of consciousness is connected with one of these energy centres in the body. Each chakra communicates through a specific endocrine gland in our bodies, and through subtle energy channels that radiate out from each chakra, called nadis. The more open, positive and integrated our chakras are, the better our energy flow is, and the more access to all states of consciousness and possibilities we have.

The seven main chakras:
1. Root - Security, survival – at the base of your spine
2. Sacral - Emotions, sensuality – just below your navel
3. Solar plexus - Ambition, courage – pit of your stomach
4. Heart - Love, compassion – middle of your chest
5. Throat - Thinking, communication – nape of your neck
6. Third eye - Intuitive understanding – between your eyebrows
7. Crown - Unity consciousness – at the crown of your head

There are also many minor chakras throughout the body, such as in the palms of the hands, and chakras of increasing subtlety above your head.

Spectrum of love
Chakras may be subtle wheels of energy, but the way they manifest is quite tangible. Take the way we love. There is predominantly first chakra love, second chakra love, third chakra love...

1. Love expressed primarily through the first chakra is about survival and territory. "You my woman. This my cave. I hunt, you cook, we no die. You no leave cave. You no see other man. You mine.'
2. Love expressed through the second chakra is sensual, sexual, nurturing, creative, and fosters the attachment that bonds the ties between families and friends. "I need you, honey-baby, you make me feel so fine." "Let me kiss your red lips and run my fingers through your soft hair..."

3. Third chakra love is about personal boundaries "I deserve to be treated well," or controlling. "I love you, I know what is best, and so you should do as I say." It's also about ideas such as "I love you because you think like I do."
4. The heart expresses love through caring, giving, supporting and empathizing. "I will do all that I can to nurture you, support you. I give you space to be free."
5. Fifth chakra love offers deep respect and regard for who you are. "I accept and honour you as you are," "I am interested in you." "I give you the freedom to follow your interests."
6. Sixth chakra love sees the soul and inner light, and loves that light. "I know your soul, I see spirit shining in your eyes"
7. Seventh chakra love knows all beings as God, as unity, as essence. "I am you, you are me, we are eternally one."

Having become aware of the spectrum of consciousness, the central channel and the chakras, we are more in a position to tweak our body-mind-energy systems into a higher level of functioning. We can do this through meditation, self-healing, intent, yoga, qigong and other methods, or through professional energy work, acupuncture, chakra clearing and emotional therapy.

2. Clearing limiting mental and emotional patterns

Just how beautifully, graciously, happily or peacefully do you wish to express yourself? Each layer of our consciousness can be cleared, realigned, fine-tuned into its optimal capacity. We no longer need to be limited by shyness or fears based on past experience, nor limited by the beliefs we learned from our parents, or picked up elsewhere.

Using therapeutic tools, some of which have only recently been discovered like energy psychology, we can clear our fears and past pain. We gradually cease to have 'buttons'. 'Buttons' are packets of unresolved past pain that we carry within us that can be triggered by any current life situation that reminds us of our unresolved past, like our lover reminding us of a parent and triggering a sullen withdrawal.

When we have cleared our past hurts, we can go into situations that used to make us feel bad and find our buttons are no longer pressed. We also cease to need to shut down to avoid internal pain.

Our emotions swing into ups and downs less, and so our emotional field becomes a more accurate instrument, able to intuitively feel those around us.

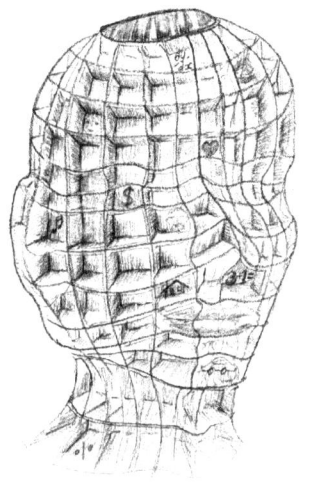

Our minds can also change. The work of our minds is to differentiate, formulate, symbolize and compartmentalize perceptions into categories. It remembers. It extrapolates on the basis of memory to create future plans and fears. It can be programmed with any kind of learning, much like a computer.

The mind believes its thoughts to be totally true and real. It turns the nebulous, free- flowing nature of existence into concepts and symbols, and puts words to the final understanding. This can be done in a way that is useful, or a way that creates fixity, prejudice and limitation.

What kind of a mind do we want? One that sees in definite black and white differences, or a mind which sees spectrums of greys? A mind that can encompass opposite viewpoints? A mind that is switched on the whole time, or one with an 'off-switch'?

As we transform, we increasingly see that a busy mind isn't as conducive to tranquillity and inner listening as a settled mind. We see that negative thinking, being self-centred, trying to control others, or feeling like a victim doesn't resonate as well with our loving, light inner awareness as positive thinking, trusting, universal awareness or cultivating equality in all relationships.

How do we do change our patterns of thinking? First by observing ourselves. After discerning the limiting patterns that don't serve us, we set about replacing them with something that works better. Of course, this is much quicker said than done. Sometimes there are emotional underpinnings such as fears based on past experiences that affect the way we think, so we need to work on the emotional side. This may be a large part of your transformation journey.

Each layer of consciousness has its own laws and ways of functioning. As our minds become clearer and more discerning, they are less likely to mix up the truths from each layer of consciousness.

While it is true that our spirits are immortal, our physical bodies will die. On deeper levels of consciousness we are unaffected by circumstance, yet on a feeling level we are affected. Even though we perceive subtle states of consciousness that are beyond time, our minds operate in a time framework.

This same observation applies to the conglomerate of ideas about ourselves that we call our self-concept or personality. As we become more comfortable with our universal spirit nature, we may re-inquire into our nature and wonder if our sense of being a certain particular kind of person is needed anymore. We could be multifaceted, adapting to whatever the moment brings. Our education, age or social standing is no longer a reason to do or not do anything, so we can respond more directly to what our spirit calls us to.

The sense of being individual rather than universal can also dissolve. What we call ego is a basic sense of separation with

the essence or source of being. The sense that creates 'me-mine' as separate from 'you-yours' This has been a traditional facet of our way of thinking, but as we open up, we realize that our individual whirlpool, and all the twigs and leaves caught up in its rotation, can come to a peaceful place and allow the water to merge with the ocean. We have less need for ownership, less need to fear, or to control.

We hold resistance and all kinds of emotions in our bodies. We carry 'emotional armour' like hunched shoulders. We eat things that don't suit our bodies; we believe stressing ourselves to achieve goals, such as earning more money, is more important than our well-being. We have illnesses. As we clear our emotions and thinking, add in a little stretching, bodywork and a good diet, our health, comfort and vitality increase enormously. As a direct result, we are happier and more open, which in turn draws more light and love to us. It's an ever upward spiral of transformation. Chapter 7 goes into internal clearing in more detail.

3. Aligning our day-to-day life with our new awareness

It is not a little more calmness or relaxed condition of the mind nor a little more creative ability nor a feeling of euphoria nor visionary experiences nor a little more efficiency in work that determines whether or not a transformation in consciousness has occurred in an individual. Rather, it is a complete metamorphosis of the personality that points to it.
Gopi Krishna[3]

Opening and deepening our awareness feels good, but it doesn't stay in a permanent way until we get the rest of ourselves aligned with this awareness. We can dissolve into a beautiful peace in one moment, but our habitual thinking comes in and distracts us back into worrying thoughts. We've all experienced coming back from a relaxing holiday, only to find we are hurried or stressed within days of our return. The lovely inner peace cultivated during a meditation retreat easily fades when we return to our less-mindful patterns.

In the same way, to sustain and maintain our increasingly open awareness, we need to live a life that is in synchrony and harmony with our inner being. As we'll see in chapter 11, this realignment includes our diet, leisure activities, relationships, career, what we read and what we choose to spend money on. <u>There is no one way this looks</u> – we are all different, and have different soul destinies.

Once we align our lifestyle with our inner awareness, we feel more congruent. The shifts in consciousness made internally are now firmly rooted in our physical, emotional and mental life. We have integrated this part of our journey.

2

Journey's Terrain

We are all of one fundamental essence. When we attune to our essence, we become aware of a time-honoured, universal truth. Our souls are all intrinsically connected to each other and one with the universal source, yet all have their unique character and life purpose.

We call our increasing awareness 'opening up', and call the process of mental and emotional clearing and alignment with our soul purpose 'spiritual emergence' – the emerging of who we are in truth, the living of our light, freedom and potential. We call it 'spiritual emergency' when this process becomes so intense we need help.

Our journey clears memories and emotions, dissolves beliefs that don't serve us, frees us from habitual actions and thinking, deepens our compassion and understanding, and gives us the courage to do what we took birth for.

A short précis of the basic process.
Certain principles underlying times of deep transformation are common to everyone. Briefly put: shifts in consciousness and changes in perception need adjusting to, assimilating, and integrating. There are ways to make it easier for ourselves, and ways we can make it more difficult. When our transformation is gentle and steady, it's not a big deal – we manage fine. When the process speeds up, we have more to be aware of.

Why do we start transforming more quickly?
There are four main reasons:
1. We consciously practice something that opens us, like yoga, meditation, prayer, qigong, fasting, vegan diets, or we go to workshops, therapists, or receive energy treatments. These all raise our frequency of consciousness.
2. Life situations, like unexpected death, financial loss or failure that challenge our sense of surety or control over life, and shocks us into waking up or changing our beliefs.
3. We have a mystical experience or spiritual awakening that boosts us into a more expanded awareness.
4. We are all connected. We move forward through each other's efforts. One person's achievement opens the door to new possibilities for others.

1. Spiritual practice tends to gradually open our consciousness in small increments while our outer life may stay pretty much the same. At a certain point, the change inside us may quietly accumulate to the point where we realize our day-to-day life no longer matches who we are inside. We look at our lives and think, "this isn't me!" We have two options: to dull down our consciousness and fit back in our previous conceptual box, or make changes to bring our daily lives into resonance with our inner truth.

Transformation through spiritual practice

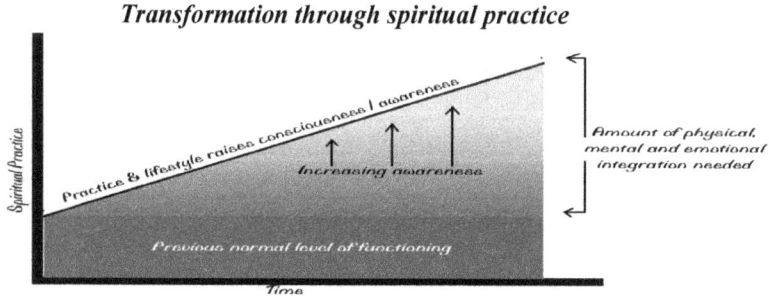

2. Life happens. Illness, financial loss, burnout, accidents, failure, and lovers' break-ups toss our carefully laid plans to the wind and shake our world. Wonderful transformation happens through these times because they challenge our concepts and shake us out of complacency.

Transformation through life situations

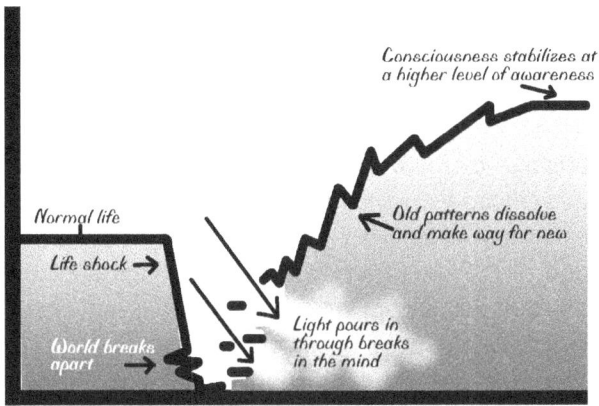

3. A spiritual opening temporarily boosts us into a more expanded state of consciousness. It is as if the effect of years of spiritual practice was given to us in a moment but without all the assimilation and integration that a steadier growth time would have offered. Assimilation is needed afterwards.

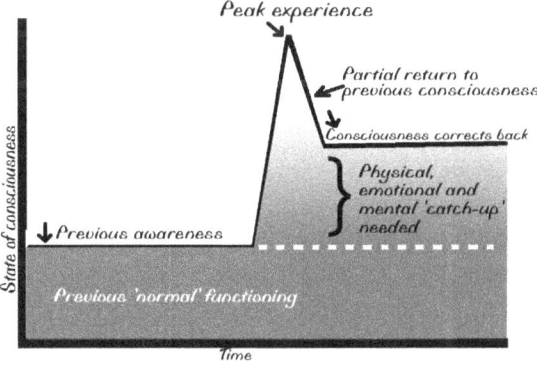

We go through a wide range experiences during deep transformation, yet listening to clients I hear similar themes and processes. Simply put, it reads like this:

1: Whether our internal process starts with spiritual practice, an unusual experience, or a life situation, deep transformation usually involves a shift in awareness or beliefs. This awareness is common to all of us. It is a guiding light.

2. People react in various ways to increased energy and openness - the reactions create a large part of what we are dealing with during transformation.
3. The more light opened to, whether due to spiritual practice, shifts in consciousness or for no apparent reason, the more shadows are revealed. *(shadows being our limitations, undigested memories, and negative attitudes.)*
4. Purification of the mind, emotions, energy field and physical body inevitably arises as part of the process. 'Purification' is about clearing the previous mental patterns that are not congruent with the new awareness. The purification may be due to high-vibration energies and openness dissolving the walls that keep intense past experiences parcelled off from our conscious mind, or due to the influx of energy washing old memories into the conscious mind.
5. During this time we are generally much more sensitive than we used to be.
6. We then need to integrate our awareness into our lives and align our lifestyle with our awareness. Purification and integration can take a while – months or years – depending on the number or intensity of the experiences needing clearing, and our ability to let these experiences go, to remain centred in spirit, and to apply positive principles.
7. As we become more heart centred, spiritually open and intuitive, previous careers, lifestyle, relationships and leisure activities need adjusting – or, sometimes, changing altogether.
8. New intuitive, healing and creative abilities often unfold through our transformation and increased openness. Some abilities are temporary and some will last. We then need to learn how to use these skills with integrity.
9. Each person expresses his or her awareness according to his or her soul nature and life direction. There is no one right way to express spirit. We find a centred, autonomous place within that is connected to the flow of spirit through us, and balance this with the lives and sensitivity of those around us.
10. The transformation process moves us from fear to love, from separateness to oneness. We become more aligned with spirit, with oneness, with unity consciousness.

Our transformation is unlikely to be as neat and defined as the transformation steps outlined here, nor will the steps necessarily appear in this orderly way. Much of the time we don't even recognize that what is happening within us is part of our transformation. We are much more pre-occupied with the content of our stories, the rights and wrongs of the situations we find ourselves in, than the wider picture of our evolution and the evolution of humanity. Also, it appears to us that we make headway forward, and then regress into troubled places, not realizing the link between opening to light and the light illuminating the shadows that need clearing.

A slightly expanded précis:
During shifts in consciousness we tend to experience:
- mystical experiences
- influx of powerful energies
- increased sensitivity
- paranormal perceptions
- resurfacing memories
- past life experiences

Reactions to the initial experiences include:
- bliss/transcendence
- wonder/awe, fear, trepidation
- confusion, doubting our perceptions
- feeling like we're losing control
- depression and estrangement
- worry that we've gone crazy
- thinking we're enlightened/the new messiah
- wondering what the *#! is going on!

.

Our work
- Increased inner listening
- Increasing intuitive understanding
- Keeping our energy, emotions, thinking and lifestyle balanced
- Finding words and ways of communicating new perceptions
- Daring to live new values
- Harnessing new skills
- Finding a way of bringing these gifts to others.

Our main internal difficulties:
- Dealing with the contents of Pandora's Box (including our 'past life' memories)

- Depression / feeling suicidal
- Undiagnosable physical pain
- Constant mental anguish
- Seeing things others can't see
- Kriyas - involuntary movements
- Over-sensitivity
- Insufficient focus
- Energy imbalance
- Being misunderstood
- Weird body sensations
- Diagnosed as mentally ill and put on medication
- Negative psychic experiences such as psychic invasion by entities
- Feeling under pressure inside, feeling heat, burning or fire, too much energy in the body, or conversely, having too little energy in the body.
- Chronic fatigue, fibromyalgia and multiple chemical sensitivity may well be found to be linked to the transformation process for some people.

Life integration difficulties
- Unable to work (dizzy, spaced out, headaches, oversensitive)
- Needing a change of career direction
- No interest in previous friends and leisure activities
- Needing to radically transform or finish a relationship
- Diet and lifestyle needs change
- Mismatch between daily lifestyle and inner awareness
- Learning to manage sensitivity
- Just wanting to be still/do spiritual practice/watch the beans grow, but our own or other people's beliefs creates resistance.

As we become aware of increasingly fine, open, loving and expansive states of consciousness, our perspectives widen, we may feel more freedom, more connected to our life purpose, more vibrant and awake. It is possible to do a lot of upward shifting and feel just fine – life just keeps getting better and better. However, from time to time we may either come across a wall of limitation, or we need a catch-up time of assimilating, integrating or purifying. We may flip between feeling invincibly and eternally free to feeling stuck or blocked, from exotic mystical energy sensations to waves of troubled emotion. If we keep our sight on the light, we move through more easily, but nonetheless these processes are rarely comfortable.

Why the discomfort?

Common reasons include:
- **Confusion**, not knowing what is going on, not having the words or a framework of understanding.
- **Feeling alone**, needing spiritual company, seeking empathic spiritual mentors.
- **Internal purification**. Issues we haven't fully dealt with emerge for clearing, pushing us to do internal work and emotional clearing we perhaps wouldn't have bothered to do otherwise.
- **Dealing with intense energies**, strange pains, heat, burning, dizziness, involuntary movements, new allergies, headaches, or paranormal phenomena.
- **Intense sensitivity** to the world around us.
- **Inability to remain grounded**, balanced, focused and able to manage day-to-day life with all this inner processing.
- **Relationships, career and lifestyle** don't fit with our new awareness.
- **New skills** have opened up that we need to learn how to use with integrity and find ways of sharing.

You are not alone. You are amongst thousands, possibly millions, of people in the midst of profound personal transformation. What people go through is related to their own particular experiences and needs. Not everything here will apply to you - you don't need to wade through the whole text. Go for the sections that interest you today.

Useful things to learn
- How to ground energy
- How to protect oneself spiritually and energetically
- How to stabilize in the new higher-vibration energy
- What can be said and not said to each person
- Understanding new perceptions
- Re-aligning your life to the new you
- Processing arising emotions and memories (with or without professional therapy)
- Finding like-minded company

We'll take each of these areas in turn.

3

Mystical Experiences

Mystical experiences are not necessary for our transformation. Millions of practitioners around the world have meditated, prayed and grown through their practice for decades without having had a deep mystical experience.

Responses to these experiences vary. Spiritual practitioners often welcome them as signs of their progress. However, when non-practicing, not spiritually interested people have an unusual experience, they may conclude there is something wrong with them. Even a long-standing practitioner can be surprised, or even shocked, by a very powerful, deep awakening.

To research this field, 110 people who felt they had had a profound spiritual experience (PSE) filled in a 4-page questionnaire. Results showed that 43% of these were not practicing in any way prior to their first experience, meaning that spiritual openings and transformation can happen to anyone, not just those consciously on a path. 15% of these people didn't even believe in spirit before the experience (although they all believed afterwards!).

It turns out most of these 110 participants had had numerous mystical experiences. What did they think triggered them? They ticked off the situations and activities they thought had in part initiated their profound spiritual experience; added up we see some are things we do to get more open (yoga, meditation) and some are life situations that happen without our conscious choice.

11% of these participants had no idea why their experience happened. The only explanation we have is 'grace' – and we have no real understanding of what grace is and why it comes to one person and not another.

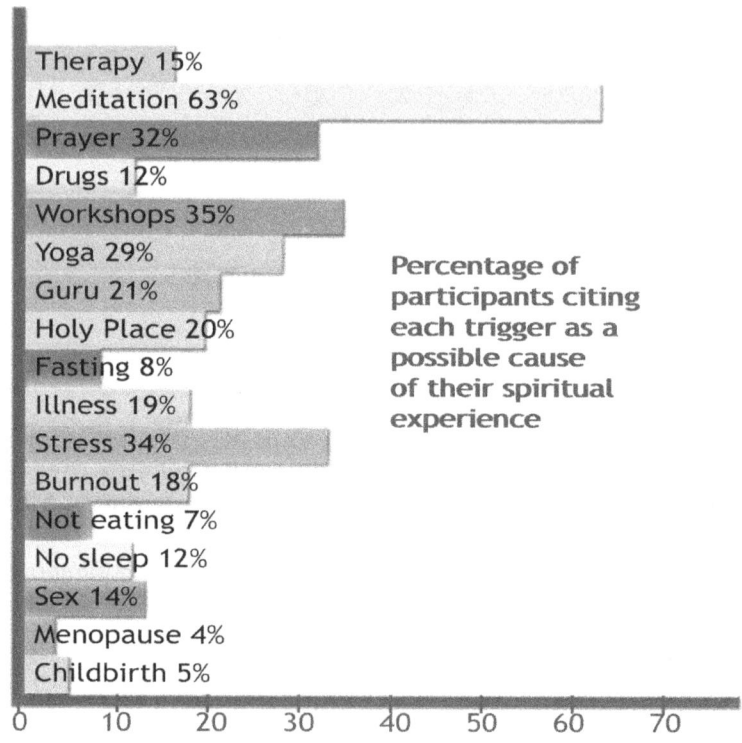

Percentage of participants citing each trigger as a possible cause of their spiritual experience

- Therapy 15%
- Meditation 63%
- Prayer 32%
- Drugs 12%
- Workshops 35%
- Yoga 29%
- Guru 21%
- Holy Place 20%
- Fasting 8%
- Illness 19%
- Stress 34%
- Burnout 18%
- Not eating 7%
- No sleep 12%
- Sex 14%
- Menopause 4%
- Childbirth 5%

30% of these people were engaged in spiritual practice prior to their *first* profound spiritual experience, and 17% described themselves as 'kind-of practicing.' They had many experiences since then. When asked what practice or activities most initiated their experiences, nearly two-thirds of them cited meditation, but many ordinary life situations were also cited, like stress, burnout and illness. Perhaps we can emotionally 'bottom out' into a shift in consciousness and arrive at much the same internal place as someone engaged in dedicated spiritual practice since both dissolve or crack the fabric of the mind, allowing light and new possibilities to flood in.

Since many non-practicing people's transformation process was initiated by an awakening of some sort, and very little is said about these unusual states of consciousness, we'll take a look at the main types to put some words to them.

What are these experiences?

The deeper our experience is, the more it eludes words. The words we write are a limited approximation. Some of the study participants ticked one or two boxes, others ticked almost every one. Added up, it looks like this:

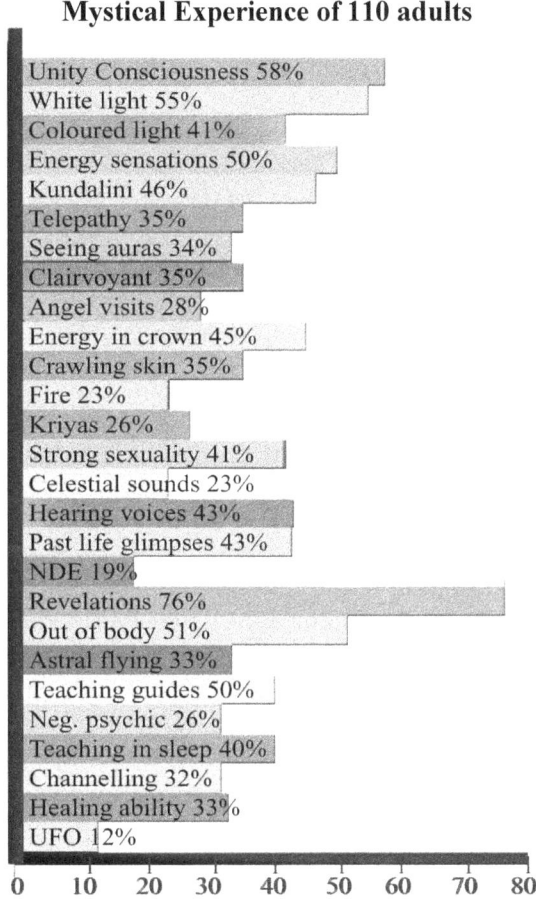

Mystical Experience of 110 adults

- Unity Consciousness 58%
- White light 55%
- Coloured light 41%
- Energy sensations 50%
- Kundalini 46%
- Telepathy 35%
- Seeing auras 34%
- Clairvoyant 35%
- Angel visits 28%
- Energy in crown 45%
- Crawling skin 35%
- Fire 23%
- Kriyas 26%
- Strong sexuality 41%
- Celestial sounds 23%
- Hearing voices 43%
- Past life glimpses 43%
- NDE 19%
- Revelations 76%
- Out of body 51%
- Astral flying 33%
- Teaching guides 50%
- Neg. psychic 26%
- Teaching in sleep 40%
- Channelling 32%
- Healing ability 33%
- UFO 12%

You may have had many of these experiences, but in case you are wondering what some of them are, these are quick descriptions.

Unity consciousness: When our sense of separateness dissolves and we feel merged with everything

White light: you see bright white light surrounding you or within you, or everything merges into white light

Coloured light: We see coloured light surrounding us or within us, or everything merges into coloured light.

Energy sensations: These include movements of energy, call it prana, chi or life force, in the body, electricity-like sensations, internal pressure,

a sense that energy is shifting, off kilter, or moving about.

Kundalini: A borrowed Sanskrit word that refers to a latent energy coiled up at the base of the spine that when aroused, rises up the spine, activating and clearing energy centres (chakras) as it goes.

Energy pouring in the crown: This in-pouring may be perceived as white light streaming into the head, or can feel like a pressure pushing in, sometimes creating heat or a sense of melting in the skull at the apex of the head.

Physical experiences:
Some experiences can accompany transformation or spiritual experiences that feel strange.

Crawling skin: Tickling or tingling in the skin.

Kundalini fire: Internal heat or pressure, often in specific areas of the body such as along the spine. Can be intense.

Kriyas: Involuntary movements – the life force or some awareness within us, moves our body without us intending to, often moving into yoga positions or hand positions we later discover are sacred in some spiritual traditions.

Paranormal perceptions:

Telepathy: The ability to know other's thoughts as they think them.

Seeing auras: The ability to see the energy field that surrounds all living things.

Clairvoyant: The ability to see things that our physical eyes cannot see, such as events in distant places, spirits and astral entities, or medical conditions.

Angel visits: Culturally we are not trained to listen to our guides, so the clear messages or loving presence of our angel guides can be a surprise for some people. We can recognize guides by their loving, wise, supportive presence.

Teachings from guides: Receiving guidance and information by listening to spirit guides.

Hearing celestial sounds: Commonly heard are choirs, flutes, bagpipes, the sound of running water, a cosmic hum, and other beautiful sounds that are not coming from the world around us.

Hearing voices: When hearing voices of people who aren't physically present, either part of us is imagining this, or we are receiving guidance (or misguidance) from non-incarnated beings.

Past life glimpses: When we experience situations through dreams, altered states and visions that are not in our current time yet we have a strong sense that the person in that other time is us, we call this a past life experience.

Near death experience (NDE): Occasionally people physically die for a short period of time and are medically resuscitated. In the mean time, they may go through a tunnel, enter spirit worlds, or are met by angels, and may temporarily experience what we would call 'enlightenment.' They are often told that their time has not yet come and they should return to life on earth.

Revelations: Insights into life and the universe.

Out of body experience: Our awareness, usually located in our physical bodies, re-locates, for example, to the ceiling of the room looking down at our own body, or flying over rooftops.

Astral flying: A conscious form of out-of-body experience.

Negative psychic experiences: Just because a being is not incarnated does not mean it is wise, loving or well-meaning. Some astral entities are mischievous. Some are even harmful, attaching to us, draining our energy, creating fear, or giving bad guidance.

Sleep teachings: We may receive inspired teachings in our sleep, often forgotten on awakening. Unlike dreaming, these lucid altered states of consciousness flow in a similar way to being awake, but the plane we're on isn't physical.

Channelling: Guidance, prophetic insight and information coming through a person, who is often in a trance, who allows this 'downloading'.

Healing ability: We are all capable of healing others, but only a few fully access this ability. During spiritual awakening, sometimes the life force moves through us, opening up our hands and other abilities that enable healing.

UFO or alien encounters: Numerous accounts of alien abduction exist. Following these abductions, people are invariably more spiritually connected and have a deeper caring for the environment.

We'll now look at some of these experiences and phenomena in more depth.

Kundalini

In India, spiritual practitioners talk of a coiled energy, called Kundalini, that lies dormant at the base of the spine.

When this kundalini energy fully awakens, it rises up the spine through a central channel, called in Sanskrit the sushumna, awakening and clearing each chakra as it goes. It can feel like gentle warmth, or a powerful surge of electricity. Energy completing its ascent up the spine is called a 'kundalini awakening. This is generally a powerful and ecstatic spiritual experience. If the energy makes it right through the crown you can have a white light experience or feel temporarily enlightened. The kundalini does not always move all the way through to the top of the head. It may stop at any point along the way. It can rise to the solar plexus, increasing personal power and confidence, continue to the heart, increasing deep love and compassion, open up the third eye to intuitive perceptions, or flow up into the head, activating the pituitary and pineal glands.

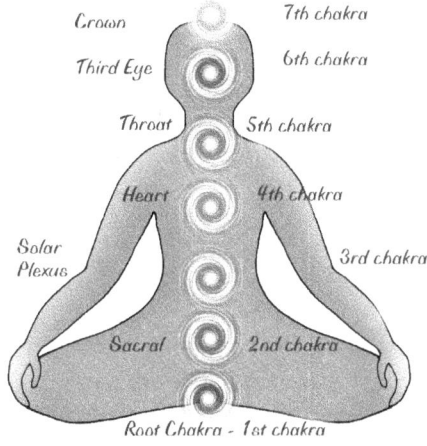

Some spiritual practitioners believe that this rising kundalini energy is essential, or pre-requisite, to spiritual awakening, yet in my pilot study, only half the people who reported experiencing unity consciousness also experienced kundalini energy rising up their spine. While a kundalini awakening experience is relatively common, it is not the only way people experience unity consciousness.

Research snippet
51 of the 110 participants in the PSE study[4] (Profound Spiritual Experience study) reported experiencing energy rising up their spines. Of these:
16 of the 51 participants were engaged in spiritual practice at the time.
13 of the 51 participants were 'kind of' practicing at the time.
22 of the 51 participants were not engaged in spiritual practice.

This pilot study draws from a more spiritually oriented sector of the population than average. It is very likely that more kundalini awakenings happen unexpectedly than due to spiritual practice in the population as a whole.

Certain kinds of yoga, such as kundalini yoga, pranayama, some meditation practices and chakra-opening techniques are practiced specifically to raise the kundalini.

Kundalini can feel like a jolt of high-powered electricity up the spine (*"it felt like 4,000 volts..."*),[2] or a slow, ascending warmth or tingling. Some people experience the kundalini energizing each chakra as it moves up the spine. Some say the energy spirals up, and for others it feels like the energy whooshes straight through. It may feel somewhat like an orgasm. We may feel hot afterwards, very spaced out, very sexual, or totally serene, depending on our nature.

Energy pouring in the crown - 'sahasraric' energy

Sahasrara energy is an intense in-pouring of energy though the crown of the head, which may feel like white light pouring in. It is possible that this is to do with receiving new information or frequencies from consciousness.

> *White light floods in all night. The crown of my head is hot, and I feel stretched to the limit by something I can't see, taste or touch. I used to kind-of dread this happening until I heard it was to do with new information downloading. Since then I started valuing the flow of insight I have afterwards – revelations that write themselves in an effortless stream on paper, all kinds of creativity, innovative steps forward in my thinking and understanding.* [1]

The attempt of all spiritual energy movements is to open us to more awareness and clear blockages. Of course, when the energy is trying to work its way through a block it doesn't always feel comfortable – it can sometimes even feel painful. The benefit is that in the long run, the light seems to do good work. Our thinking is upgraded through these 'down-loads.' Our energy fields, meridians and chakras are increasingly clear, open and able to conduct more energy.

Out of body experiences

This occurs when consciousness leaves the body, sometimes hovering above the body, moving effortlessly to distant places around the world, or going to different planes of consciousness. The events perceived track logically. They feel real and lucid, as if they are actually happening, rather than the disparate events that come during dreams, or the familiar modes of our thinking and imagination. When flying, we see everything vividly. We look down on rooftops and treetops. Some people have checked what they have seen, for example when astrally visiting a friend's living room, and found that they were seeing what was actually there at the time.

We astrally fly freely without gravity having any effect. It is wonderful to sense this freedom of your spirit to move outside the bounds of this limited, gravity-bound body.

It's an odd thing to find yourself looking down at your body from the ceiling. You know for sure afterwards that you are not just your physical body! It is a social habit to think we are so finitely located. A wide spectrum of consciousness and spirit inhabits our bodies. Some people have reported travelling in a light body to distant places, flying over cities and landscapes on the way, and finding that what they see at distant locations is quite accurate.

One way to know when we have 'flown' into astral planes is by the clear bright colours we see, which may remind us of the vivid, pretty colours used in some cartoon animations. Perhaps some animations have been inspired by the artist's flights to astral planes!

The weird thing is not that we are able to leave our body or astral travel, but that we have become so focused and condensed in our physical bodies that leaving our locations so rarely happens. Our spirit essence is not confined to this physical body!

Seeing lights, hearing sounds

In certain states of consciousness, you can find your awareness filled with beautiful lights or sounds. White, golden, or blue light is especially common. Seeing a golden egg at the third-eye, an expanse of deep blue or bright blue light emanating from a central core are all common experiences.

In some traditions (Surat Shabd Yoga, Eckankar) these colours and sounds and the planes of consciousness or frequencies on which they resonate, are quite well documented. In these traditions such experiences are cherished as signs of attainment. In other traditions, for instance, many Buddhist lineages, practitioners are encouraged not to make much of these passing experiences, or even to disregard them, since all formed experiences fall within the realm of the ego-mind. In these traditions, light and sound experiences are considered distractions from the final goal of union with the essence of spirit, especially when practitioners become attached to the experience(s).

Another kind of experience is to perceive, with open eyes, solid objects to be composed of light. Sometimes our vision changes, allowing objects which previously seemed so solid, to be perceived as fields of light or energy, called auras. Auras (energy fields) may also be seen around people, plants and animals.

When out of the ordinary experiences happen, it is not unusual to wonder if one is going crazy.

> *I had completely unravelled and had no idea why. I no longer had a grasp of reality. My mind was so empty and unstructured I couldn't hold simple directions in my mind.* [2]

It is not crazy to be temporarily in an altered state of consciousness and see and hear unusual things - it happens to many people. It is a bit crazy to go around telling everyone what has happened, or sit in meditation hoping for a 'far-out' experience – especially since we tend to imagine what we want to see. It doesn't serve us to cling to the experiences and hanker for them again and again; we end up living in the past. These openings come and go with their own logic, and our wishing for them puts us in the very desire-based ego-mind, which closes off our vision.

If you start to mix up the planes of consciousness, believing that this solid physical plane works the same way as the subtle energy or light planes, some people may think you are crazy. There is a view of reality that people (albeit unconsciously) agree to share. If you see things in another way, that's kind of OK for open-minded people if you can still relate to the shared, agreed-on reality. People who can't operate in the agreed reality are outside society's mental box and so deemed 'crazy' (unless of course they are intelligent or charismatic enough to convince others of their way of seeing, in which case they are thought to be geniuses or prophets.)

Hearing Sounds

The most commonly experienced sound is a fine, high-pitched resonance. Some say it is the cosmic sound of the universe, others say it is the sound of the tiny bones in the ear vibrating or the sound of blood cells brushing against the ear drum. Many people find that the resonance becomes louder during meditation.

Other commonly heard sounds include the flute, the hum of bees, running water, thunder, bag pipes and a choir of singers.

> *The night sky was filled with a choir of angels singing, wrapping me in their love* [2]

Past lives

Experiencing past lives is quite common. These flashbacks could come as visions during meditation, lucid dreams or raw, emotional experience as if the memory was currently being lived. These experiences can be quite useful, often offering explanations or even resolutions, for unusual relationships, connections between people, fears that have no logical explanation, and unexplained talents. Often seeing the context of the past experience is enough to clear current issues - you see that the situation belongs entirely in another time and so there is nothing to fear in the present.

> *I had this inexplicable fear of speaking about anything spiritual or unusual. I started wondering why. Shortly after, images started coming up during meditation. I saw myself being tortured by the Inquisition, and then thrown on a fire. I could smell my burning flesh. It was horrifying. At other time I saw myself jailed, flogged to death for being a witch, ostracized and cast out by my whole village for giving a sick person a herbal medicine. I was left in no doubt as to where my fears came from. With relief I realized these incidents don't belong in this time. With the help of an intuitive, I put these experiences in the past and gradually found a new sense of safety in this current time. Speaking of spiritual and unusual things is OK now.* [1]

Near Death Experience (NDE)

Occasionally, perhaps due to an accident or surgery, people die for a few moments and are resuscitated or medically brought back to life. These people go through the first stage of a normal death process – they detach from their physical bodies, their lives flash before them, they enter into a state of consciousness where they feel deep release, expansion, peace, and a love so awesome that the experience cannot be conveyed by words afterwards. Often they pass through a tunnel or a transitional realm, moving towards a light, and through the light into deeper realms of existence. Stripped of their ordinary programmed minds, their life purpose, the meaning of life in general, and many other deep truths are revealed to them. Much of this is remembered after resuscitation. Some lives have been radically transformed by these deeper perceptions. People have a powerful conviction of the reality of this NDE experience, a clearer vision about their life purpose, and a loss of fear of death.

Occasionally people visit realms where non-incarnated beings are obsessed with desire or anger, and much wisdom about human nature is retained after the NDE experience.

Near death experiences and spiritual openings share many similarities, both in the transcendent experience and in the after effects. Some people change their attitudes and have to learn to manage friends and family who expect them to be as they used to be. There may be difficulty carrying on previous life patterns and roles after a deep awakening. These people often feel alone, and have no one who understands them or shares a similar experience.

According to Gallup Polls, about approximately eight million Americans claim to have had a near-death experience (Mauro, 1992),[5] a third of whom also had deeply transformative experiences.

Alien encounters and UFO sightings

> In September 1996, the Gallup Poll Organisation asked 1000 representative U.S. citizens, "Have you, yourself, ever seen anything you thought was a UFO?" 12% answered "yes."

Researchers have studied over 1700 cases of alien encounters. These experiences are included in this section because of the powerfully transformative effect of being abducted by aliens. After return from the spacecraft, the abductees find they are more deeply concerned for the well being of the planet, and have much more sensitivity and concern for the environment and human life. Their lives change in some of the same kinds of ways as the people who have had spiritual openings. Even though people are usually afraid at the time, the abductions are often spiritually transformative in the long term.

Many people claim to have seen UFOs or aliens. Some believe that some kinds of aliens are not as physical as we are, but are light bodies, which is why people have reported seeing them move through walls, so it has been speculated that these kinds of aliens are seen only by people who are intuitive or psychic to some degree.

Although people who claim alien abduction occasionally have some mental illness, clinical tests show that as a group, the psychological health of people who report alien abduction does not differ significantly from the population as a whole.[6]

Do aliens exist? When Whitley Strieber published "Communion," a book about his abduction experience, he received over 250,000 letters from people who wrote about their own similar experiences.[7]

Rumour has it that U.S. military pilots must sign a form pledging their commitment to not divulge to the public if they see a UFO. If true, what does that say?

Negative states

Occasionally people enter fearful or hellish states where they experience darkness, beings that mock them, demons, evil beings, or fire and brimstone. Negative and hellish realms seem to be created from the fears, desires, fixations and unresolved trauma people experience in day-to-day life. The hatred and fear becomes larger than life since these planes are not limited by the constraints of physical matter. However, in many of these cases, when God's name is called, angels are contacted, prayers said, or there is conscious, firm rejection of the darkness, the fearful scene radically changed.

This client drawing is about breathing in sunlight, breathing out the darkness. She describes the sentiment of this drawing:

> *Taking in, accepting, the good -- kindness, tolerance love -- repels the bad --evil, hatred, fearfulness, pain, morbid shame; clearing out the bad makes room for the good.* [2]

How often do distressing or negative experiences happen? Most research has focused on near-death experiences. George Gallup's study of NDE survivors found about 1% reported hellish experiences, although some others experienced distressing experiences.[8] P.M.H. Atwater found 105 out of 700 had 'painful' experiences (around 14 %.)[9] She commented that it tended to be people with suppressed guilt, fears and angers and people who believe in punishment after death, who had these experiences.

Revelations

We have been brought up to see life a certain way. When our awareness expands, we see things differently. Our expanded awareness allows us to see life from other points of view. In deeper states of consciousness, we see from outside the usual limitations of time, space and duality. We come to realize that we are all love, that we have a common essence, and that we are all integrally connected as one being.

> *I was sitting at work one morning, in the most boring temp job I have ever done, typing a pile of invoices on an electric typewriter. At a certain point there was a power cut, so we had to stop for a while until the power came back As my mind was idly meandering around this, I looked at my typewriter, with its grey plastic casing, and all of a sudden, out of nowhere, I suddenly 'saw' it for the very first time. It blew my tiny mind, as if I suddenly 'saw' reality. I 'saw' the very fact of existence, as if arising out of the matrix of nothingness. It was the most utterly incredible, miraculous, ecstatically exciting experience ever. I looked at the other people in the office, and they blew my mind. The very fact of their being, their existing, was utterly incredible.*

> *As I watched one girl pottering about the office, I had this sudden urge to rush over, shake her and shout 'Don't you see, it's incredible, it's a miracle!!' I could hardly contain myself with this intense, outrageous energy and ecstasy rushing through my body.*[2]

Powerful and sudden insights can radically alter our way of seeing. In the moment of seeing, the truth of the revelation is so clear and apparent we cannot imagine seeing any other way. Later - even moments later - our ordinary thinking can step back in and say, oh, come on, if I remember yesterday making an appointment for tomorrow, time must exist. In this way we discount our own perceptions, quickly reverting to the usual way of perceiving the world.

> *Men occasionally stumble over the truth, but most of them pick themselves up and hurry off as if nothing had happened.*
> Albert Einstein

It is especially easy to discount or invalidate our perception when we see all around us people whose perceptions are different from ours, thinking in the same way. It's a stretch to think that they are not necessarily right because they're the majority. It takes an astute mind to keep our revelations alive and awake and integrated within us, yet be aware of and responsive to the way of thinking of the society in which we live.

Awakening, Unity Consciousness

The deeper into consciousness we go, the more unformed and abstract it appears. These kinds of experiences are very profound; there is not much that can be verbalized about them.

If you get this rather awesome sense that nothing has really ever come into existence or become anything ever in all time and space, you're right. You can hold this deep truth in the heart of your being and still function quite fine on the physical plane. There's a smile inside – a sense of humour about life and its funny ways.

We see that what is meant, in essence, when we say 'I.' is universal Beingness. This perspective is our fundamental truth, but we are usually too entrenched in duality, too focused on our individual selves to notice it. Someone who remains permanently in a state of unveiled awareness is called an enlightened being. It is a rare and special thing.

Oneness feels expansive, light, and loving – unless you are the kind of person who gets nervous about stepping into the unknown, or are afraid of losing your sense of individual self. If you are afraid of losing yourself, don't worry - you won't disappear forever. The ego is tremendously resilient, like a rubber duck that bobs back however deep you dunk it. Even if you temporarily lose your ego it will likely be back in force all too soon (alas!) If this reforming didn't take place so automatically, there would be a lot more Buddhas walking our streets.

If you feel anxious, apprehensive or afraid of this openness, reassure yourself that you are only opening to Yourself – to your higher Self. It is all You. If these words don't mean much to you, read some of the ancient scriptures that speak of this unity, such as Ashtavakra Gita. In time, the mind (which is usually the part of us creating the resistance) gets used to the openness. We gradually get used to dissolving in eternity, and used to somewhat reforming afterwards.

This higher self is imbued with fulfilment. It is for these reasons that sages and saints throughout time have maintained that this state of consciousness immediately releases us from unnecessary mental and emotional suffering. When integrated, this awareness is the basis for living in true love, compassion and wisdom.

It is easier to transiently touch deep states of consciousness than to maintain them. Few step into the light and stay there right away. Most people drift back into a state of consciousness more like they used to be. So once we connect with our inner being, the art is to remain connected. Part of this is about aligning the rest of our life with our inner awareness so our outer life resonates with our inner awareness. This requires long-term, dedicated attention to both inner awareness and the details of our character.

The openness can be lost in a moment by thinking, "Wow – look at this!" The ego steps in, and recreates the separation. The ego would like to claim, either subtly or overtly, that this realization is its own special insight, that it knows, that it is God. The expression of our usual ego nature is not congruent with oneness.

Changing your spiritual practice

If you were engaged in spiritual practice (e.g. meditation, prayer, yoga, chanting or qigong) prior to a shift in consciousness, you may need to change the way you practice. Simply put, you are now in a different place, and your practice needs to change accordingly.

You particularly need to review your practice if you are the kind who practices diligently, or follows laid-out teachings and precepts designed to open consciousness. The discipline that got you here – such as getting yourself up early enough to do your morning practice, staying on your meditation seat for a prescribed amount of time, using effort to transcend your individual nature or remain on a specific diet – may not necessarily be the best thing for you now. It is important to constantly tune in and check in with your own awareness, especially if you are in a spiritual group that upholds particular ideals and practices.

Through disciplined practice we can train our minds, purify and strengthen our bodies, balance our energy fields, and clear past emotions. Grace opens us beyond where our own efforts can reach. Once open, `you need to align with your openness. This requires ongoing, intuitive, gentle inner listening. It means going with your inner sense, rather than going with what you think or have learned to do. It means putting aside your striving – when you're at a mountain peak, why keep trying to climb?

Be sensitive. Listen. No one can do this for you. You are starting to step beyond mass teachings into establishing an autonomous inner centre of wisdom, and your own direct access to truth. Disciplined practice can help, and can also obstruct your process.

If the openness fades such that you feel you are in an 'ordinary' state of consciousness again, you may feel a need to resume your previous disciplined or precept-oriented practice to again open to the direct experience of light. The great paths, teachings of masters, and scriptures are there to bring you to a place of direct inner connection. When this connection is experienced, your highest awareness is a profound teacher.

Contrary to the implications of some New Age and spiritual ads, 'MysticalExperience' is not for sale, and cannot be bought. You can go to your expensive "Intensivo-Kundalini-Shaktipath-Pranayama" yoga retreat, you can travel to the Himalayas and contemplate deeply with a shaved head for years, but you may or may not get the advertised enlightenment. If we could just go out and buy a mystical experience, the small print at the bottom of the 'MysticalExperience' package might say,

---

Mystical Experience Package Money-back guarantee:

The contents of this package are guaranteed to change your life whether you want it or not. This package may come to you even if you didn't purchase this package or have any intent to do so. Guarantee applies even if you have no interest in the product. N.B. This product is not a virus.

WARNING! May cause intense awe, bliss, anxiety or fear depending on previously loaded software and available RAM.

May well cause a spaced out feeling, sensitivity, and psychic ability.

DISCLAIMER   The contents of this package are unlikely to be understood by you or anyone you know.

SMALL PRINT: We are not responsible for your life, thinking and beliefs, whether positive or not. Consult your doctor before using the contents of this package, but know that there is little you or your doctor can do to stop things being as they Are. The content of this package is more powerful than you are. Learn to live with it.

N.B. You won't get time to read the small print

Frequently asked questions

Are spiritual experiences necessarily transformative?
Most people are deeply changed by their experiences, but some people are less changed, or even unchanged. You can open to a deep experience, or deep meditation state, and remain much the same in your thinking and personality.

> *Spirituality was for me an escape from my suffering. I would have benefited from psychotherapy before going into sadhana. Although these experiences resulting from intense sadhana were transformative of my consciousness, they did not heal my traumas and emotional wounds, or the neurosis of my personality.[2]*

> *"If there is one thing I've learned, it is that "experiences" only serve to show that reductionistic scientism is incorrect. If they have any other purpose (and they well may), I don't know what that is, and I don't care to speculate. My profound intuition is that life itself - all the events of our lives, especially the small and ordinary - is ultimately the best, most growth-enhancing "experience".   PhilipSt Romain [10]*

Does an experience make you a better person?
How should we define 'better'? Someone everyone likes more? Someone who is more productive?
   A deep spiritual union can temporarily give us a clearer sense of who we are in truth, a glimpse into deeper states of consciousness, life and the universe. How that insight is integrated depends entirely on the person because we have free will. We can choose to commit to love and light, or to personal power and furthering our self-interest.

Does an experience make you a happier or more blissful person?
The inner connection, when it is current and directly experienced, comes with an inner sense of bliss and perfection. Until the inner openness is established constantly at a sufficient depth, we may not necessarily feel happier about life. Invariably there is an increased sensitivity to all the idiocy and crassness in this world, and to our own inadequacies that was not present prior to the experience.

Does an experience make you a wiser person?
If you have the kind of mind that can encompass and integrate deep states of existence with every-day life, and can remain centred and detached yet keep an open compassionate heart, you will likely grow quickly in wisdom. If you can put words to all this, you can share this wisdom with others – again, not a given. Will be you be wiser about your own nature, human nature, or the ways of the world? It depends on your power to observe and be present with these areas of life.

Does an experience make you enlightened?
After a brief shift in consciousness, we have a deeper insight than we had before. This is a great gift. Until our awareness is permanently open, we are not enlightened; we are people who have had a glimpse of enlightenment or a subtle realm of consciousness or light. There are many wonders of having these profound experiences, and there also are some pitfalls.

Are openings a good thing?
Openings give you wonderful glimpses into your inner nature. They can provide brief glimpses of enlightenment, and a clearer idea of where you are heading. This is a great thing when your mind is open to the expanse of your inner being. Some people are totally freaked out by such glimpses and become anxious, while many others are elated, inspired, and radically transformed through the glimpse. So the question: are openings a good thing is a subjective one – are they something your psyche is open to? Do you welcome the New?

Openings can speed up your transformation, 'fast-tracking,' whether you choose to or not. This is a bonus when you welcome the expansion; it's a challenge when you are already more open than you can currently handle or when you don't welcome the purification that inevitably follows as your psyche, emotions and energy fields catch up with your new perceptions. With good information, inner listening, and a willingness to allow yourself to move into your highest potential, openings are generally a gift.

Why don't these mystical insights happen more often?
These realms of consciousness are within everyone, and are equally available to everyone. The reason they usually remain concealed from our vision is because we tend to be so very focused on and preoccupied with the material world that all the subtle realities are

screened out. When your focus changes, the veil is removed and the vision opens, or re-opens, to depths of existence that you had largely forgotten. Why the veil parts at some times rather than others, quite out of the blue, is a mystery. People can meditate for years without ever having a mystical experience, and someone with no spiritual or religious interest can enter into a profound experience while walking the dog.

We have the ability to balance, purify and centre our body-minds so we can receive the light, knowledge and energy well, but we cannot actually open ourselves beyond a certain point. We can only say that it is grace that is operating – the hand of God, unseen, and unfathomable.

It is not at all important whether you have experienced anything unusual or not. You can have a very profound awareness of your spirit without any unusual experiences occurring. Your ability to listen and tune into your innermost heart is more important than exotic moments. The descriptions of unusual experiences are included so that those who have had them can recognize them, name them, put them in context and know that they are very much part of human experience (i.e. 'normal, not 'crazy'!).

Are mystical experiences dangerous?
In essence, openings are doorways to your true nature. Are they dangerous? Well, is your true nature dangerous? Our mind's resistance, fear of the unknown and wish to stay in control makes openness feel dangerous – it is dangerous to the ego-mind's control machinery.

Is this purification a problem?
The majority of people can cope with the purification, especially when they understand they are in a transformative process with positive end results. In the long term, people feel decidedly all the better for the clearing they have done.

When the psychological walls that keep past traumas out of our conscious minds melt, which often occurs after a deep opening, the traumas tend to flood into our conscious minds. This is great if you feel up to it – if you are ready to clear your past so you can move on. Even a small amount of this kind of clearing can feel like a problem when we don't understand what it is, what it is for, when we resist, or when we think it is happening at the wrong time ("why now?!").

Do I need the supervision of an enlightened master?
Yoga books and scriptures invariably state that meditation and yoga should only be practiced under the supervision of an enlightened master. It sounds good in print, but let's face it – how many people actually have a fully enlightened master? There are nowhere near enough to go round! Those who do have a master rarely have someone who is accessible near their hometown, or even on the end of a phone line. Well-known enlightened masters are way too internationally busy to give ongoing personal supervision.

There is also another factor that people don't reckon on. Just because a master has amazing light, knowledge, or the ability to open us to deeper states of consciousness, it doesn't mean he or she necessarily knows how we will react to the openness, intense energies or ensuing purification. Many spiritual teachers simply do not know what guidance to give other than the teachings they have already given – which are often focused around how to open consciousness, not what to do when it does open.

A yoga intensive weekend or a ten-day silent meditation retreat, excessive yoga or breathing exercises, and other strong practices are quite likely to deeply open your consciousness – they are supposed to. These days, anyone can sign up for yoga and meditation classes, intensives and retreats, without prior preparation or purification. If you've got the bucks you can go. Guidance and support during the retreat varies, depending on the teacher or leader. Guidance and support after the retreat is often non-existent. You're on your own.

If you are on your own, feeling troubled or confused by your inner process, and are seeking guidance, make a practice of sitting for periods of time in receptive stillness, gently requesting your awareness to guide you. Be receptive to subtle answers, synchronicities and other indications. If receptive, you could ask your angels and spirit guides. If you cannot do this, (i.e. you sit receptively and nothing comes), one option is to find a **reputable** psychic who can channel this awareness for you. If you take this route, listen to the guidance offered you with 'an inner ear'. Rather than taking everything as fact, ask yourself, does this guidance have the ring of truth? Try the advice. Does it work? Does it feel right?

Keep listening, moment to moment. Moments change. Yesterday's advice doesn't necessarily apply to this moment.

Is my experience someone's fault?
It might appear that a certain practice, therapy session or life situation has triggered the opening, but if you think of the number of times these practices or sessions happen without an opening, there has to be some other ingredient(s) involved. Since there are millions of people receiving teachings or energy work and practicing kundalini-awakening techniques who have never experienced a powerful opening, clearly these awakenings do not have any reliable cause.

Is there anything I can do to prepare for an enlightenment experience?
Many people are not fully integrated in the body. They live in their heads or in the sky and don't have their feet on the ground. One good preparation is to work on your grounding – the balance and integration of your lower chakras and connection to the earth. This is especially important if you don't have a well-grounded type of makeup. Make grounding part of your daily routine or spiritual practice so that you can maintain good balance. If you are not well grounded, energy can build up in your body, spinning in your mind and emotions, making you feel oversensitive, vulnerable to picking up everyone's negativity and bad feelings, and not earthed enough to manifest your spiritual inspiration on this earth plane. When well grounded, the energy you open to flows through you more easily, and the emotions and vibrations surrounding you conduct through you, constantly releasing into the earth, so they don't build up inside you.

Yoga helps clear physical tension. Yoga was created to maximize the ability of the physical body and energy fields to receive light in a balanced way.

Does prior spiritual practice and belief in spirit have anything to do with the ability to handle an opening?
Those who are atheistic or disinterested in spiritual life may possibly be less prepared for the expanse of consciousness they open to, but even those who have read extensively and have a good understanding of higher realms of existence feel unprepared when these realms actually open. Nothing you can read or think is anything like the real experience.

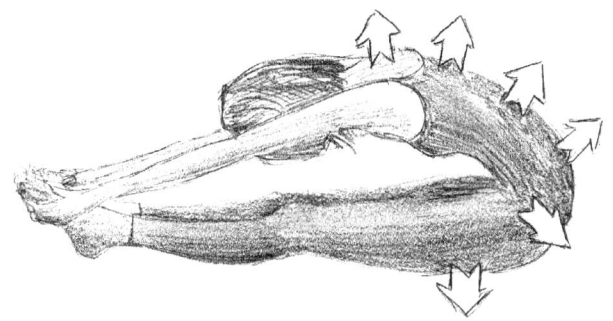

If you know you have past trauma which is likely to emerge, you might like to seek out a good therapist who can help you through when the time comes. If you feel your energy is out of balance, check the self-help sections on page 62.

Should I tell my friends of my experience?
If you have the right kinds of friends, it can be enriching to share your perceptions. There are a few cautions here that you may not initially suspect in your newfound wonder and enthusiasm after an amazing experience.

> *I found approaching 'just anyone' with these types of experiences, left me open to very negative reactions that somehow dirtied an incredible experience and made me feel they could put my very soul in jeopardy. I learned to be very discreet with whom I shared my stories. When I first realized that not everyone had these experiences, I searched for someone who could understand what was happening. I assumed religiously devoted people would definitely understand and in my early 20's I approached a devotee born again Pentecostal woman. I found out quickly that there is a big difference between religion and spirituality. Although I have met very spiritual religious people since then, that first open-soul discussion was a really BIG eye-opener.*[2]

There is something about putting words to these kinds of subtle experiences that make them something other than they are. The fluidity and openness gets can easily get consolidated into the linear words of language. However well you word it, the words are not the openness itself. Take care not to confuse the actual experience with the words you try to put to it, lest you put the experience in a box of conceptualisation.

Be observant of your motive for telling your experience – it can easily come over like a spiritual one-upmanship even when you don't intend it to, especially if you are enthusiastic. Many spiritual paths actively quell the telling of experiences.

You may well imagine that your friend will have the same awe and wonder you have, only to find a stony faced, fearful, suspicious reaction without empathy, resonance or understanding of what has happened and how you have been affected. Sometimes your Presence is the best way of bringing other people to a place of sensing this openness – letting the experience be quietly constant in your heart and awareness, allowing your actions to come directly from your awareness.

All this being said, if you come from a place of pure intent with your listener in mind, it could be a wonderful experience for your listener to have a taste of your experience.

I haven't had any mystical experiences. Is this a problem?
We don't need exotic experiences in order to grow. We can become kinder, happier, more open, loving and wise without ever having colourful mystical experiences. One the other hand, it's possible to have wildly exotic, deep experiences and still be neurotic, unkind and fearful. Exotic experiences are not ends in themselves. These experiences give wonderful glimpses into other realms and new possibilities, yet don't in themselves necessarily create more happiness, spiritual maturity or awareness. Moment to moment loving awareness, dedication and compassion are essential keys.

4

Our Reactions

Our feelings and overall impressions are generated not so much by *what* we experience, but *how we react* to these experiences.

The first part of this chapter focuses on our reactions to shifts in consciousness, and the second half focuses on our reactions to finding ourselves in profound transformation. In both cases, reactions range from 'love it!/wow!/gratitude!' to 'hate it/fear it/resist it.'

If you are experiencing only love, joy and bliss, you likely don't need this chapter, but you might be interested in reactions to openness from those around you on page 79. If you've had a weird negative experience, like finding yourself in some hellish state or experiencing negative psychic entities around you, try page 177. For strange physical phenomena like kundalini fire see 101 and kriyas, read page 98.

Responses to the mystical experience and altered states

The previous chapter took a fairly positive look at mystical experiences. This section is about feeling depressed, disquieted, or troubled by openings, shifts in consciousness and the transformational process happening within you.

However mystical the experience, or profound the transformation, the experience itself is usually transient. From then after, it's our usual ol' mind that does the thinking about it.

Take any incident, and watch each person's response. If a loud boom unexpectedly resounds through a crowded shopping mall, each person reacts differently.

Nervous Jane panics, looking up fervently, "Oh my God, the roof is about to fall on us!"

Procrastinating Fred strokes his chin beard and ponders, "Hmmm, now what could that be?"

Spaced-out Felicity anxiously wonders, "Did I just imagine that?" She searches people's faces for confirmation.

Eager-to-please Greg rushes around to see if anyone needs his help.

Elderly Maude mutters, "That's it – the war has started! I knew it … Quick! – Everyone! – get under a table!"

The boom was a high decibel, low frequency vibration with no inherent meaning. Everyone heard the same sound. The extraordinary diversity of reactions of each mind reflects each person's way of thinking, which in turn is coloured by their past experience. Jane once saw a roof fall in, crushing people under it. Maude had lived through the Second World War. Greg secretly wishes he were a superhero. Felicity's mother constantly reprimanded her, 'It's just your imagination." One boom, five overlays.

Mystical and transformative life experiences work the same way. What we are mainly dealing with is not the often fleeting experiences that happen, but the way our physical body, emotions, and thinking respond to them. Ten people can have the same experience, and each will respond differently.

Returning to the image of the crowded shopping mall, and replace the BOOM! with a satori, a sacred moment of pure enlightenment, what might we see?

Jane has tears flowing down her cheeks. "It's so beautiful!" she says. Then her joyous face tenses and she stutters, "Oh my God, I'm losing myself. I don't know who I am. Help me someone!"

Fred has a disquieting moment that he doesn't understand followed by a deep-rooted wave of nervousness. He bolts to a nearby booth, grabs a cup of coffee and downs it, in a furtive attempt to make the quietness go away.

Felicity breathes a sigh, "I feel so at home. This feels so right" She smiles warmly at the crowds of people around her that usually make her feel tight, fearful and claustrophobic. "Why am I always so afraid of people?" she wonders, "They are all light!"

Greg throws his arms wide and announces loudly, "Everyone! Listen! You must follow me. I know the way! I ... am the MESSIAH!"

Maude is silent. She finds herself contentedly reminiscing about ambling through a sunny meadow of flowers when she was 4 years old, which somehow felt just like this....

Much of what we experience during spiritual awakening and profound personal transformation is due to our reactions to this process. Our sense of difficulty is largely fuelled by these reactions.

When our 110 study participants were asked how they felt about their spiritual experiences, we find a mixed bag. As you can see in this chart, the most popular response was "mixed" – they literally ticked off a whole bunch of these reactions, wonderful, yes, weird, yes, pleasant, yes, fearful, yes...

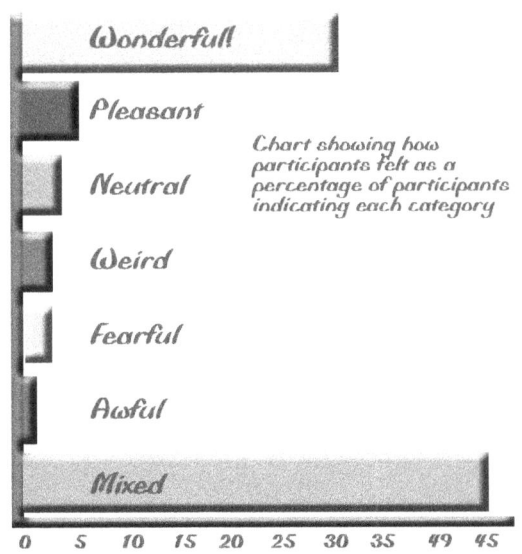

Chart showing how participants felt as a percentage of participants indicating each category

Percentage of participants indicating this response

New awareness stretches our minds out of their structured 'boxes.' It often pours in high frequency energy, opens our hearts, and brings up memories to help clear out fears and lingering memories. All of this is good in the long run, but since we aren't used to it, we may want to close up to avoid painful memories, rather than face them to clear them. Also, we desperately don't want to be different from those around us, so we try to 'normalize' rather than openly greet new possibilities. Fear is the main power behind these responses. These reactions have little to do with the new state of consciousness or the self-actualisation we would prefer to attain.

Responding to energy

So, what do we do with these energies, the internal clearing, and the different states that are happening? Later on we'll look at spiritual emergency, when the experience or transformation becomes overwhelming and help is needed. The next chapter looks at weird energy sensations, and chapter 7 looks at internal clearing – the part to which we often have most resistance. Here we'll explore our basic reaction to the fact that something different is happening, something that we may or may not be comfortable with. In this chapter, I am assuming that what is happening is kind-of manageable. We'll run through our major responses, first to unusual states of consciousness, then to aspects of purification.

Mystical Experience
Reactions range from:

I always knew I was special – I'm the Messiah!
Wow – something great has unfolded!
I am present with what is.
This is OK...I think...
I don't know what this is
I don't trust this, it's weird
I hate what is happening – it should go away
There's something awfully wrong with me that this happened!!

What we see is a continuum from the heightened ego through excitement, tranquillity, confusion, distrust, resistance to self-condemnation. Self-condemnation is the ego-opposite of feeling very special, both being self-focused responses. Most of these responses are so full of reaction that the state itself is covered over.

I always knew I was special - I'm the Messiah!
In a certain way, we can say that everyone is special, everyone is God/Allah/Buddha inside. Can we live this awareness, breathe it, and be love in each moment? That is what counts.

> *I began to always feel that I was preparing for an ultimate display of power & vulnerability and it was going to change the world in one all-inspiring moment. I was sure that I was going to change the world. Was it the ability to love? I had this new power and needed to know what to do with it. Sometimes I thought I could transform into the new "Jesus" or maybe I can become the new world leader. (Talk about a GOD complex) I thought that I would be the most perfect (I was sure other candidates around the world would be desperate for this job so I wasn't sure I would have the job) tour guide for aliens visiting earth because I had this brand new perspective.*[2]

Even subtle version of the Messiah complex may send people's eyes rolling, leaving us feeling misunderstood, like the world is pooping on our enlightenment. But what is maybe more difficult still is that some people buy the claim. "Yeah, you're *really* special, I want you to be my Spiritual Master." Until enlightenment is fully established, and plentiful wisdom and self-observation is cultivated with it, what goes invariably comes down.

I have actually met five people who felt they were reincarnations of the Messiah. Three of them lived in the same town, a town that was predominantly Buddhist – go figure! Messiahs aside, I have met scores of people who feel spiritually special to the point that they feel they should be looked after or served, in contrast to the Taoist adage, "after enlightenment, chop wood, carry water."

Wow - something great has unfolded!
True – it has. Value it without getting too excited about it. Breathe this new energy into every cell in your body – right down to your feet. Allow your mind to be oriented into a more positive and loving way of perceiving. Stand strongly, but not necessarily loudly, by your perception. Become the light and love.

I am present with what is.
This is the least reactive state of mind – you are fully present with what life is unfolding in you. Acceptance. Trust in spirit. Trust in the process. No issue.

This is OK...I think...
Perhaps the energies and states of consciousness feel OK, but you're your mind isn't sure and is starting to doubt. Focus on love, light, and your most positive conclusion. Our minds can swing both ways – into doubt and fear, and into optimism and self-actualisation. You can choose which. Whatever you attend, your mind becomes, so choose wisely. Replace negative thoughts with their positive opposites. Return your mind, again and again, moment after moment, to light, love and optimism, and light will become your reality – if you choose it.

I don't trust this, it's weird
Ask yourself, if you your friends had been through something similar and talked about it frankly, if you'd seen documentaries on TV, and soap operas about what people go through inside, would you still feel weird?

Another question to ask yourself: if you bought a plane ticket to the most exotic place in the world you could imagine, and you stepped off the plane into a world that felt just the way your hometown does, would you be disappointed?

Isn't it amazing that something new is happening? Why not trust it – it feels a whole lot better than mistrusting. When you've finished the book you'll likely find this easier.

I hate what is happening - it should go away
Spend a little time inquiring, with loving curiosity, into your resistance. What are you resisting, and why? What do you wish for yourself? Could this process be in any way part of your long-term aspiration?

When we attend resistance and fear, the mind shapes itself to these forms. In the same way, if we guide our attention towards our spirit nature, love, and trust, our minds will become more clear and peaceful.

To the extent that we don't feel able to trust the process or when we don't feel like we chose the process (at least on some unconscious level), we may feel victimized by it, subjected to it.

> *There's something awfully wrong with me that this happened!*

The converse of messianic specialness is that you, (*you <u>alone</u>*), have been singled out for this weird process because there is something wrong with you (*you alone*). Ask yourself, 'is this really true?' Do you buy these egoic thoughts?

Negative self-preoccupation can contract you into a gloomy hole, and drag you into depression and stagnation. Rather than dissolving the ego and moving into new possibilities, we reinforce the ego, and contract. Observing our minds' patterns with self-acceptance and gentleness helps. When we become too self-focused, break the preoccupation by getting involved with others – volunteer, do team sport, party, get involved in a cause you feel passionate about helping.

Responding in a useful way brings us to our potential much more quickly than us getting in our own way. Altered states of consciousness and major internal clearing are big enough projects without our mental and emotional overlays clouding the picture.

> *Acceptance, love, trust and a simple, present mind works better than fear, distrust, expectations and mental analysis.*

Reacting to the purification processes

If you've opened to a deeper state of consciousness or are in a deep transformative process, theoretically, it should feel good, right? In practice, most of us alternate between loving peace and bliss, and anguish or resistance.

Ideally

Ideally, we are all totally open, balanced, grounded, fluidly adaptive to change, accepting, able to listen for inner guidance, and totally trusting our spirit essence. Ideally, when new energies open, we tune in, sense what is happening, and quietly make any changes needed in our lives. Ideally we monitor our physical, mental, emotional and energy fields, knowing when to receive energy work, do some yoga, or do qigong to rebalance. When past traumas resurface, ideally we are able to be with the intensity of the experience, allowing it to express itself for a few moments, and then able to let the pain and emotions go - forever. We then move on to a new fresh moments uncluttered by the past, stepping ever closer to our spirit light and self-actualisation, trusting our intuition and our spirit guidance. We are grateful for what we have learned through the experience.

Do you know anyone as ideal as this?!

It's worth aiming for these ideals, but practically speaking we have to accept that we all feel considerably more resistant, confused and non-accepting than is ideal. We don't just 'flow' in 'loving acceptance' – we resist, grump, moan, complain, and wish things were other than they are. We get in our own way. We think, "I want to be free, I want to be a vehicle for spirit light", but then we think, "I want my freedom to look a certain way, feel a certain way," and when reality doesn't match our expectations we think something is wrong.

It isn't particularly helpful to feel like we're a victim of life to blame life, or our transformative experience, or other people for getting in our way. Nor is it helpful to strive so very hard to make things go the way we want that we go against our very soul. Could it be that life is our teacher? Could it be that our friends, enemies, everyone we encounter are all our teachers; and our life situations are all there to help us understand ourselves better and deepen our awareness? Every moment is an opportunity to unfold new awareness.

When past memories surface, we can be present with what is coming up, or we can try to avoid seeing it, diverting our attention in any way. We can raid the fridge, phone a friend, surf the net, read... In the short term, it alleviates the immediate tension, but in the long term, we find ourselves perpetually on the run, unable to settle and simple Be in silence. How much better would you feel if through facing the memory and doing a little clearing process, that there would no longer be a past memory trying to call your attention to it? More on this on page 116.

What is transformation about?

Essentially, transformation is about moving from fear to love. Fear expresses through constriction, anxiety, closure, suffering, hoarding, stress and limitation. Love expresses through openness, freedom, caring, honesty, sharing, happiness, gratitude and unity. Love and fear are our two root feelings.

Fear ⇨⇨ Love
Closed ⇨⇨ Open
Denial ⇨⇨ Honesty
Fixity ⇨⇨ Fluidity
Judgment ⇨⇨ Acceptance
Suffering ⇨⇨ Happiness
Grudging ⇨⇨ Forgiveness
Blame ⇨⇨ Gratitude
Individual ⇨⇨ Universal

Why bother transforming?

Because we feel MUCH better afterwards. Freedom, love, acceptance and self-actualisation simply feel much better than limitation, fear, judgment and blockage. So what if while shifting to a new state of consciousness some 'stuff' is coming up. Let it come up and clear through. Like water moves down river, life flows. This doesn't mean we don't meet obstacles, but fluidity most easily dissolves them and moves us on. We remain free from whatever we cleared. Less personal baggage = more opportunity.

Contradictions

When unfamiliar perceptions, energies or states of consciousness unfold, part of us wants total, ecstatic union with the divine and part of us is afraid of this divine merging – afraid of losing ourselves. The loss of our usual sense of individuality, mind and personality is a joy for the spirit yet feels like a death to the ego.

After an unusual spiritual experience, part of us may feel kind-of enlightened, while another part thinks, "This is weird, I must be going crazy." We tell all the wrong people about what happened and how it makes us feel like we're losing our minds. We were hoping to ease our confusion by sharing, hoping to have someone tell us, "Hey, quit worrying. You're fine!" but instead we managed to create the very thing we were most afraid of. We sowed the seeds of fear in everyone around, now they are thinking we are indeed going crazy (which they weren't thinking before), and that that some day they might too (which they weren't thinking before). Everyone ends up in fear and resistance.

It's easy to be wise when we're not in the situation. "Stay close to your heart and trust spirit," the wise one says. True enough. In reality, this means breathing a lot, taking lots of pauses, stopping to reach behind the mind's reactions, and attentively listening for inner guidance. It means having the steadiness, conviction and strength of mind to counteract the ego's habituated gravitation towards contraction and clinging to the known. As a way of understanding this onslaught of fear and contraction, we may have to constantly remind ourselves that the ego-mind always wants to be in control, and will do anything to maintain its place as the ruler of our lives and firmly in the driver's seat. We may have to return again and again to an affirmation that reminds us to let go and trust – such as "Thy will be done, not mine."

To move swiftly and 'cleanly' through profound spiritual transformation and times of deep personal growth, it can be helpful to make a decision.

The 'mainstream' life we have grown up in is about earning money, owning lots of objects and property, saving money, and buying security in one form or another. The way we have been socialized, it doesn't really matter whether we evolve spiritually or not, or even if we are happy, healthy and fulfilled or not. Success, for many people, is having a prestigious job, a good-sized house in a good neighbourhood, a big car, nice clothes, and the latest electronic devices.

Now, whether you enjoy these things or are indifferent to them, if striving for the social ideal isn't compatible with your soul path, you may need to make some new choices.

Your values are what drive your life. What do you choose to have your life be about?

Some important questions for you are:
What is your main time/energy priority?
What values are most important to you in your life?
To what extent will you sacrifice your life direction, health, happiness and creative flow for, say, financial security, intellectual qualifications or fitting in with a relationship?

Pick up a pen, and clarify your direction.

Blaming God for changing your life
In some cases, the intensity of the transformation, inner experiences and purification temporarily breaks up someone's life. Do we react? You bet! Under this circumstance, we might feel ripped off, angry with God, life, the universe or oneself, and blame any identifiable causal circumstance. It is not always easy to adjust to losing your memory, not being able to think straight, read, plan, and being too sensitive to go places (which can happen temporarily during intense transformation).

> *"It's easy to live in the present when my memory is gone – it's all I've got!"*[2]

It's challenging to let go and trust a process that dissolves your usual mental clarity when cognitive dexterity, independence and being in control are so highly valued by mainstream society, especially if we were used to having a good clear, accurate mind before. We must accept that these things sometimes happen. Resistance only slows down the transformation and healing. It is helpful to value the process that you're in, even if you didn't plan it.

A little known quirk of life is that sometimes the mind needs to melt, undo, or even fall apart for a while so that it can rebuild in a more conducive way. We have no place for this in our society. We are supposed to be perfect, in control and on time, consistently, all of our lives.

If part of our process is a temporary lessening of mental ability, reach to welcome the more intuitive abilities coming in. If you had a good mind before, it will return – generally with more clarity and intuitive depth, a mind that is now more in the serve of spirit – but sometimes the process takes a while.

In the meantime, blaming, getting angry, feeling ripped off and other natural human reactions don't get us anywhere – except to cause us to feel bad. It works better to value the transformation process and its gifts. One gift of a change in mental ability is to shift us out of our reliance on the mind, and move us towards living more from the heart, intuition and emotional felt-sense (basically because this is what we're left with when the mind is out of the way). Losing one's usual mental acuity is excellent at showing us how identified we are with the mind and its abilities. The mind is a primary foundation of the ego-machinery. As our identification shifts or dissolves, we can be more centred in knowing ourselves as spirit-essence. What a gift!

Because our upbringing has instilled certain intellectual, material and social values, we don't place great value on personal growth, health happiness, and spiritual connectedness. Society celebrates the bachelor's graduate, honours the PhD degree, yet huge shifts in personal development go without acknowledgement, let alone ceremony, and sometimes are negatively valued.

Society congratulates someone entering medical school even though we know this means 7 years away from home, long hours studying in libraries, anguish over exams, followed by internships that wreck natural biorhythms, and graduates with a huge debt. When entering a 7 year personal growth process, these years are looked down on by many as 'wasted', as if we were a failure during this time because not much money was earned, no houses were bought, and no certificates were added to the wall. When emerging from a 7-year period of personal growth with new intuitive and creative skills, the skills are rarely attributed to the gestation period. The relatives say, "Ah, finally Susan has got her life together. It's about time!"

The multi-layer approach
When we're feeling uncomfortable and reacting, it often helps to pinpoint where exactly the trouble actually lies. Is it emotional? Mental? Physical? <u>Where</u> in your body, chakras or energy field do you feel it?

A multi-layer approach is useful to help locate the discomfort. When we focus on the layer of us that is the seat of the discomfort, and use the right kind of therapeutic tool for the job, we can clear or heal it more easily. We might as well hit the nail directly on the head; and naturally, using hammer is easier than a saw. Conversely, when we work on another layer, it helps, but it isn't as direct.

For example, arising childhood memories may trouble us. We can think about the memories, talk for hours on the psychiatrists couch, sue the wrong-doers, and still the root emotions lie within us. Alternatively, we can pinpoint that the essential problem is that we have emotions that need to be released; we can set about releasing the emotions using a good body-centred emotional therapist and save time and legal fees. Focusing on the emotional layer is more effective than the mental layer in this case.

When we realize, "Oh, I'm thinking just like my mother. My mother always hated change", we sense where our discomfort lies. Blaming our mother doesn't do much to help us move on. Observing our patterns, envisioning ways of being or thinking that we are more comfortable with, and gently, patiently bringing our thinking in line with our vision can help.

Pinpointing the layer where the trouble lies streamlines the healing process. The cause of a troubled mind might lie in food allergies; a digestive problem might be caused by anger held tight in the solar plexus.

When we are in reaction, resistance or denial, we block this whole inquiry. When we fight what is or forever wish things were different, we can't even make the first step into this inquiry.

The ease with which we handle unusual experiences and deep transformation has a lot to do with letting our reactions go, being present, and accepting what is.

Others' reactions to us

We have looked at our reactions to our own experiences and inner processes. We don't live in isolation; people around us may also react to our state of consciousness or state of mind, and we may react to their reactions.

Loving, light, open and free

When someone is exceptionally loving, light, open and free, some common reactions from those around us include:

Acknowledgement and acceptance: "This is wonderful! I celebrate your path, may you always be in this light and awareness"

Envy: "Why does this happen to you not me? I also meditate, I eat well, I… I…"

Fear: "You're weird. You're not the way you used to be. Maybe you've gone to the devil. You're dangerous."

Clinging: Now you're free, you don't need me. You may leave me. I don't trust you."

Guilt: "I too should be open but I'm afraid to be. I don't want to be around you because you remind me of the awareness I have turned my back on to be financially successful."

Pragmatist: "Come down from your pink cloud. Life is about work and responsibility. Get real. Knuckle down to work like the rest of us."
"What if everyone thought like you? Who would earn the money and run the country?"

Denial: "well, look at you. I suppose you think you're so special now you're all blissful. Well, you're not special. You're the same old (x--) person to me."

Fearful, depressed or anxious

The basic response to any negative state of mind or consciousness is, "I hope this doesn't happen to me!" Our minds want to feel sure this won't happen to me, so they categorize all the reasons why you have brought this fate on you and others are exempt.

This works the same way female jurors are more likely than male to blame the woman for her rape ("it was her behaviour, her clothing, her being out at that time). If no fault lies with the woman, rape can happen equally to any and all women, and this is a frightening thought – a thought that can be (somewhat) alleviated by thinking she brought this on herself.

The same thing happens when we go through a deep or painful process during transformation. Someone who doesn't understand the long-term benefits thinks this process is a terrible thing that should have been avoided. Rather than being supportive of the process, you are blamed for being in it.

Ideally we remain unaffected by the comments of those around us, whether praising or blaming. We remain true to our inner knowing, steadfast on our path, compassionate to those around us who don't understand, able to discern other's reactions and know they are not necessarily about us. This ideal is tall, and not easily attained when there is already so much going on inside us, but after reading these paragraphs hopefully we can recognize other's reactions, name them, and remain more centred and able to remain steady on our paths.

5

Handling Sensitivity

While becoming more open, we invariably become more sensitive. Why?

Reasons we may be feeling more sensitive.

- ❖ We're like radios that have started to pick up more channels. We used to be relatively closed down, with fewer frequencies available. The range of frequencies we sense has increased, and we're simply not used to it.
- ❖ We are more alive, more in the moment, less switched off, less defended. We Feel.
- ❖ The new openness melts away – or strips off! – the intellectual and social masks we used to use to handle, or deflect, the world around us. We feel naked, unprotected.

- ❖ Our eyes are more open. We see more. We can no longer avoid perceiving things as they are (rather than the way society or the media would like us to see them).

Typical sensitivities include:

- ❖ Background sounds: The whir of computers, air conditioning, fridges and strip lighting.
- ❖ The energies in shopping malls.
- ❖ The suffering of animals we farm and kill.
- ❖ Our effect on the environment.
- ❖ Synthetic fabrics, their energy fields, and the chemicals they off-gas.
- ❖ The effects of different colours.
- ❖ The effects of cigarette smoking, alcohol, drugs and meat eating.
- ❖ The vibration of our food, and the person who cooked it, how old or stale it is, how many synthetic chemicals are in it.
- ❖ The effects of TV, thriller movies, and newspapers to create fear and social anxiety.
- ❖ The aimlessness of idle social chitchat, gossip, soap operas.
- ❖ We may need to become vegetarian, or only eat raw food or organic food, or more grounded food than we used to because of new sensitivities to particular foods.
- ❖ Sensitivity at the cellular level shows up as allergies, sometimes multiple chemical allergies, which can be very disabling. Many people become allergic to chemical perfumes and body-care products during profound transformation.

There is nothing wrong with you, or the transformative process you are in, just because you are more sensitive.

These sensitivities will likely change in time.

❖ The key to handling sensitivity lies in cultivating grounding, a strong inner centre, inner listening, and responding appropriately to your perceptions.

❖ In time you learn to handle the increased sensitivity.

❖ With more time, this sensitivity can be harnessed as a new skill.

How grounding can help us handle our sensitivity

Grounding helps us handle sensitivity. There are two main uses of the word 'grounding'. One is a more psychological definition – to be cognisant of what is going on around us, to be in, or connected to, consensual reality. The other is 'to be energetically connected to the earth beneath our feet, to have all our chakras equally open and strong, to have our feet on the ground, to be connected to the earth plane.'

These words don't mean exactly the same thing. Office workers who sit at computers all day are cognisant of what is going on around them, but they are not necessarily energetically grounded. Many have lost touch with their feelings, their spirit, and their connection with nature to the point that they no longer notice when they need to breathe, walk, stretch, drink water or eat. They are not energetically grounded.

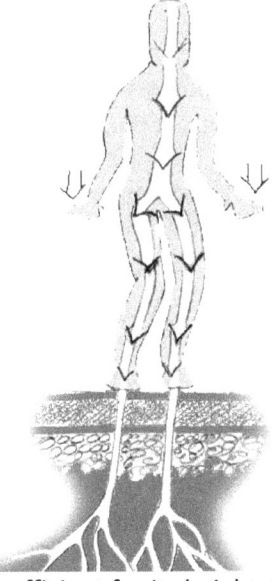

Grounding does not mean the same as 'closing down.' It means, quite literally, to have one's feet on the ground, to be energetically in the body, living in the present, relating to immediate surroundings, and to be energetically integrated. We can experience tremendous light with ease as long as the strength of our connection to the earth matches the amount of light we're open to. Opening to more light requires more grounding. A tree can only grow branches up into the sky to the extent that it is firmly rooted in the earth. When a trees root system isn't sufficient for its height, it can topple.

Grounding helps with over-sensitivity, dealing with emotions, staying connected to one's physical body, and remaining integrated and functional at work.

'Closing down' means closing down the higher channels, such as the crown and third eye chakras, when energy is pouring through. If your kundalini is really wild or the states you've opened to are far too open, closing down can be useful, but in general, it isn't as useful as energetic grounding through the feet.

The medical profession generally helps people 'close down' through drugs. Medication is certainly not the best or only way of becoming more grounded, but can be a useful option under certain circumstance. Other quite ordinary, common sense activities and techniques can be highly effective if introduced in a loving, companionable way.

What can we do to become more grounded?

- **Nature**: Be with trees. Stroll in shady woodland. Walk barefoot on grass or earth. Lie face down on the earth and connect to the earth through the belly. Do gardening.

- **Diet**: Eat well, eat regularly, and eat consciously. Proteins, root vegetables, brown rice, onions, garlic and dairy products are grounding foods. Salty dense foods (olives, miso, meat) tend to bring us into our bodies. Sweets, fruits and stimulants tend to be expansive. Sugar, alcohol and caffeine are least grounding.

- **Physical and emotional nurturing**: Being in soothing, gentle environments where we feel safe enough to relax fully and fully inhabit our bodies are likely to be more grounding than abrasive, over-stimulating, stressful or fast moving situations. In general it helps to avoid places you don't feel relaxed in, like noisy, crowded, busy or demanding places. It may be helpful to watch and read films on wildlife, gardening or indigenous communities, and limit watching violent films and thrillers. Similarly, it may help to limit contact with people who are busy-minded, demanding, quarreling or competitive and choose the company of people who are kind, gentle, and positive if possible.

- **Movement, grounding manual work:** Puttering in the garden, weeding, digging and other contact with soil is excellent. Doing ordinary things can be very consoling and settling. Clean the house. Stack wood. Peel vegetables. Sweep floors.

- **Contact with water helps some people:** Go swimming. Wash clothes by hand. Soak in the bathtub if you find this helps.

- **Music**: Music has great influence. You can play music that resonates with your own vibrational frequency, or use music to fill in the frequencies you are missing. For example, listening to the upbeat music you danced to as a teenager might be just the thing one day; listening to soothing classical music helps another day.

- **Clothing:** Comfortable clothes in natural fabrics are usually more conducive for a comfortable energy flow. Choose colours which help to balance you – earth tones for grounding, red to bring in more vibrant activity, blues and greens for cooling.

- **Body contact:** Massage, hugs, being held, making love with someone you love, and dancing can bring us into our bodies.

- **Creative expression:** Participation in projects which engage your energy and interest – art, music, creative writing. Journaling helps keeps the rapidly changing moods and thoughts in perspective.

- **Visualization**: Envision energy travelling down your legs to your feet and right down into earth. Imagine the rich, dark brown earth below and route energy into that earth. Energy follows thought.

- **Listening: Be responsive to your perceptions.** Respond to your sensitivity as much as is practical. The fact that mainstream people are perfectly fine with the things you are sensitive to doesn't invalidate your sensitivity. Listen and respond!

When you <u>can</u> make a change in your environment, for goodness sake, do so! Make a list of all the things that feel uncomfortable and quietly set about finding alternatives. If you sensitive to your computer, replace your cathode ray monitor with an LCD screen and put your noisy tower in a large closet and close the door. If the city is too busy and intense, move to live in the peaceful countryside if you can. Notice your sensitivities and respond to them. Replace synthetics with natural fabrics, buy organic vegetables, meet your friends in a juice bar, and throw out the TV… What is more important, your comfort or your ideas?

For situations you can't immediately change, such as established work environments, the attitudes of your parents, or world pollution, the next best thing is to find the skills to manage your sensitivity better.

Managing sensitivity
- **Get real:** Honour your sensitivity rather than negate it or pretend it isn't there.

- ❖ **Be discreet:** Make as little 'issue' of it as possible. Act, quietly and decisively rather than ruminating, complaining or continually telling everyone about it.
- ❖ **Work on your grounding.** The more connected to the earth you are, the more sensations run through you rather than accumulating in you. You become a conduit, the experience flowing through your body. You feel in the moment, and then move on. Check your resilience after doing some grounding activities like walking barefoot in the woods, weeding your garden, sending energy through your tailbone in meditation. The earth-connection helps create a strong inner core, which stabilizes the changes happening in your mind and in the world around you.
- ❖ **Buy protection and wear it:** Hang crystals on lengths of cords so the crystals hang protectively over each chakra, if you find this works. Wear a protective 'purple' plate, which create a positive, protective energy field when you're at the computer. Wear health magnets. Place symbols that you feel are protective on your person. Wrap your belly in silk or wool. Wear sunglasses to help keep out other people's 'vibes.' Protect the crown of your head with a hat.
- ❖ **Shields:** Create a protective field of light and intention around you to shield yourself from the emotions and energies of other people.

How to create a shield
- ❖ Be clear about what you need to be shielded from. (e.g. other people's tension, anger, dull energies, etc.)
- ❖ Also be clear about whether you want a total barrier or a partial screen that will let through, say, joy and love, but screen out anger and tension.
- ❖ The shield can be made out of light of any colour (white, gold, multi-colour), or of a mirror-like substance that will deflect some vibrations and receive others.

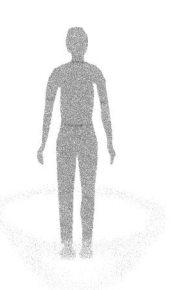 Clearly envision placing a plate of the shield substance under where you are sitting or standing. Extend this up around you, either envisioning plates, or a coil that works its way up and around you.

 Take time using the power of your vision to methodically build the shield walls up from this base all around you, front and back and to each side, covering all your body, and finally over your head. In your envisioning, don't leave any part of you uncovered.

- ❖ Send your intention to this shield. "Please screen out anger and tension but let through joy and love".
- ❖ Throughout the day send energy and intention to the shield to keep it strong.

    If you do not visualize well, it may help to draw what you want. A stick person representing you, surrounded by an oval bubble in the colour you want, will work fine, as will a full-colour artistic rendition. Write your intention for which energies you want the shield to screen out or let through. Use your intention to transmit the message of your drawn image to your energy field.

    Put on a shield before you go out anywhere, especially before going to places which are likely to have uncomfortable energy and vibrations.

Protective crystals

You can hang protective crystals over your throat, heart and solar plexus chakras. You can use any number of crystals. Intention is part of how they work. While there are tomes written listing the effects of each crystal, there is some variation between authors, so obviously the effect of a particular crystal is somewhat personal. If a crystal feels good for you, it works. You might try an amethyst or lapis lazuli for your throat, or a rose quartz for your heart. Some crystals come with a hole drilled through, others have a ring set in. If the crystal you want to wear has neither hole nor ring, you can buy a wire clasp. Crystals can be hung on linen thread, leather thongs, or metal chains.

Cloth wraps

Wrapping silk or wool cloth around your lower abdomen helps protect you from vibrations. Shawls work well. Silk is less bulky than wool and can be worn under your clothing – no one will notice. It might be possible to conceal finely woven wool shawls underneath clothing in the winter. Otherwise, just blatantly wrap the cloth around, covering from your waist to your hips. If some explanation is needed, you can figure some response, like 'the extra warmth helps alleviate my back pain.'

Fitting in

As far as the people around us are concerned, we look like we always have, so why should we feel any different? You try to explain to your friend and hear, "Hey man, just drop it! Get a life!" All transforming people are in the same kind of boat. Some are lucky to be surrounded by more aware, understanding and loving people than others. Some have more resources than others. Yet our boats are much the same in that they are turning towards the light in a world that appears to have most of the population avidly sailing in the opposite direction. It's not easy being different.

Our awareness may change such that we no longer feel like we fit in with our family, friends, or our spiritual group. Sometimes we feel totally alone, the only one seeing this way. Everyone else seems enthralled by a world focused on money earning, spending and acquisition; a world dominated by materialistic, 'scientific' thinking; a world tied to the clock. Once you start opening up, you will likely lose interest in this focus, and will be enthralled with a subtle world which many people have no way of perceiving.

Your life values, spiritual practice and time-energy priorities are also likely to change, and you'll likely be looking for leisure activities which resonate more with your new way of being, along with workshops, training, and groups.

For some reason, many of the things that people think of as cool or fun are not conducive to health and intuitive awareness – like fast food, thriller movies, beer, coffee and computer games. You may well feel like moving away from low energy, spiritually disinterested people in preference for friends who have similar energy and interest – if you can find them. You may well need to spend more time alone, in Nature, or in meditation. Your relationships or ways of relating with partners, family, friends and colleagues may change. You may not mind, but they likely will.

After your perception changes, changes in your values, life purpose, relationships and career direction may well follow. Big shifts in consciousness can radically change your life.

It's enough for you to adapt to all your new sensitivities and awareness, but then on top of this, you have people around you complaining, "Why aren't you like you used to be?" Your sensitivity may well be perplexing for both yourself and your companions.

Options for dealing with your old acquaintances are:
You can
- try to look like you used to (pretend)
- try to avoid those people (hide)
- you can be honest about your new perceptions and let people choose whether they want to accept you or find other company, and accept whatever flack or acceptance comes your way.

When we are well centred, directly experiencing ourselves as perfect and complete, needless, strong and autonomous, then dealing with others is less of a trial. Since this centred state of being is usually the outcome of transformation rather than something we all start out with, we might not find any one of these options particularly easy.

Cellular sensitivity - often called allergy
Acute biological sensitivity can feel like a major handicap. The list of places, people and situations that feel excruciatingly uncomfortable can grow long, leaving us with few comfortable options. For more

information and help for your specific condition, consult your medical doctor or a naturopathic doctor.

How to handle sensitivity:
First, find out what you are sensitive to.

Trial and error
Keep a diary of what you eat, drink and breathe, and how you feel over a few weeks. In time, the patterns should emerge, provided there is enough variability in your lifestyle that the allergens aren't a constant presence in your life.

Kinesiology - muscle testing
The principle behind kinesiology (muscle testing) is that a substance which doesn't suit your body weakens your muscles. Hold an outstretched arm at shoulder height and have a friend gently press down on your arm while you offer resistance. From this you get a reading of your general arm strength. If you put a piece of food on your tongue and then your friend presses down on your arm, you'll know by the relative strength of your arm, how your body feels about that food. If the strength of your arm remains the same, you have no problem with the food. If it weakens, you are allergic.

It doesn't work quite as well, but if you don't want to put the substance on your tongue, holding it over your solar plexus can also provide a reading. As an alternative to pressing your arm, your friend can test the strength of your index finger and thumb pressed together. If the link can be easily broken, you are allergic to the substance being tested. If the finger and thumb circle remains strong, you not allergic to the substance.

Go through your fridge and cupboards, testing each food in turn, and you'll get an idea of your body's reaction to these foods. If you test many substances in a row, allow for muscle fatigue. If your muscles test really weak to something, try again later after a rest, just to verify.

Typical food sensitivities include sugar, wheat, milk products, yeast, corn, chocolate, coffee, food additives and soy. Many people have found that completely omitting sugar and dairy from their diet cut down their allergies to a manageable level. Some people were completely relieved from allergies through this (admittedly boring!)

change. If you like your sweet treats, you may have a tough choice to make between your overall health, well-being, personal transformation and energy levels, and your transient tongue-stimulation.

If you really like sweets, try stevia as a natural alternative sweetener. Creating a more alkaline environment in your body may help reduce sensitivity for some people. Replacing cooked foods with fresh, organic vegetables and fruit can do this.

To avoid dust mites, try wearing a fine silk scarf over your nose and mouth and vacuum, bank rugs outside, shake out blankets, and wash bed sheets and upholstery covers regularly.

The effect of air pollution can be lessened by wearing a carbon mask, made for roadside cyclists and runners and sold at some outdoor sports shops.

Your sensitivity to chemical perfumes may be more intense after you've eaten sweet foods, drank milk, inhaled dust mites, and driven in your car (breathing road pollution) if you are sensitive to these substances.

Avoid what can be avoided, including not going to places you would otherwise enjoy, because your body will react. You can choose to not tax your body rather than choose to do what you would have otherwise wanted.

6

Weird Sensations

When we open spiritually, we may receive more energy, often of a higher vibrational frequency than we're used to. We tend to think of 'more energy' as simply having more 'battery power' or personal power. We rarely think of this energy as a powerful force of purification.

> *I think now, in retrospect, the energy I was flailing about with could have been put to very good use had I the correct teachings. Now, whenever those feelings return, I see it as a sensitive energy time and try to ground myself and enjoy the ride rather than feel afraid. I used to look at other people and how they socialize with great envy. "Oh, why can't I function like those around me!?"*[2]

During spiritual transformation, we don't necessarily stay within our usual parameters of feeling and perception. It is quite common to experience unusual energy sensations, involuntary movements, headaches, or strange pains which elude medical diagnosis. We'll take a quick look at the range so you can identify them, and either come to accept them, or take steps that will help you to feel more comfortable.

Pain that eludes traditional medical diagnosis

Pain can arise in many places in your body, or even in places above or around your body (in the energy field). Try telling that to your G.P.!

These pains can be disturbingly intense. Energy sensations and pain can be so strong that even people already having extensive spiritual and medical knowledge have checked themselves into hospital emergency centres. Later, after medical tests show nothing, they finally conclude that the sensations must have been due a kundalini awakening. Suffice to say, strange pains aren't that always easy to diagnose.

Some of this pain is caused by bottlenecks in energy pathways. Like roads that were built 50 years ago to handle a low volume of traffic, when the traffic volume increases, cars uncomfortably build up at junctions. Similarly, our nervous systems might be doing fine at 50 watts of input, but at 250, the energy is bunching up in any place not sufficiently open to handle the flow. At a 1000 watts, it the build up can hurt. Acupuncture can offer immediate help. In the long term, we might consider looking into what emotions and memories we are holding in that place in our body to create the constriction.

Pains that shift from one place to another are more likely to be energy related, but there are also some medical conditions that display shifting pain.

Energy, also known as chi, prana, life-energy, can also bunch up in the chakras. When the heart chakra is too constricted for the amount of energy flowing through it, it can feel like a thick dull pain in the chest. Undiagnosed pains in the heart following kundalini awakening are invariably energy related, but if you are at all uncertain or concerned, go see your medical doctor and have an ECG (electrocardiogram). Science has the tests. Worrying isn't useful.

To help clear the heart, lightly rub up and down the bottom of the sternum. Relax, breath, and envision the heart opening like a flower. Envision energy flowing and connecting from the heart to the head and then down to the lower body. Breathe any congested energy from the heart to other places in your body. If you know how, do Reiki on yourself. Tap or press the heart meridian end points. To clear energy excess energy from the heart, sweep with your hands from the heart, re-distributing the energy through your arms and body with your hands (or get someone else to do the sweeping).

Energy can also build up uncomfortably in other chakras. When the throat is constricted, energy can create intense tickling or coughing. Annoyingly, this is particularly prone to happen just as we are lifting into a lovely meditation. The energy catches in the throat, and an irritating cough sends us spluttering, eyes watering, to grab something to drink. You can help clear your throat through thumbing. Place your hands upside down around your neck (i.e. pinky side upward under your ears, thumbs in the dip at the nape of the neck). Gently sweep your thumbs from the nape outward. At the same time, ground your energy by breathing it down through your pelvic floor into the earth.

A combination of light massage, acupressure, energy grounding, visualisation, breathing and relaxing the body helps keep energy flowing well.

Energy related pain usually clears fairly quickly. Intense physical pain rarely lasts for long. The suffering created from our mind's resistance can creates more long-term difficulty – sometimes more difficulty than pain itself. Be assured that however odd or unpleasant it feels in the moment, the next moment is a new moment.

If you have weird pains in your body that are persistent or worry you, get a medical check-up. If your doctor finds nothing wrong with you, don't conclude that you are a hypochondriac! Medical instruments cannot pick up energy – they are designed to pick up physical and chemical symptoms. If tests are clear, the chances are that this undiagnosed pain is energy trying to clear a place of resistance or blockage in your body, especially if you have had a spiritual awakening or you are in the midst of psycho-spiritual clearing.

> *I was sitting in front of my computer at work one day when the first and most intense crown-chakra symptom got me. It wasn't so much that it was just pain. I mean.... okay, it WAS pain. But it was the novelty of it that struck me. It felt like someone had taken a long rod of SOLID energy about the circumference of my index finger, and was inserting into INTO the top of my head. I mean, right through the hairy skin and through the bone and downward. I mean my physical head, nothing "meta"-physical about this! I slapped my hand up on top of my head in astonishment, but felt nothing with my hand. It went away after about 15 seconds. But my "crown chakra" -- which I had never 'felt' before -- hurt like HELL for the rest of the day.*
>
> *I'd like to put a pretty "we're all evolving, how transcendental!" sort of label on this experience, but the reality is just that it is anywhere from a mild ache to it hurting like a sonofabitch and requiring drugs to make it go away (Excedrin to the rescue!).[11]*

Headaches

Most headaches are caused, at least in part, by muscular tension. Migraines are due to a disrupted blood circulation to the brain. If your headaches are persistent and worrisome, ask your doctor for an MRI (magnetic resonance image) if you are worried. It might also be worth having medical tests for food or chemical allergies, sinus pressure, hormonal imbalance, and other health disorders.

However, if the MRI and other tests show nothing, get to work on grounding your energy, and clear energy blocks in your neck and shoulders.

Sit with yourself, do some inner listening to sense what the underlying causes of the constrictions are.

Common transformation, energy and lifestyle related causes of headaches include:

- Energy constrictions or blocks from neck and shoulder tension, preventing the free flow of energy from your crown into the rest of your body. This is exacerbated when a lot of energy is flowing in through the crown.
- Not being grounded enough so in-pouring energy has nowhere to go.
- Pushing yourself to keep going when you need to be still, going against your inner needs, striving to meet up to expectations, any activity or orientation which is contrary to your inner needs or intuitive knowing.
- Eyestrain, such as reading or looking at a computer monitor for hours.
- Expansive and diffusive headaches in the forehead and temples are sometimes due to sugar, coffee, or alcohol. They can also be due to insufficient grounding.
- Underlying beliefs. Likely places to look: believing you should be in control, living up to other people's ideals, trying to be better than you are, and not accepting yourself as you are right now.

Dr. Lee Sannella, M.D. writes about headaches:

> (One) case had severe headaches, but these stopped as soon as she ceased trying to control the process and simply "went with it." Te pain, in other words, resulted not from the process itself but from her resistance to it. We suspect that is true of all the negative effects of the physio-Kundalini process.[12]

Energy blocks

Belief: "I have to stay in control" - the voice of the ego-mind. Not trusting life, control is held in the neck and shoulders. This block keeps you firmly in your body, and away from higher states of awareness. Rising energy has nowhere to go. It hits the block, circulates in the back of the neck, sometimes spilling out of the back of the neck. The block invariably creates tension headaches. We can *hear* this block – it gives the voice a tight, grating often shrill resonance.

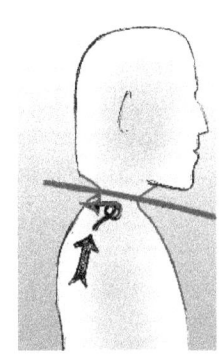

Underlying belief – "I'm not safe here." or; "I don't want to be here."

The soul finds safety by withdrawing from the physical plane, cutting off access to the feeling centre of the body. You can watch the world like an owl from the safe branch of a tree, intellectually aware of what is going on, but uninvolved. It's another way of staying in control – by being absent from anything that may not suit your preferences or sensitivity.

Belief: "I must conform" This kind of block arises when you are spiritually open but feel you need to operate in the world as everyone else does – to be on time, meet your deadlines. You cut across your natural life flow. Energy rising and energy pouring in through the crown has nowhere to go. Headaches and shoulder tension are likely.

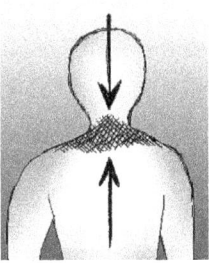

Kriyas

The word kriya is the Sanskrit word for action. In this context, kriyas refer to spontaneous movements, movements that happen without any apparent will, as if the body is moving itself. It feels as if energy is moving the body without the mind's intervention. This is not uncommon in altered states of consciousness or when more energy than usual is flowing through the body.

Sometimes people are as-if propelled into yoga postures, even if they are not familiar with yoga. Luckily, there seems to be intelligence to the propelling energy – there is no record of anyone being hurt. It's likely the energy seeks to release blocks or kinks in the body or energy channels through movement or stretching. Perhaps this is the physical body's way of expressing directly from its own cells, a natural movement arising from the movement of life force in the body that needs no intervention, control or comment from the mind.

> *One night shortly after my peak Kundalini opening, I tried to meditate. Suddenly, my body began to list sideways. I decided to just let go, rather than control it. Soon I found myself rolling on the floor, and being pushed in and out of strange positions. These movements still continued, 1 year later, whenever I relaxed. My head would sway from side to side, my arms would shoot about, and my face would be pulled into strange expressions, as well as other kriya phenomena occurring. Overall, the kriyas have been beneficial. I have less pain from the fibromyalgia that I had for many years. I frequently feel a warm, soothing, yet stimulating energy during the kriyas. Interestingly, I have sometimes observed people at spiritual events like seminars or toning, having kriyas, in which their arms shoot up, or there heads sway, or their two hands are propelled into prayer position. I wonder if they know!* [2]

Crawling sensations on the skin

It feels tickly and weird, like spiders crawling, or tingling electrical sensations in your skin. While these crawling sensations could be a case of B6 deficiency, if you've had your B6 checked out, and you have other kundalini related symptoms, chances are the tickly, crawly electrical sensations on your skin are due to energy moving. It may feel weird, but if you let it do its work, it will finish its activity in time.

Weird energy

It can sound mystical and enticing when you read about unusual experiences, yet feel rather strange when they actually happen to you. You might be having visions, seeing lights, hearing sounds, having kundalini energy shoot around your body, or feeling other weird sensations in your body, and while part of you feels high other parts feel something weird is going on.

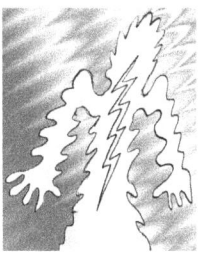

> *The moment my head touched the pillow a large tongue of flame sped across the spine into the interior of my head. It appeared as if the stream of living light continuously rushing through the spinal cord into the cranium gathered greater speed and volume during the hours of darkness. Whenever I closed my eyes I found myself looking into a weird circle of light, in which luminous currents swirled and eddied, moving rapidly from side to side. The spectacle was fascinating but awful, invested with a supernatural awe which sometimes chilled the very marrow in my bones.*[13]   Gopi Krishna

Strange perceptions and phenomena happen, and can feel pretty weird at the time. They very rarely stay. Their nature is transient.

If we could see the bigger picture, we would likely see that these are energies freeing up energy pathways, and energies that are out of balance and need integrating. There are also phenomena that shake us out of our ordinary, static ways of seeing and being. We work to remain well connected to the earth (grounded) and connected to the flow of spirit through. These unusual energies will change in time.

Kundalini fire

Kundalini fire is not just a hot body. It is definitely not the feeling of a hot body on a hot day! Kundalini fire can feel hot – like baking hot on a winter's day, or hot patches, often on the crown of the head, base of the spine or in the shoulder-neck area. Sometimes it can feel more like being under pressure – like there is more energy inside your body than it can handle.

If you have this 'fire' you may well also feel 'on the edge,' as if ready to combust at any moment, and very sensitive. The sensitivity can rise to almost excruciating levels around sources of heat and emitters of radiation such as lamps, sunlight, electric heaters or wood stoves. Discomfort can also arise after eating the wrong kind of food (generally heat producing foods), or being around high energy people. Kundalini heat may give us unusually red cheeks or red-rimmed eyes, skin that is hot to the touch particularly in areas of the body where energy has accumulated or is flowing less freely. We may feel very uncomfortable without any obvious physical heat, feeling more like we're under pressure.

Explanations:

Eastern scriptures say, 'Kundalini (a Sanskrit word) refers to a coiled energy that lies dormant at the base of the spine.' Even after reading this, people are left wondering what exactly is this kundalini energy, and if it is it the same as prana, chi or the life force? We have only vaguely defined these energies. There seems to be one fundamental energy, call it life force, prana or chi, which manifests or appears differently according to the way it interacts with our body-minds. We might call it 'prana' when it moves our breath, and chi when it flows through meridians. We call it yin when it is female or expansive in nature, and yang when male or contractive.

Ayurvedic doctors talk about people having enough prana, udana, and upana, specific life energies needed to regulate breath, digestion and elimination. They also talk about having too much or too little vata, pitta or kapha energy. When you have too much vata you become airy, light, sensitive, or intellectual, whereas when pitta is strong you are physically active. When you have too much kapha without pitta and vata you feel stable, although rather inert or even sluggish.

Chinese doctors will talk about having excess kidney yang, a metal imbalance, or too weak shen, the joyous energy that is associated with the heart. We feel it when our energies run a certain way and we become fearful, or lacking in heart-joy, but we have few English words to explain this feeling or other energy perceptions, and lack ways to define our perceptions and feelings. We have a sense when our life force is strong and when we could do with more of it, and that's about it for many people.

We call this life force 'kundalini' when a large packet of prana / chi/ life-force rushes up our spine all at once. These days the term 'kundalini' has widened out to include any strange energy phenomena such as a feeling of electricity buzzing through an arm or leg because we just don't have another word.

Causes of the fire

When you pass energy through a channel or wire that has constriction in it, such as light bulbs and heating elements, the place of restriction will heat up. Through massage, acupuncture, or letting go of mental resistance, the constriction in our bodies dissolves allowing a freer flow of energy.

Another fundamental cause of kundalini fire (and many other transformational problems) is lack of trust. If we lack trust in the world around us, and also distrust this strange spiritual energy moving in us, we find ourselves neither able to ground our energy by connecting to the earth we distrust, nor are we open to the spirit that we distrust. We get stuck in between, wedged in our resistance. Cut off from the two main places of energy flow, our life force is unable to flow freely. Energy accumulates in our bodies because it simply has nowhere to flow to.

Sometimes the fire is due to imbalance or not listening well enough to our physical and energy-related needs. For example, we need to be still for a while, but force ourselves to keep going, finish some work or project. The striving creates constriction, blocking the energy flow, creating burning or discomfort. Sometimes even a few moments of stillness is sufficient; you can continue the work afterwards – in a more natural flow.

Sometimes this fiery energy is part of a process of spiritual purification (the kundalini appears to literally 'burn' through energy resistance, habitual patterns, limitations and held memories.) While very uncomfortable, it's doing its job. Yoga helps clear the energy pathways.

Do your best to welcome the process and allow the kundalini to do its job, rather than adding to the resistance (and fire) by resenting it and wishing things were different.

Dealing with kundalini fire

Observe carefully the effect of various foods, energies, situations and people. Through observation we may discover spiritual practices that don't really suit us the way we are right now. We may become more aware of the effects of coffee, sunlight on an uncovered head, synthetic clothes, and heat producing foods, non-conducive work or company. Our observation will give us the best clues as to what is likely creating the fire. When we observe a negative effect, we simply make mental notes of what to do in the future. Written notes can help us at times when the fire gets so intense we cannot think what to do. These notes can also help guide a caretaker if need be.

The most important help is intuitive listening. Tune in. Respond soon. These kinds of energies are fast and light, and can change like the wind with a single thought or contact.

- Something that helps is to <u>drink a lot of water</u>. Lemon juice and other cooling liquids work even better. This may seem bizarre, but cola soft drinks help some people. Perhaps cola works for the same reason that it sells – it energizes the body, makes us feel more physical, and perhaps closes the chakras and those roaring higher channels a little – a worldly drink.
- Sucking an ice cube helps when the fire is in the head. The ice cube can be placed in the mouth so it cools the soft palate, which is just below the pineal and pituitary glands. When the fire is in the crown of the head, a bag of crushed ice, or a package of frozen green peas can be placed on the head.
- Wearing white or cool-coloured (blue or green) clothing may help. Wearing natural fabrics is always helpful, since synthetics create a force field that is disturbing to energy flow even at the best of times. Synthetic fabrics have a negative charge, which deflects away the healthy negative ions in the atmosphere. (Negative ions are part of why you feel good at the sea or around large bodies of water.)
- Breathing through your left nostril is cooling. You can softly plug the right nostril with cotton, or close that side of the nose by hand.
- Sitting with just your hips in cold water – the colder the better, even ice can be added – is surprisingly helpful, even when the fire is in the head. The cold water cools the kundalini at the base, soothing the fire.
- Take cool showers (not too cold since very cold water stimulates more energy)
- Squeeze your neck with a cold, damp washcloth to help release tension and heat in your neck where it invariably builds up.
- Swimming or immersing in water can be helpful, though not if the water is hot.
- Choose less stimulating activities and environments.

- Stretch gently.
- Breathe through the left nostril. An easy way is to put some cotton in the right nostril for a while.
- Walking barefoot on dewy grass is cooling and grounding.
- Get a massage.
- Cold water on the feet, the back of the neck, the top of the head and forehead helps. Squeezing the neck through a cold, damp washcloth helps release tension and heat in the neck, where it invariably builds up. In extreme cases, a cool shower can help.
- Eat cooling foods, like green leafy vegetables, salads and fruit; and grounding foods like mashed potatoes, and root vegetables. Butter and dairy products and rice are settling for many people.
- Spend time in Nature and in buildings built of natural materials (wood, stone). Avoid electromagnetic fields (for example around dimmer switches, transformers and high voltage electricity wires. Sometimes jewellery inhibits energy flow, particularly when it is metal.

Avoid
- Spicy foods, fried foods, sugar and hot drinks are best avoided, as is coffee. Cereal coffees also create heat, but at least they are less stimulating.
- The fire or heat sometimes ends up accumulating in the liver, especially when living in warm climates. In this eventuality, cover the liver area with a small, wet towel. In addition you can gently massage the area, drawing out the heat, rinsing the towel when it gets warm.
- Temporarily discontinue spiritual practice that increases energy (focused meditation, pranayama[a] etc) Soft intuitive practices may be continued if they feel comfortable. Pay special attention to maintaining a good grounding link with the earth.

Energy swings
When energy is free flowing and light it can change very quickly from fiery hot to chilly cold. We need to be much more attentively tuned in, and respond to our perceptions without delaying.

Left-right side imbalance
Sometimes one side of the body goes numb or left and right sides feel different from each other. An energy worker can help to balance things out.

Energy pouring in the crown
There's a lot of talk about kundalini energy rising up from the base of the spine, yet energy can also pour in through the crown of
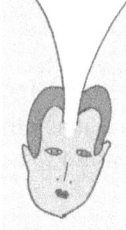
the head. It is called sahasraric energy. It can feel like white light pouring in, or stronger, like light or energy burning its way in. It can be painful. The pain may extend several inches above the head, or be in the crown itself, which invariably feels very warm to the touch. Energy may flow behind the eyes to the occipital and neck and down through the body. When the neck isn't open enough, the energy tends to get stuck in the head creating pressure and headaches. It can feel intense.

Moderate amounts of sahasraric energy feel light, clear and insightful. When more sahasraric energy flow in, it feels fine when the energy channels are clear and the energy flows right through, grounding into the earth. When insufficiently grounded, or when the energy channels aren't sufficiently clear to handle the voltage coming through, energy can build up in the body. It can feel like being under pressure from the inside. This can be surprisingly uncomfortable. No one will understand why because you'll look just fine.

What is happening?
Possibly this is one of the ways new information and vibrational frequencies are received. It can be useful to record any revelations and inspiration that comes through during these times.

Shiatsu and acupuncture help clear pathways and move sahasraric energy through. Ordinary massage, squeezing and pressing the body and limbs, working the energy through to the feet also helps. Reiki, a flow of healing energy that passes through hands that are laid on or near the body, generally adds more energy, which at these times may well be an uncomfortable overload.

Electric currents
Sometimes kundalini or life force energy can pass through you with such power and swiftness it feels like a strong electric

 current. It rarely lasts more than seconds or a minute, but it can be surprising at the time. These energy surges will not necessarily recur. There is no record of anyone being harmed by them, even though they feel quite intense.

After you've been through a few weird experiences, you kind-of get used to it. You realize that you can go into some pretty unusual states of consciousness and still return to something reasonably familiar afterwards. You learn how to handle them. If you don't like them you learn how not to trigger them. Surfing the Net you realize you are not the only one having them. If you're lucky, you make some friends or e-friends having similar experiences. It's great to have someone who understands to call up and tell about your latest occurrence. It's even better to find someone with some practical know-how to help you stay on an even keel, and who knows what to be concerned about and what isn't much of a problem.

With time we intuitively learn to balance spiritual energies. We also learn to manage the energy/openness edge – knowing where it is, the signs of approaching the edge, and how to pull back from the edge. If we open too much too quickly, we can be swamped with too much energy, which amplifies every imbalance and constriction in the body, mind, energy or emotional fields Time, energy and resources permitting, we can fast-track our way through the growth process, selectively using professional energy workers and therapists as needed. When our resources are more limited, it is worth managing our openness to the extent we can.

Slow down, or stop altogether, your spiritual practice if you find yourself opening to too much energy. Grounding practice should be continued, or started, if this is not a regular part of your daily routine. Insight meditation (Vipassana, mindfulness meditation) is a more physically integrated practice than most meditation techniques, and could be continued if you find it balancing. Most other forms of spiritual practice create a lot of high-vibration energy – that is what they are supposed to do. It's great when you need more of that kind of energy and openness, and overkill when you don't.

If you are part of a spiritual group that has a strict discipline to be followed by all members, and your 'spirituality' is measured by your attendance and constant disciplined practice, you will have to find a way of explaining your absence at these sessions. Following along with a group when you are too open can be very uncomfortable.

If you carry beliefs which are discordant with your inner awareness, for example, believing that you will fall from grace if you don't continue regular spiritual practice even though this practice makes you uncomfortable, you have a choice between your concept and your comfort. There are some discomforts that benefit from 'pushing through.' Energy overload is not one of these situations. In the short term, it is better to do some gardening or housework, or relax with some soothing music. In the long term, work on grounding, remaining receptive and relaxed, being in the present, and do yoga, qigong, energy work or visualisations to open up the energy pathways so energy flows unimpeded. Take time to sense the underlying mental and emotional resistance that is creating the blockage or imbalance in the first place. The clearer your energy is and the better grounded you are, the more energy can flow through you like a brook – or a wide river – giving you the vitality, energy and inspiration for all kinds of creativity and good work.

Distortions in time

One moment of time as perceived when you are very open can take an extraordinarily long time to pass. No one in a normal time framework will understand. For example, if you're left alone, after the first minute, you may feel abandoned; after the second, you may feel like you've been abandoned forever; and after the third, feel that

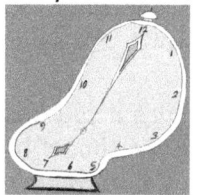

there is no hope to live for. Similarly, a day living with kundalini discomfort can feel days long; after a few days it is as if the discomfort has been lived forever and there is no hope of anything ever being any different. Part of this is due to living more in the present than you are used to, which means that what you are currently perceiving and knowing is all you know. Under normal circumstances, memory tempers and modulates current experience, making it less intense.

Also time can pass extraordinarily quickly. You close your eyes to meditate for a minute, and find three hours just disappeared. Days can slip by and hardly be noticed. Altered states of consciousness don't always track in our normal time-space logic continuums.

7

Internal Clearing

It would be great if the full power of enlightened awareness opened in us and just stayed. It would be wonderful if we could just drop all our old, weighty issues, all the painful memories, all sense of insecurity, and simply walk out into the light. In theory we can, and in brief moments we do, but the weight of our conditions inevitably seems to draw us back into our limited patterns, like gravity returning us to the earth.

Attaining permanent, perfect enlightenment after one experience is a spiritual myth. Jesus, Buddha and other masters all went through a fairly extensive process before they arrived at the state of being that attracted the large crowds.

Spiritual transformation isn't just about experiencing love and oneness during an awakening or when sitting on our meditation seat (although it's a great start!); it is about bringing every facet of our body-mind into alignment with this truth. Until this clearing is done, life situations trigger our past patterns, returning us to less enlightened states of consciousness, or our increased life force amplifies our less enlightened characteristics like power, control, egoism and sexuality.

The vast majority of people need considerable internal 'house-cleaning' – emotional, mental and physical purification, adjustment and integration before being able to live steadily in a higher state of consciousness. Even after a profound opening, it often takes a while – often years – before our lifestyle and thinking fully reflects our inner awareness. It takes considerable purification to create a body-mind capable of conducting light-spirit-energy and perception at a high frequency in a balanced, integrated manner.

Having done this internal 'house-cleaning,' the possibility that beckons to us is permanent transformation - to be able to step out into the light and never step back.

This chapter outlines some ways to clear the skeletons out of our emotional and mental closets, along with ways to make our physical and energy bodies fit for our new awareness.

We'll look first at some issues surrounding our resistance to growth, then explore emotional clearing, and finally look at working with the mind. Physical illness is briefly addressed.

Resistance to the process

We like it when we are clearer and freer, but do we want to go through what it takes to get there? Not necessarily, especially when the clearing causes pain, discomfort, or disrupts our plans and expectations.

It's like wanting our dishevelled closet to somehow perfectly reorganize itself without having to empty it out and sort it through. If the contents of the over-stuffed closet tumble out of the closet demanding a clean up, we'd likely stuff everything back in and live with not being able to find anything, rather than taking the time to sort things through.

We want total freedom, but don't necessarily want what it takes to get there. To the extent that we want our unfoldment to fit neatly inside the parameters of the conceptual box that keeps us bound, we will have all kinds of resistance to what is happening within us. We need to cut through social ideals that we should all be perfectly 'normal' and optimally functional at all times, and to cut through the rosy spiritual myths that promise quick-and-easy enlightenment. If we can let go of these myths, our internal clearing will proceed more gracefully.

What spiritual books often don't tell you:

> ## *Light reveals shadow.*

The more light we open to, the more vivid those shadows appear, if only by contrast to the exquisite light we have opened to. Living a mediocre, mundane life on half energy is like living in twilight or the grey of a cloudy day – there isn't enough light to create shadows.

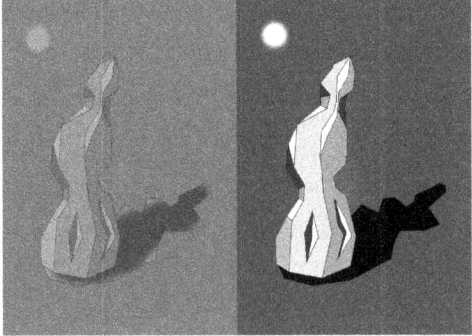

If we live in sufficiently mediocre states of consciousness, we can avoid looking at all kinds of things. As we increase our light and energy, our light reveals our shadows. Part of what feels uncomfortable is an alternation between opening into an expanded, blissful state of consciousness, followed by smacking a wall of grey conditions that has up until now prevented us from living this openness.

Perhaps you thought that once you opened to the light you would just stay there. While this does occasionally happen, what is far more common is light alternating with times of darkness – sometimes for years – until we clear enough shadow to be able to stabilize into constant light.

Clearing shadows is very much part of the transformational process. The good news is that it takes far less energy to clear your past pain once and for all, than it takes to hide from it for the rest of your life. We feel so much better after we've dropped that baggage!

In the short term, while being excellent and growth-full times, no one likes pain. You buried that pain for a reason. While this shadow clearing is in process, you may well feel troubled and fragile and wish it would all just go away and leave you alone. If you are reading this chapter, the chances are something like this is happening. If it's happening, you might as well welcome it.

If you are 'processing,' clearing your shadow right now, you're not alone. Millions of people are currently going through all kind of internal processing, clearing and purification; they just don't talk about it. When Jesus took 40 days in the desert, it wasn't all roses. Buddha went through all kinds of anguish before he attained nirvana. Krishnamurti suffered intense physical pain throughout his life. None of these great masters arrived at their enlightenment without internal processing. This aspect of spiritual development has been played down to the point that people going through major transformation do not have enough information to know what to do.

Transformation is like other areas of life. Think of what an athlete or gymnast goes through in the vigour of training. We see on TV the awesome accomplishments of those who make it to the Olympics. The broken bones, aching muscles, despondent morale and general anguish that occur on the way to reaching their potential are rarely televised, but nonetheless a reality. Why should the aspiration to our highest spiritual potential be any different?

We have been sold a kind of 'suburban' spirituality – something we can routinely fit in with our 9:00–5:00 schedules that can be scientifically proven to be beneficial to today's work ethic and money focus. That's okay – most of the time we can do all kinds of classes, workshops and retreats and keep up our jobs. Sometimes spirit has other ideas. The interesting thing is that in the long run, these 'other ideas' take us to a fulfilment we would never have dreamed of with our 9:00 to 5:00 thinking.

Spiritual teachings do say, "Take heed! Do not practice without a spiritual master!' Yet they omit to mention exactly what could happen without the spiritual master, what to take heed of, and more importantly, what to do if whatever-it-is does happen. Part of the 'marketing' of these paths is through rosy myths such as, 'once you join this path your guru/master will oversee your development and protect you from all troubles.' This thought is helpful for creating a peaceful trusting mind, but isn't an accurate statement or teaching.

> *A yoga student asked her teacher why he didn't ever talk about the difficulties of kundalini openings and transformation. His reply was, "you have to understand – this is a business."*

Religious and spiritual paths have always had needs to meet, books to balance, roofs that need repair, and ministers or teachers who need feeding and clothing – no different from any other human endeavour. Perhaps the time has come to state that it is dishonest to hide the integration, adjustment and purification that may be needed. Humanity has now evolved to a place where there is no longer any point in hiding the internal clearing, for business or any other reason.

We now know enough about self-healing and evolution to recognize the positive effect of clearing shadows.

One problem with the 'glossy' approach is that it gives a false picture. Profound transformation is always rosy when it's the real thing. If you are given the impression that your spiritual practice is supposed to only bring you more happiness, bliss and peace, when you go through turbulent times you cannot help but conclude that something is wrong – wrong with you, wrong with your teacher or wrong with the practice. Rather than accepting that shadows are part of the path and learning to work with them, you can end up at odds with the fundamental aspects of your practice or transformational direction.

Blaming diverts our attention from the work that really needs to be done. Instead of inquiring into the shadows and finding out how best to clear them, our attention focuses in useless places. This erroneous focus slows, or even halts, our progress.

Other things that spiritual books rarely tell you:

Meditation can melt the walls that keep out subconscious material. Past hurts and traumas we used to be able to hide from, are likely to surface in time. In the long run, it is excellent for our personal development. Our past memories are running our lives, but we can't see what is creating our difficulties because these memories are tucked away in our subconscious. It's difficult working with something that is out of sight. When the material is in the forefront of our conscious awareness, we can work with it.

We go to intensive spiritual workshops and retreats, receive guru Shaktipat, undergo intense therapy, raise our consciousness and deepen our meditation to become more blissful and at peace. What the advertising doesn't tell you is that all this powerful uplifting energy may also wash the seeds of your past experiences into your conscious mind for clearing. As already said, this is great for clearing your old stuff – to get it out of the closet, into the open and let it go, but it rarely feels good at the time. It's a package deal, and this is part of the package. We might as well expect some purification, and welcome the process.

> ***More energy = more clearing.***

If you've been really high and open and you hit a dark or morose time afterwards, you haven't fallen from grace. It's the shadow that light has revealed, part of the process that will take you towards more sustained light in time. Keep your attention on the light while simultaneously acknowledging the shadow (pain, limitation, memories etc.)

True inner fulfilment and self-actualisation doesn't arise through *trying* to be all smiley and happy on the surface while stuffing insecurity, fear or darkness in the closet recesses of our subconscious. Our social masks are surface presentations, often a pretence. To tidy your closet you have to at least briefly see all the old, crumpled things you had stuffed in it – to see your shadows. You don't have to dwell on the contents – in fact really, endeavour not to dwell on them – it's unnecessary suffering. However, you just cannot clear them by jamming the closet door closed on them and pretending they're not there. We've all tried it, and found that it takes immense effort to keep all those experiences shut behind a door. Much better to air it all out and let the dross go.

Purification, alignment and integration happen on all the layers of our consciousness: physical, emotional, mental, and in our subtle energy fields.

Emotional Clearing

We have all buried unresolved past hurts and troubles into our subconscious minds. Opening to light strengthens our connection to who we are in essence – prior to our having emotions and thoughts. This inner sense gives us the most stable and centred basis for our emotional clearing.

As we open, the increased energy can pour into our minds and emotions, amplifying anxieties or troubled memories. This light also dissolves the walls that keep subconscious material out of sight. Emotional troubles which were previously unnoticed can become a tidal wave demanding our full attention.

As an example, say on your first day at school the class bully grabbed you by the neck and threatened to beat you up if you crossed his path. The incident was too sudden and threatening to be processed at the time, so it was parcelled off into your subconscious to process later, and was forgotten. Years later, as an adult you are still creeping around your place of work hoping you won't be seen. At a certain point, this limited way of being would become unacceptable to your expanding consciousness. The memory would either be revealed in your meditation or sleep, or the next time a life situation triggers this, like your boss suddenly looming out of nowhere and hovering over you, instead of reburying the dread, you inquire into it and clear it.

We can't be totally open while there is a part of us that we need to keep closed up and out of sight. In the short term, we would rather stuff all our memories back in Pandora's Box, jam the lid of our subconscious back down, and hope our discomfort somehow goes away. However, the process of emotional clearing is key to our total transformation.

What emerges from Pandora's Box?
When Pandora's Box opens, what emerges from the subconscious is partially digested childhood memories, guilt, sadness, anger,

other long past situations. The juxtaposition of time can feel pretty weird.

The feelings that we have stuffed away can be sufficiently intense that without spiritual guidance, some people feel depressed or hopeless. These memories don't necessarily stop at this life – we may spontaneously remember our previous deaths and other hurts and insecurities.

We add to our challenge by resisting the process, not wanting to let go, not wanting to face painful memories. We slow the transformation by clinging to the way we used to be, rather than moving on.

If you want to avoid dealing with your emotions
Avoiding emotions isn't healthy, and it takes a lot of time and energy. But we all have a pretty good idea how to do it, if only subconsciously. We all know how to stay busy – we occupy ourselves with TV, surfing the net, video games, phoning friends, chit-chat, magazines, going to

bars, drinking alcohol, reading tabloids. or working around the clock. Sounds familiar?

Eating meat, junky comfort foods, deep-fried food, and starchy, stale and packaged food helps distracts us and generally lowers our energy and vibrational frequency. Releasing lots of energy through sex will reduce energy for most people. We can also adopt atheistic ideas, pooh-pooh our own perceptions, laze around, or procrastinate. We can also discontinue spiritual practice and meditation or, alternatively, practicing a meditation technique which is about transcending the physical, emotional and mental fields, facilitates being disconnected from the body, mind and emotions. In other words, doing the opposite of mindful, attuned, listening spiritual practice.

While not particularly healthy, these paragraphs are not entirely facetious. We can slow our process down. The transformative force is strong, but for those who vehemently wish the process would 'just go away' there are choices. A combination of the above will undoubtedly lower our vibrational frequency, distract our attention, and take our time and energy, leaving little to sustain a transformational process. In time, unless your spirit is very persistent, the inclination to transform may possibly fade away – if this is what you want.

If you think you just want the process to 'go away' inquire within yourself whether this is your ego-mind's wish, or your soul's.

If you can get your transformation to stop, is this recommended? You are free to choose your life path, but it is worth considering that when you go against the grain of your soul you risk being at odds with yourself, out of balance, feeling spiritually sickened by the lower vibration activities. You may feel bound to continue pacing your treadmill, constantly diverting your attention, endlessly running to distract yourself from the process your soul calls you to do, but it does takes a lot of energy. Some people hardly dare to relax because they so want to avoid their internal process. This creates a ripe ground for illness. When illness creates sufficient discomfort, we may finally be coerced to focus on the inner work we could have resolved in the beginning – and remained healthy.

If you figure you'd be happier without your limitations and old memories, you might as well do what is needed to drop your baggage. If you're going to drop the baggage, you might as well do it now, and enjoy living the rest of your life that much lighter and freer.

What is truly transformative?
If you want to permanently clear these emotions:
The quickest way of clearing emotional pain is through holding simultaneously in your awareness the light and clarity of your inner being *and* the emotional feelings in your body (N.B. <u>without your story line</u>). When you are in touch with this inner openness, emotion has no substantial ground to root in and will evaporate like mist in the morning sun. Finished.

Although this can be written in one sentence, it takes some practice to be able to do this. The two major pitfalls are:
- **Falling into an emotional trench** (i.e. unable to remain centred in light, and becoming sucked into the pain).
- **Merging with the light** and leaving the pain behind. In this state, the pain no longer exists or feels relevant in the loving light of being. (Unfortunately, the pain feels just as relevant when we leave the transcendental state, so this isn't a permanent solution.)

Emotion is felt in the body. It is sensation. It needs no explanation; just because the emotion doesn't make sense to your mind doesn't mean the emotion isn't there. Emotion is different from thought. Your mind can think, "I don't care!" but emotionally you care a great deal.

Held emotion is an energetic patterning that has stayed in the system because it has not been released. We stuff these undigested feelings into our subconscious where they become demons we try to avoid. The feelings are released by fully feeling them, by perceiving it with the full presence of your awareness.

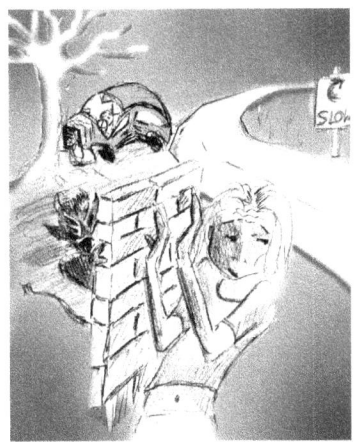

To access your emotions, bring up a snapshot of a traumatic incident. This is a snapshot of a memory from Jenny's teenage life when she had borrowed her parent's car without permission. Wanting to get back home before she was noticed, she nervously took a corner too fast, and totalled the car on impact with a large oak. Find a snap shot of your experience.

Don't think about it the situation, just revisit the felt-sense of the situation, and be with the place in your body that responds emotionally to the snapshot. You could ask yourself, where in my body do I feel this? What colour texture or density is this feeling? Rate your emotional intensity, on a scale from 0 (doesn't have any impact at all) to 10 (the most intense feelings

you've ever had).

It may not be the incident itself that is the baggage you are now carrying. In Jenny's case, sure, being in hospital all bandaged up was a shock. She was in physical pain for months. Jenny's real pain, and what is still running her life, is the guilt of her disobedience. Her parents have long since forgiven her, but she has never truly forgiven herself.

Pure emotion does not easily find its way into words. That is one measure of how close to the core of the issue we are. The surface, or mental, level of an emotion is the verbal story about it. As we go deeper into the emotion, it is perceived more and more as an abstract felt-sense. When we reach really deeply into it, emotion is found to be of the same essence as the awareness that is watching.

It is our bodies, not our minds, which hold emotional pain. Anger might sit in your solar plexus, maternal attachment in the naval area, security at the base of the spine, loss of love in the heart. When emotion is felt in the throat, the emotion may not actually be located there. The throat creates a collar or band that keeps the feelings down, and prevents those feelings from being expressed. When the collar dissolves, you may well feel the emotion in a place elsewhere in your body.

Practical tips for going about this process
- You need a fairly strong inner connection or centeredness so that you won't nose-dive into an emotional pit. If your gut sense is that your feelings will overwhelm you if you access them, then: either find someone who can be at your side and speak on behalf of your higher self, reminding you of your light-spirit nature; or do this clearing at another time. It is better to watch a movie or spend time in company than dive in your troubles when you feel unsteady.
- Wallowing in emotion is also to be avoided since it empowers and strengthens the structure of the emotion, which is the reverse of what you need.
- If you are steady and clear, create a safe uninterrupted space to be in for a while. Lock the door, disconnect the phone, put a 'do not disturb' note on the door, or do whatever else is necessary to ensure your uninterrupted peace and quiet.
- You may like to meditate first to strengthen your inner awareness. Don't transcend – just align with spirit, and strengthen your sense that your spirit nature – who you really are – has never been touched or affected by anything that has ever happened to you.
- Sit or lie somewhere comfortably where your body can completely relax.
- In the full presence of your awareness, get in touch with the emotion. Feel it. If the emotion is an intense one, just turn a corner of your attention to it at first. Keep close to the awareness that your essential nature has never even taken birth, let alone experienced any pain. In this awareness, there is a sweetness - the sweetness of the presence of being - that pervades even the most intense experience of pain.
- Any resistance to feeling, such as a sense that 'I can't handle this,' 'I don't want to go through this,' 'I don't want to live,' is dealt with similarly, as a felt sense. You feel the sense of not wanting to live any more, and you feel the resistance to feeling. All of this is consciousness in one form or another. It is all imbued with the perfection and sweetness of existence when reached into with a daring heart. These emotions can be processed too.

What continues to run our lives is not the past situations, but the decisions we made about those situations.

I had a lot of asthma when I was a child, and people didn't notice, didn't get me medication, and yet expected me to be as strong as my siblings. My way of making sense of this was to assume that I wasn't worth looking after. This belief unconsciously weakened my self-esteem throughout everything I did. In a therapy session half way through my adult life, when I heard, "every child deserves to be looked after," my immediate reaction was, "oh no, not all, not this child!" I was absolutely assured of this. When the therapist pressed the point, I was swept with dismay, sadness and despair.

The situation that caused the pain may have occurred long ago, but it is not the past you are dealing with, but the feeling currently present, right now, in your body. There is no need for reconstructing a 'past.' You look out at life through eyes tinted by the emotions you carry in your system *right now*. Everything you see is tinted. You may think that the tint is associated with a particular history, but the tint itself has no reference other than held feeling that you currently carry. Be with the feeling in full awareness and it will gradually release. When the emotion is released, your past will seem like a storybook that has been gently returned to the bookshelf after years of hanging in front of your face.

After being felt with your full presence, emotion passes swiftly, like a cloud swept by a spring breeze, and life moves to a fresh moment that is open, free and fully present. Once you've stepped through the eye of the emotional hurricane and experienced the clarity and lightness of being as your baggage melts away, you will look forward to the next opportunity to have something come up that you can clear. The elation of the post-storm lightness will inspire you to more emotional clearing.

Sometimes you don't realize that you've really cleared an emotional issue until you are in a situation that usually presses your buttons and are surprised to find you are now steady and unaffected. It also happens that sometimes you think you've cleared something, and find your old emotions triggered again by a life situation.

When you can stay a few days in your mother's house, prepare food with her, hear her critical comments about yourself and your life, and not have any buttons pressed, you are well on the way!

Working with deep trauma

If you have a lot of issues to clear, start with the easier ones to get in practice. Before tackling a deep and troubling trauma, envision a place where you feel really safe and cosy – it may be your bedroom, perhaps with your lover, or a favourite woodland nook. Create a really clear image of this place. If you start feeling swallowed up and overwhelmed by the intensity of the memory you are dealing with, leave the memory and go to your safe place.

If you have a friend – preferably an aware or spiritually attuned friend – who can be at your side, creating a safe, accepting space, this helps greatly when dealing with very troubled memories. Your friend can remind you of your higher nature, guide you to your safe place if you get out of depth, lend a shoulder to cry on, and hear you in full awareness.

Professional help

Good professional help may help cut the lengthy process of internal clearing and can be worth its weight in gold. Body centred, emotionally oriented therapists, and energy workers might be helpful professionals to consider. Skilled energy workers can read directly from your body and energy field, bypassing the need to talk about your troubles. A few sessions with an intuitive, skilled professional can save long periods of trying to do it all on your own. E.M.D.R. works especially well.

E.M.D.R. - clearing past trauma

Eye movement desensitisation response is a relatively new and very effective therapeutic method practiced by professional therapists and some psychiatrists, which can clear past trauma much more quickly than conventional methods. It works like this:

First you establish a safe place by bringing to mind a place where you feel comfortable and safe, such as your bed, your favourite woodland or a hideaway attic. Next, think of the trauma you would like to clear and bring to mind a snapshot of the incident. Rate the level of trauma from this snap shot of the incident from 0 (doesn't bother me) to 10 (overwhelmingly troubling). While keeping the snap-shot in mind, rhythmically move your eyes left and right for a few minutes, following the therapist's hand, (or, alternatively, you can tap your left and right knees or listen to a sound through headphones that alternates from one ear to the other.) The alternating left-right stimulus links the hemispheres, and helps clear the impression. You will know when to stop. Rate the trauma again from 0 to 10.

Other impressions associated with the trauma may come up during the eye movement, which sometimes stimulates an underlying layer of experience. Another phase of eye movement will help clear this layer. The idea is to bring the intensity down to zero.

If at any time the trauma feels too intense, go to your comfortable, safe place and be there for a while.

Other things that help:
Intent
Firmly decide that you want to move on, to let go of the past and to heal.

If you experience reticence in letting go, look to see what your pay-off is for holding on. It might be something like, "I can't let go of this painful memory otherwise I might allow this situation to happen again." You could ask yourself, what do I have to give up or strengthen in order to let this memory go? It might be I need to give up always being the 'nice guy' or the peacemaker and dare to say 'no' when you need to.

Clearly envisage, with as much detail as possible, how you would like to be. Offer your prayer to the sky or God, and ask that your prayer be fulfilled.

Look at what each situation teaches. Often we can leave behind and move on from experiences when we have learned from the wisdom they offer.

Creative expression
Keep a journal. It really helps to keep the daily ups and downs of your life in perspective. Your journal won't mind if you complain on and on – you can dump all your negativity there. You can also capture the high moments, the times of lucid clarity when you know exactly what is going on, and why it's happening, and when you see the light at the end of the tunnel. Preserving these insights on paper helps you through troubled days.

You don't have to be an artist to express how you feel on paper. Get a set of wax crayons, and a pile of printer paper, and just let yourself go. The very smell will remind you of how good it feels to scribble with abandonment. Draw your anguish, your inspiration, your light and your shadow. Giving a form to abstract feelings helps clarify them, and allows feelings to communicate to other parts of yourself.

Make music. Write music. Sing. Make sound. Shout, cathart (purge your difficult feelings), sigh and groan. Find songs that lament the way you feel, or write your own, and sing them with feeling, releasing the emotion as you go. Sing songs that lift you up or remind you of good times.

Dance to music that is descriptive of how you feel. Dance to keep your energy moving, to move the places where emotions stick, to stomp the released emotions into the ground. Move in any way that releases your body. Breathe. Open your chest, swing your pelvis, and keep your energy moving.

Read. Read the experiences of others who have lived similar situations to you – you'll pick up all kinds of insights from their perceptions. Read books that offer insight and clarity. Read books which draw your attention to who you are as light-love-spirit.

Try sandbox therapy. Get a box or tray and put some sand in it. Shape the sand. Place objects in the sand which symbolically represent your emotions, psyche, fears, or situations in your life. Any objects you don't have can be modelled out of plasticine or flour dough.

Be with your world a while. It is surprisingly helpful to see a manifest 3D depiction of facets in your inner world.

Be with the different characters and symbols you have represented. Turn the tray around and see what it looks like from the other side, or from the point of view of one of the pieces or sand shapes. What message do the various characters or objects have for you?

> *The sand box was full of people, furniture and animals. Then she spotted a sandalwood Buddha, and made room for him. We paused as we took in her world. "Actually, you know, I don't really need all these people now the Buddha is there. Can I take some pieces out?" I told her she was the creator of her world and so could have it any way she wanted. She cleared a wide area around the Buddha, smoothing the sand, and put in rocks and trees to the side of the clearing. "You know, it's just become very clear to me – I need to spend more time in my garden."[14]*

Take a photo of your world. Sit with it. Make any changes you would like so it is just the way you want it. Build another world when you next feel inclined to do so.

Cathart
Anger is a strong emotion. Sometimes the best thing is to get it out and release it physically. Running and other taxing exercise can sometimes do the trick. Some gyms have punching bags that you can safely lay into. Alternatively, punching a large pillow can help vent anger and frustration. Punch as if you really mean it.

You can pick up some second hand plates, and smash them. The sound is satisfying, but the disadvantage of this approach is that there is a lot of cleaning up afterwards. Alternatively, you could go to a quarry and smash large rocks – less availability, but much less clean-up.

If you can find a place that is sound proof or distant enough to not disturb others, primal screaming, howling like a wolf or shouting might help express and release anger. The more aware you are throughout all of these activities – the more fully present – the better they will work.

Bach Remedies
Many people find Bach Flower Remedies help clear emotions. They can be purchased inexpensively at your health food shop. They have no known side effects.

Which remedies?
- If you are experiencing hatred, envy, jealousy, greed, anger, revenge or suspicion, try the remedy Holly.
- Crab Apple is good for when you feel unclean, self-disgust, or repulsed by yourself.
- Gentian helps a negative outlook, despondency, and when you are feeling depressed by your setbacks.
- Alternatively, the remedy Gorse is good for feelings of despair, when you feel like nothing can be done to help, or when you give up hope.
- If you tend to be stuck in the past, Honey Suckle helps. Willow helps dissolve the resentment you feel when you blame others for your misfortunes.

- ❖ Pine helps when you blame yourself, and feel self-reproach and guilt.
- ❖ Mustard provides relief when you feel deep gloom for no particular reason.
- ❖ Rock Rose helps reduce terror, panic and nightmarish feelings.

There are many more remedies. Health food shops often carry leaflets so you can easily identify the remedies for your emotions. Books about Bach Flower Remedies are stocked in most alternative bookshops.

How to use Bach remedies: short term use (1-2 days):
Put three drops of your chosen remedy(s) in a glass of water and sip it frequently. Up to three remedies can be added together in a glass of water. Alternatively, you can put one drop of the chosen remedy directly on your tongue.

Long-term use (3 days or more):
Take an empty dropper bottle and add three drops of each remedy you choose. Up to six remedies can be used together. Fill the bottle with 80% spring water and 20% brandy or cider vinegar as a preservative. Take the mixture at least four times a day, putting two or three drops on your tongue.

Visualization
If you want to clear or unblock an area, you can use visualization, as a way of focusing your intent. The kinds of images you use depend on what you can picture easily. You might envision the blocked part of your body in a colour like black or red, and through your intent, envision the colour transforming into, say, blue or gold.

You can also envision an area that is closed or blocked opening up like a flower. Envision anything that is held being released and clearing to a safe place well away from your body. You can envision bathing the energy field surrounding your body in coloured light. If you need to energize, you could choose a bright, vibrant colour, if you need to settle, you could choose a soft cool colour.

Crystals
Crystals are used to clear energy, protect the chakras, and to heal. There are also stones that work to revitalize each chakra, such as Garnet for the root chakra, Carnelian for the second chakra, Citrine quartz for the solar plexus, rose or green quartz for the heart, Lapis

lazuli for the throat, moonstone for the third eye, amethyst for the crown, and clear quartz above the crown. Clear quartz can also be used to amplify your energy and intent.

> *I remember when I first moved out here, I was dealing with a lot of grief. By a strange sequence of events, I ended up wearing an amethyst ring. I found out later that Amethyst is a great stone for healing this type of emotion. I also found clear quartz would help me energize and make things more clear, including raising my vibration. Two more stones I found helpful to remove heaviness were Peridot and Aquamarine.[15]*

Many books detail the properties of each crystal, and you can also use your intuition and simply use what feels good.

Dealing with Fear

Fear is a very fundamental emotion, often felt in the pit of the stomach. From the time we come into existence as individual consciousness, there is a fear of returning to simply Being, a fear of emptiness, fear of the unknown, and fear of death. To put it another way, we want to continue being in existence, continue being someone, and continue following our preferences.

The Patanjali Yoga Sutras state that we are made up of fundamental duality (avidya), ego (asmita – sense of individuality), raga (attraction to what we feel sustains our existence), dwaysha (aversion to what we feel threatens or takes away from our existence), and abhinivesh – the fear of death, or the wish to live. In other words, because we think we exist as separate entities, we seek to preserve these entities. So we want things that support us and we don't want things that we feel don't support our existence. This is a powerful, fundamental psychology underlying everything that we feel, do and think.

Fear is counteracted by love and trust. Like all emotions, you don't have to get into the story line. If you feel fear when you sit in the dentist's chair, place your hands over your solar plexus, breath into this centre, and it will cool out.

If you have fear of known things such as death, illness, madness, poverty, losing friends, the Bach Remedy Mimulus helps. If you don't know what you're afraid of, or if your fear is nebulous, and there is little you can definitively pin the fear on, try Aspen (fear for unknown reason).

Don't worry, no one's watching
Your internal clearing is largely invisible to others. Your inner world may be full of all kinds of strange energy sensations, shifting pains and the ghosts of distant, unresolved memories. Yet if you wish, you can put on a social face with a fair assurance that people won't notice, if that's what you want. Most people are wrapped up in themselves, their plans and their thoughts. Many people hardly know what they feel themselves, let alone have the sensitivity to sense someone else's feelings. So unless you draw attention to your inner state, you could carry on your job and leisure life while going through all kinds of inner turmoil, yet your outer life remains pretty much the same. This can be quite helpful, offering an element of comparative constancy while your inner world radically alters, although it can feel like Jekyll and Hyde are living side by side within you.

You can slow down, or ignore the process for a time, but usually it continues until it is finished. For this reason, it is best to help your inner process as much as possible by giving it time-energy priority and professional support when needed. Resisting the process creates needless difficulty. It may not feel like this is what you wanted, but on some level, you welcomed this transformation or you would still be half-asleep, hiding your traumas, and concealing from your true potential like so many other people do. Happily, in time, all that arises clears, leaving us feeling much lighter.

Ways we avoid clearing emotion:
The internationally popular 'ignore-it-and-it-will-go-away' approach only works for so long. Putrid smells arise from even well buried garbage.

Procrastination. Time helps you find perspective, it allows you to get used to having a part of you that hurts, and it provides a new moment to focus on, but it doesn't heal your wounds.

Denial is a coping response. In the short term it is definitely more effective than sinking in the dark. In the long term, denial tends to bury your issues so that you have to consciously dig down to find what is silently running your life.

Dwelling on the circumstances surrounding the pain (called here the 'story line') is another way of avoiding it. You can tell the story of your suffering again and again, (weighing down so many ears in the process!) but the pain will still be there. Why? Thinking distracts you from real feeling. It is easy to avoid the intensity of feeling by thinking about the feelings. If you find your mind is an endlessly stuck record, repeating a pattern with no resolution, it is because your emotion remains untouched.

Psychotherapy enables clarifying, labelling, and reframing the problem in terms your mind can encompass. While this may sometimes seem useful, if you afterwards you are still troubled, a more emotionally based, body centred therapy could provide a better alternative.

Since denial, transcendence, dwelling in the pain, dwelling in the story line, and avoidance through distraction, don't work to clear the emotional pain from your system, what works best?

Make your transformational process a priority
Reduce stress and activity. Sleep, rest, and give yourself time and space to grow in. Wherever possible, cut back your work-load, domestic responsibilities and other pressures. Free up time, by reducing social and extracurricular activities. Give value to your inner process. Give yourself as much time as possible to 'be' in, to get 'undone' if you need it, to diary, and reflect. Redirect your spare cash for therapy and energy treatments when you sense this will help you along. Consciously say to yourself, "I'm ready. I will do what it takes to become free."

8

Working With Your Mind

When our minds tumble with thoughts
Our minds tend to be busy at the best of times. Through spiritual practice and awakening, you open to more energy. That energy can flow into your emotions, your sexuality, your heart, or into your mind. When more energy flows into your mind, it can be flooded with a million thoughts, imaginings, memories and plans. It is especially noticeable when you try to meditate. In the short run, you may well find times during your spiritual practice when your mind is more stirred up and agitated than you have ever known, especially if you don't know how to handle your unruly mind.

What is happening?
- ❖ You are spending a lot of time doing mentally busy activities such as study, using a computer, and planning. When you use your mind a lot it becomes active, and you have to work at settling it down afterwards. It is possible that you might be busy studying or planning as an unconscious form of avoidance, as in the point above.
- ❖ An influx of energy has washed seeds of unresolved situations into your conscious awareness.
- ❖ Avoidance: Your mind is avoiding feeling, avoiding the vastness of being, busy trying to keep control, or busy living its preferences.

If, by a redirecting attention, your ruminations vanish, you don't have too much of a problem. However, if your mental teeth have become well embedded in issues and cannot let go, you may well wish to make your mind a more comfortable place with which to live.

What do you do with this busy mind?
When your thinking is solid, busy, unremitting, there are three main solutions. The best is to bring your mind back to stillness and clarity through meditation, taking time in nature, breathing and relaxing.

If this feels unmanageably difficult, an interim measure might be to read beautiful, divinely inspired, peaceful words, words that will hopefully return you to a place of more inner peace and clarity through their meaning and resonance. You could also listen to beautiful music, listening with your full awareness to every instrument, every sound, every feeling the composer was communicating. This listening brings attention into the present.

If you are truly present in this moment, this very moment, you'll find there is no room for a written, spoken or thought sentence in it. Sentences spread out over time, each word symbol coming one after the other. A sentence cannot fit in the present moment.

If you are just too busy-minded to even try to settle, the next best thing could be to pour that busy mental energy into an uplifting project or study. This puts your mental business to good positive use, but obviously won't actually cure the situation. The root of the trouble remains, but it's a relief to take a short-term break from it. Taking a break is better than dwelling in discomfort. Making a choice to use your mental energy positively helps strengthen your commitment to choosing to be happy. The very decision to not dwell in unhappiness helps break your ruminating patterns. Every time you choose the positive over unhappiness, your spirit strengthens.

Transformation takes the reigns of our unruly, 'chewy' minds and refocuses them. With practice, we can train ourselves to focus our attention on a tranquil state of being that exists prior to our thinking. Our minds take the shape and quality of whatever it attends. If it focuses on awareness, it will become open, fluid, and at peace. Every time you have the courage to turn away from the mind towards awareness, you lessen the power of your mind over you. In time this builds into tremendous strength and mastery.

A really busy mind may not easily focus on something as abstract as awareness. Return to page 133 in chapter 4 for more details about how to calm a busy mind, or see below for additional tips.

Quieting the mind

- Repetition of a mantra or verses – a soft lilting repetition that focuses our attention.
- Singing. There is a reason why every spiritual tradition around the planet throughout time uses some form of singing. Our voices will open us up, and make us feel good. For the time we are singing, we are with the song rather than our mind.
- Humming is simpler, but works really well. Humming resonates throughout the body, throughout the bones. You can open all your chakras by focusing where you direct your hum.
- Pranayama and other breathing exercises help focus our minds and increase energy. Since the mind and the breath are closely linked, as our breath becomes steadier, our minds will follow.

One time-honoured breath technique: start by breathing in for six counts, suspend your breath for six counts, breathe out for six, then suspend your breath for six counts. Every few rounds you can increase the count – to seven, eight, nine etc. As the count increases, you need increasing amount of attention to maintain the breathing technique, especially when mastering the breath so it is totally even and steady. There is little room for thought. During this time your mind gets a break and has a chance to unwind a little. Conscious breathing increases your energy, allowing you to live above the grip of the mind more easily.

Aligning your mind with your inner being

If you feel perplexed when your thoughts and actions differ from your love and awareness, when you act in a way that is not in accord with your inner truth, your mind is likely in the driver's seat, acting automatically in habitual patterns. These patterns can be changed through ongoing observation, honesty, and intent. Introduce a pause between the situations and your reactions. In that pause, empty yourself for a moment, tune in to your heart or inner awareness, and speak or act from There.

Stubbornly ingrained patterns may take longer, but if you keep patiently observing, pausing, re-tuning, and speaking from a deeper place within you, the patterns will change. In time your mind will come to resonate with the nature of your inner being.

Transforming conditions
The task of transforming your non-conducive mental habits, and transforming our identification with these habits, can take a while. We can identify with our inner awareness (which has no conditions) as who we really are, while moment-to-moment observing impartially the way our minds have been programmed to respond. Who we really are isn't our thinking. Thinking is a layer of us that has been shaped by circumstance. Part of spiritual transformation is to bring this mind into resonance with our inner nature – so our mind 'takes the shape' of our loving, free soul essence rather than our social programming.

Transformation happens through ongoing honest observation. Our departures from being the kind, loving, generous people we are in essence come from all kinds of hidden agendas and unresolved wishes. True observation happens through residing in the clarity of spirit nature, and perceiving with the non-judgment awareness of your spirit-nature.

Counterproductive mental habits
Wallowing in past memories, sadness or troubles strengthens these emotions and patterns of thinking. Thinking about the situations in our life that we wish were different, wishing they weren't there, labelling them, applying psychological processes, escaping into imagination, or denying their existence by putting attention elsewhere, does not transform our limitations. Thinking about conditions and labelling them can actually reinforce them and make them more part of one's identity.

Leaving behind our human experience by transcending in deep meditation or escaping into daydreams and fantasy appears to offer temporary relief, in the same way watching television does. Transcendence, while not particularly transformative in itself, may strengthen a connection with spirit.

We can gently and lovingly observe our negative thoughts and replace them with the opposite tendency. If in the next moment, as another negative thought come, we gently and loving replace the negative thought with its opposite. With diligence, over time we can gradually upgrade, or overhaul, our minds.

Re-writing the script
If you find your mind repeatedly running story lines that make you feel bad (the stuck-record syndrome), one way of moving forward is to rewrite the script. For example, if your parent's divorce saddened you, go back to that time, and change the way you responded. Rewrite yourself as a person with better resources, increased wisdom, a steady inner centre, more ability to communicate or receive help, or the ability to not take the situation you were in so personally. If the rewritten story feels better, adopt it. Breathe it in as your new reality. Both the happy and the sad stories are equally just stories in the mind. Both are imagination. Since only the present moment is real, the past and future are extrapolations of our mind (i.e. imagination). We are free to choose what we want from our imagination. We might as well imagine beautifully.

Putting your life in perspective
You might wonder why you deserved so many traumatic events in your life, but if you could take a look under other people's veneers, you would no doubt find events that felt just as troublesome to those people. Life is rarely smooth. Everyone has experienced gains and losses.

As we become more connected to spirit, we realize the gifts that difficult situations bring. Strengths and skills are often built through adversity. Some of the best healers came to the gifts through their necessity of finding their way out of extreme pain, or, avoiding death.

Prayer
Despite appearances, it is not we who are running this life show, but some greater power, call it God, Allah or Beingness. When you pray, you re-connect to this presence, you let go a little, you surrender your pain or perplexity. Ultimately, our spiritual practice is bringing us from 'my will be done' to 'thy will be done.'

Affirmations
Negative mind patterns can be undone by consistently replacing them with their opposite. Affirmations are phrases or paragraphs that instil your mind with love, trust and healing. You can write them out, print them in pretty fonts, and put them on the fridge door, in the

bathroom, beside your bed, or anywhere else where you will see them.

> *I never linger in the mind of discord and always quickly return to my peaceful loving heart.[8]*

> *Always and everywhere, I trustingly surrender to my present heart of feelings and the universe, the task of guarding and protecting myself and others against all forms of abuse and violence, in thought, speech and deeds, past, present and future.[16]*

Bach Flower Remedies for the mind
- Agrimony - helps when you are hiding your tortured mind behind a cheerful face.
- Scleranthus – helps reduce indecision, uncertainty, swinging between extreme emotions, and lack of inner balance.
- Sweet Chestnut – is helpful for mental despair, anguish, and hopelessness.
- White chestnut – aids thoughts that go round and round.

Byron Katie's method of freeing the mind
If you find your mind rotating in dissatisfaction with other people, Byron Katie, author of Loving What Is, has a helpful method which quickly frees the mind from its stuck records of suffering.

The essence of her thought is that we suffer when we expect people and situations to be other than they are. She calls this non-acceptance 'arguing with reality.' "When you argue with reality, you lose, but only 100% of the time."

You can free yourself from suffering by questioning your thinking. Katie's method is as follows. Write down the things that bother you. Be petty and judgmental, and write them exactly as you feel them. For example, "my partner should be more understanding." Next, for each item, ask yourself four questions:

1. **Can I really know this is true?** (It feels like it's true!)
2. **Can I really know that my partner should be any way other than s/he is?** (Well, no, I guess everyone is as they are.)
3. **How do I feel when I think the thought that my partner should be more understanding?** (I feel frustrated, and despondent.)
4. **Who would I be without this thought?** (I'd feel fine. I'd be at peace.) Can you think of any sane, healthy reason for continuing to hold a

thought that makes you feel frustrated and irritated? (…No… (Penny drop moment) – Wow, it really is my thinking that is making me suffer over this. If I'm fine without this thought, …)

The next step is to turn the thought around. Would it be equally true to say that I should better understand my partner? Or that I should understand myself more?

It is not easy to see that we have beliefs, concepts and judgements, but it is very easy to judge our neighbours. We can easily see where everyone else is at fault. Since we project on to others our own internal way of seeing and believing, judging our neighbours is a good way of finding out how we tick. When we see our thinking as it is, when we cease to project our expectations, our suffering melts away.

For more details on this method, see www.thework.org.

To clear memories through focused contemplation

When you feel discomfort and you sense there is an experience behind the discomfort buried in your subconscious, if you put your full, one-pointed concentration (sanyam) on the emotions as felt in your body, or on the seed memory (sanskara) you can get access to the situation that created the memory, (which may or may not be in this life.) Having brought the memory to the conscious surface of your mind, it can be more easily cleared. Fear due to past situations can be released by gently putting the experience in the past where it belongs, clearing the ties to it, and affirming that the life you now live is far away from the past situation. Now, step out into your new fearless world.

Energy Psychology Emotional Clearing Techniques

Energy psychology clearing techniques are based on meridian and hemisphere dominance findings. Gary Craig's Emotional Freedom Technique (EFT) is the most popular of these techniques. His formula, which he calls his 'recipe,' starts with correcting any negative polarities.

1. Find a short phrase to symbolize the problem you'd like to clear. Let's say you are still trying to get over the trauma of a car accident. There are two parts to clear – the guilt at taking your parents car, and the trauma of the accident. Start with the guilt.

2. Rate the intensity of this guilt feeling from 10, worse feeling I ever had, to 0 – I don't feel anything at all.
3. I then rub what Gary Craig calls 'the sore spot' – find the notch at the top of your breastbone, go down 3" and out to one side (either side) 3". Rub there as you say this phrase: "Even though *I still feel guilty*, I deeply and completely accept myself as I am." Replace the underlined script with the issue you are working on. "Even though I ____, I deeply and completely accept myself as I am." While you rub the sore spot.
4. Tap each of the following points in turn 7 times as you repeat your core phrase (in my case, "*still feeling guilty*".) The points are:

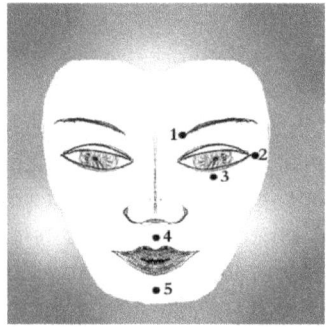

1. Inside edge of eyebrow (Bl-2),
2 Outside of eye (GB-1),
3. Under eye (St-1)
4. Under nose
5. On chin

6. Under lower edge of collarbone (K-27)

7. 4" below armpit (Sp-21)

8. under left breast (Lv-14)

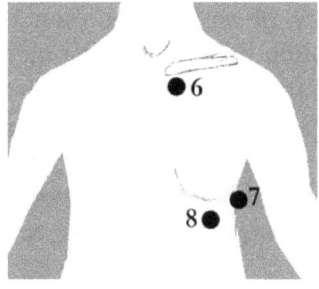

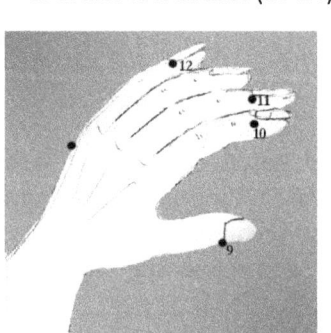

9. Outside edge of thumbnail (Lu-16.
10. Thumb side of index fingernail LI-1
11. Thumb side of middle finger (PC-9)
12. Out side of little finger ((SI-3)

5. Tap a point between the outer two knuckles, half an inch back from the knuckle edge (TH-3) while you: close your eyes, open them, look down and right, look down left, roll your eyes one way,

roll your eyes the other, hum a line of a song, count rapidly from 1 to 5, and hum the line of the song again.
6. Run through the 12 points again, tapping each 7 times as you repeat your reminder phrase (my example is, "*still feeling guilty.*")
7. Rate the intensity of the feeling (as in the second step). A light problem might have already cleared. Otherwise you can repeat these steps, finding phrases to capture different aspects of the feeling you'd like to clear.
8. At the end, you can 'tap in' a positive thought, "I am healed," "I am love and light".

Gary Craig has done an incredible job of making this effective technique available for everyone. Visit his web site http://www.emofree.com/ for a free manual with more details and information about this technique.

EDxTM is a more sophisticated version of EFT, using kinesiology muscle testing and more specific acupuncture points. TFT is another technique based on these principles.

Other techniques to clear the energy fields

We can help clear, purify and balance the subtle energy channels (called nadis in Sanskrit) that run through our bodies through ancient yogic breath exercises called pranayama. Pranayama literally means 'prana,' life force or chi + yama, to master.

The combined movement and breath of qigong exercises balances energy, promotes energetic grounding, boosts the immune system, and strengthens the nervous system. Qi means life force or breathe, gong means technique.

Medical qigong is a standard therapy used in hospitals across China as part of their health care plan.

The soft martial art form, T'ai Chi, while was not created for health or energy balance as such, has some of the benefits of qigong. Practitioners find T'ai Chi leaves them feeling more balanced and grounded. It is like a moving meditation.

Energetically depleted areas of our energy field can be energized by laying hands on that area and allowing energy to flow in through the palms of our hands (like Reiki). The effect can be enhanced by directing our breath, using intent, or by visualizing light flowing in of a colour that would balance or complement the area. This method of visualization can extend out to the whole auric field, or energy field surrounding the body, creating more balance, and clearing scars and old memories from the field.

Physical illness

Transformation can occur on many different levels. Sometimes a mental or emotional block will resolve or clear by manifesting as a physical illness. Unresolved personal issues that have been ignored can demand attention through illness that they wouldn't otherwise get. Suppressed grief can emerge as asthma, anger can emerge in boils or abscesses, a refusal to release old memories can manifest as constipation. Why one person's grief manifests as illness and another person's grief doesn't is one of life's mysteries. Perhaps at certain times in our evolution we are simply called to clear or rebalance some aspect of us, and this is the form it takes.

Transformation moves us towards more health and balance. Western medication can alleviate the immediate symptoms, but the underlying condition remains unchanged, and may re-surface as another medical condition until the cause is addressed or cleared up.

Disease dissolves structure. It is a teaching because it shows where attention is needed. It is a puzzle. The key to the puzzle unlocks, or cures, the disease. Listening is the key.

Roots of disease

- Loss of connection with your spirit nature.
- Unconscious life patterns and habits.
- Continuing to live in unsuitable relationships, jobs and environments.
- Not honouring the call of your spirit. (Sometimes spirit will find a way of shouting at you!)
- Unprocessed walled off emotions creating energy blocks and resistance. Organs and body tissue at the place of the block will not be able to get the energy they need to function properly and will start to lose vitality and finally become diseased.
- Becoming physically ill may be the only way you can get the quiet time needed for your process.

Certain physical conditions seem to be associated with, or tend to accompany, spiritual transformation. The participants in the PSE pilot study ticked the following boxes of conditions they had noticed during their transformation period, with the following frequencies:

Headaches	16%
Chronic fatigue	22%
Food intolerance	24%
Fibromyalgia	8%
Chemical sensitivity	12%
Digestive problems	23%
Flu-like symptoms	13%
Joint pain	22%
Immune problems	6%

Chart showing percentage of participants experiencing each condition

Are these figures much higher than the national average? They seem to be around two to three times higher. One in every 12 Canadians aged 12 or older has been diagnosed by a health professional as having migraine headaches.[17] The prevalence of adults diagnosed with Chronic Fatigue Syndrome in Canada was 199,746 in 2001, and 341,126 in 2003.[18] A study by White et al.[19] suggests that 3.3% or 825,000 of Canadians have Fibromyalgia, supported also by Dr. Elizabeth Badley who indicated that 822,000 Canadians had been diagnosed with FMS in 1994.[20]

Condition	Percentage of pilot study participants answering reporting this condition	Percentage of Canadian citizens with this condition
Headaches	16	6.6
Fibromyalgia	8	2.7
Chronic fatigue	22	13.6

It is possible that these conditions are linked to, or more likely to occur, during profound times of transformation. Further research would be needed to clarify why.

Physical purification and clearing

Our joints and muscles hold the tension of all our stress and resistance to life. Yoga helps release this tension. If you are in the midst of a lot of change, keep stretching! Keep clearing tension from your body. The stretching helps free up blockages in the energy channels and circulation. The release helps move out those dark moods.

Our bodies also accumulate toxins from chemicals, food additives and pollutants. These toxins can be cleared through a combination of fasting, special diets, cleansing herbs, enemas and colonics. Check with your G.P. or naturopathic doctor to make sure that these practices will be safe for you.

Numerous details can be found in specialized books. A wide spectrum of possibilities are available. For example, when fasting, we can fast on water alone, on lemon juice with maple syrup and a pinch of cayenne pepper, or on juice. Fresh, organic, homemade juices are full, liquid meals. They feed the body while giving the digestive system a break from solids.

When fasting is combined with cleansing herbs, the body is given a great opportunity to release toxins, which are flushed out by drinking lots of water.

Enemas can be very helpful. Many emotions are stored as molecules in the liver. Coffee enemas (made from fresh ground coffee) can help release toxins from your liver. A water enema rinse is done prior to the coffee enema, and another water enema follows after the coffee to rinse out the coffee.

For a more thorough intestinal rinse, a professional colonic treatment can clear your system well.

Raw vegetables and fruits are fine, vital foods that raise our vibration and can radically change our consciousness. We get to observe how well we accept this higher vibration by our food choices – after a fine salad, do we pine for a chocolate brownie to bring us to a more familiar vibration? Although the raw vegan food nourishes our bodies, often our emotional and sensual cravings continue to hanker for our favourite treats. By not indulging in these treats, we can explore the emotions and desires that run us. So a raw vegan diet raises our vibration, clears out the body, and helps clear issues that we usually bury by diverting our attention into taste gratification.

What we put in our mouths is something we can control. We are made of the frequency of our food. What vibration, freshness and vitality do we choose?

9

Sleep, sex, food & changing moods

During spiritual transformation, some very basic and essential aspects of our lives may not be running the way we are used to, such as our sleep patterns, our appetite for food or sex, and our moods.

Changing sleeping patterns
Sleep patterns can change greatly when there is increased spiritual openness. When life-force or kundalini energies are moving strongly we may not need to sleep much. If no tiredness builds up, we can enjoy the increased number of waking hours we have each day. We can meditate or practice yoga, work on energy grounding, journaling, or reading while the rest of the world sleeps.

Needing hours of extra sleep each day
Transformation and integration of new states of consciousness takes a great deal of energy. Some say the DNA in every cell throughout the body changes. It's a lot of change, and much rest and sleep may be needed from time to time. It is not uncommon for people to sleep 10, 12 or even more hours each day while undergoing deep internal work. If you find you need a lot of sleep, why not give yourself the time. All you need to do is go to work, eat, and use the bathroom, and get the sleep you need at this time. It won't last forever.

Waking up between 2:00 and 5:00 a.m.
A lot of people either wake up, or have dreams in which spirit guides appear to be teaching them something, between 2:00 and 5:00 a.m. It seems to be part of the transformation process for many people. Teaching, downloading new information, and re-alignment often takes

place during this time. You may need to either go to bed earlier to make up for the waking hours, or take a nap later in the day.

Inability to sleep:
Maybe you want to sleep but can't. If you feel wired, fried, unable to function well, removing coffee, chocolate, alcohol, tobacco and tea from your diet, (especially avoiding consumption later in the day) may help.

Ginger, rooibos tea, kali tea, onions, sweets and spices are also stimulating. TV, thriller movies, fast-response computer games, hours of studying, and worrying also rev up the mind. If you are still unable to sleep, perhaps your restlessness is due to a busy mind, too much energy, fear, something to do with your bed or bedroom, or a biological condition. Kinesiology muscle testing may offer a way to find out.

A busy mind:
If your mind is busy, listening to relaxing music or a guided relaxation CD might help you unwind. Repeating a mantra can be soothing to the mind if it suits you. Yoga can release physical tension. Long full diaphragmatic breathing helps. And, well, there is always the old visualization: counting sheep...

Biological:
Ask your GP to check your thyroid levels – an overactive thyroid can cause sleeplessness.
Some medication contains stimulants, such as medication for asthma, allergy, coughs and colds.

Fear:
Fear of what will be revealed to you in your dreams, fear of the dark or the unknown, may prevent you letting go into a deep sleep. Be with what is happening. Invite the fears into your conscious mind so that you can work with them.

Energy:
Going for a run or brisk walk earlier in the day might 'use up' excess energy if too much energy kicking around might be a cause of restlessness.

Receive an energy treatment from a good, grounded energy worker and see if this makes a difference. If you sleep well after the treatment, you have a clue to the cause of the sleeplessness. You may find activities like walking in nature or gardening, could bring about the same kind of internal energy.

Pillows and mattresses with magnets embedded have helped some people.

Bedroom:
Try re-orienting your bed. Many people sleep more deeply aligned north-south, and dream more sleeping east-west. You might feel more comfortable putting at a distance from your bed dimmer switches, the base of a wireless phone, cell phones or other appliances giving off an electromagnetic field. Switch off all appliances, so LED and other lights aren't flashing, creating subliminal stimulation. Use curtains or blinds to filter out city lights or car headlights. Switch off humming machinery.

Drinking chamomile tea in the evening may help. Valerian tincture can be calming. Try a relaxing, candlelit warm bath with soft music before bed.

If none of these suggestions work, spend relaxing, time while awake giving yourself energy treatments, repeating mantra, and deepening your awareness as you lie down, at least resting your body.

Changes in sexuality

Sexual energy can increase or decrease. For some people, as their higher chakras awaken, they are less interested in being in their emotional-sexual-physical bodies. Their energy naturally ascends, transcends or gravitates to subtle states of consciousness. These people may lose all interest in sex for a while. This can strain a relationship, especially when their partners used to enjoy a sexual relationship and don't understand why the change has come about.

When you open to more energy than you are used to, the energy is going to flow somewhere. The energy can flow into your mind and you'll become interested in all kinds of ideas, reading and discussions. If it flows strongly through your second chakra, you'll either be channelling the energy into creating amazing art, music and poetry, or you'll want to be in bed with a lover.

For some people, as their energy levels increase, their sexual appetite becomes voracious. Most spiritual literature advises against constantly releasing this energy, instead advising that this energy be drawn up the spine. Someone with a sushumna (central channel running up the spine) that is clear (either developed through steady meditation practice or naturally so) could re-channel this energy. If the energy cannot be easily channelled upwards, it would be better to release it, than be obsessed with it. Workshops and books on sexual tantra can be helpful.

It is not uncommon to experience a very intense sexual drive, and times when obsession with sexuality overcomes the best intentions to meditate. On occasion, sexual energy can be sufficiently strong to overwhelm the usual social, gender, and moral code, and can have embarrassing consequences. Like so many areas, this is rarely talked about, especially in spiritual circles.

> *I've found when seeking help sexual subjects are not often spoken about and I wonder if this is because of embarrassment by teachers and also those going through the process as well. I've found the sexual energy/awakening very strong and it interferes just as much in trying to live my life on a daily basis. Spirituality/kundalini awakening brought up many sexual problems due to guilt, shame...strong desires for sex and experimentation in sexual experiences. This may have hindered my process in some way, I'm not sure....and it's very hard to get people to talk about it when asked for advice etc.[2]*

Through tantric practice, this energy can be cultivated to flow up through the central energy channel, the sushumna, running up your spine. The energy can also be channelled through the heart into healing. There is information in sacred tantric texts in the Buddhist, Hindu and Taoist traditions which can help transmute sexual energy into spiritual energy.

Blocks to sexuality:

Sometimes a drop in sexuality is due to unconscious beliefs and/or energy blocks. Energy blocks often form in bands around the body

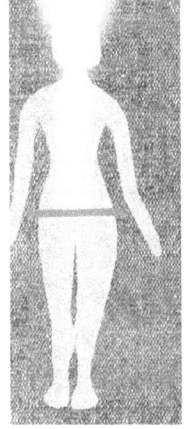

Horizontal energy block(s) across the abdomen may be fuelled by underlying beliefs like: "To be spiritual, to be pure, one must avoid sexuality," "Sexuality is sinful or wrong" or "I don't want to feel."

The energy resistance or impasse keeps you away from your feeling-sexual centres and your second chakra so you that can live in the upper part of your body. In the short run this block allows you to ignore these areas of your life, but you cannot easily hide forever. To be grounded, whole and complete you need to feel, be alive, and have complete energy flow throughout your body.

Changes in eating patterns

Not needing to eat

Periods of time can pass when there seems to be little need to eat physical food, as if breath and the life current are sufficient. There is no problem with eating lightly as long as you listen to your body and eat when it asks you.

Not needing to eat at all is likely to be somewhat temporary. In the meantime enjoy the freedom from shopping, cooking and dishes! Be careful not to make a concept or a public proclamation that you no longer need to eat – you'll end up with a contradiction when next you are hungry.

Eating huge amounts without putting on weight

Transformation can burn calories. Kundalini fire can burn mega-calories. If you're not putting on weight, and you don't have parasites or absorption problems, it's likely your body needs the food. Enjoy!

Eating large amounts and getting fat

If you are eating a lot and putting on weight, you may be eating to avoid feeling, to avoid looking into areas you need to look at. It may also be that your over-eating is an unconscious ego ploy to thwart your growth by diverting your attention, lowering your vitality, and tying your physical body more to the sense and the earth plane. When the instinct to reach for food comes, stop, feel, and catch the emotions and/or fleeting images and perceptions that arise when you don't immediately gratify the eating urge. What is it under there? What are you avoiding?

Sometimes people instinctively put on weight to keep their new sensitivity safe – with an extra layer of fat for protection. If you are comfortable being bigger, and feel healthy enough, fine. If not, work at more energy grounding and energy protection.

Feeling spaced out

If you are feeling dizzy, spaced out, unable to engage with the life around you, day-dreamy, or distant, if your friends describe you as

being 'on another planet' or 'not all there', the chances are your upper chakras are more open than your base chakras. You may also be feeling over-sensitive. You need to strengthen the first and second chakras, root into the earth, and draw the light energy from your head down through your feet into the earth. Return to page 82 for more details.

Lack of mental clarity

If your memory isn't as sharp as you are used to, it may be due to lack of grounding. Some people find the herb ginkgo biloba useful because it closes down the third eye chakra, limiting us more to the mental field. Lack of mental clarity may also occur because your mind is too busy or preoccupied to be fully present. If there is a lot of mental clearing, reorganization of beliefs and general 'processing' happening, this may be using up a lot of available mental RAM (available mental resources), creating an ongoing distraction at a subtle level in the mind.

Therapy can help speed up the internal clearing process. A skilled therapist can help bring the subconscious material into your conscious awareness so it can be dealt with more easily.

Many people have joked that they are living fully in the present because they have insufficient memory to remember any other time. If you are clear and bright in the present moment, this is quite a good place to be, once you get used to it. Notebooks and palm pilots can assist the storage and retrieval of information.

Being fuzzy, distant, and without memory feels disconcerting. Emotion-centred therapy and clearing the energy fields may help, as may drinking more water, eating a diet that is high in fresh, uncooked vegetables, and exercising outdoors.

Despondency

No matter how many years you have been working on yourself, when your unresolved issues surface, the crying lament is, "I haven't got anywhere! I'm in just the same place I have always been."

It feels like this because each time that grey place comes to the forefront of your attention, it carries the same emotions and pain with it. That's why it feels like you haven't changed. You may have moved on, in so many ways, yet this little part of you that hasn't yet been resolved, is still painted with familiar emotional colours.

Take heart. The moment you re-connect with your expanded light self, this light state also feels just the same. ("This is the real 'me' – I have always known that I was light and love...") The nature of this state is eternal, so once you tune into it, it feels like you have always been there – you have always been free, clear, expanded and aware. In truth, in your inner being, you have always been free. The real You hasn't changed a bit.

When we are in oneness, we feel blessed and light. When in separation, we feel limited and disconnected. This is the same for all of us. What is unique to each of us is that when in separation, we each fall into a particular 'pit' or story line. This story line is our essential duality or expression of separation. It might be, 'my mother abandoned me,' 'the evil uncle raped me' or 'the world is wrong and needs to be put right.' So for a while you feel wonderful, fluid, buoyant and unlimited, and then your sense of separation creeps in, and in separation, this is your story. It feels like you have not moved on, whereas in your awareness, you have moved on. It's just that the patterning of your separate conditions and story operates in much the same way as it has in the past. This too can change through your inquiry, and using techniques such as EFT, and the Byron Katie method to undo your patterned ruts of thinking.

Depression

Depression can arise when a current life situation reminds us in some way of something from the past that is painful. Rather than face the painful memory, we wall the memory off into the subconscious. If we have a few memories we don't want to revisit, we end up  in a sealed off place where we don't want to look left, right, up or down because we might feel something we want to ignore. We have closed ourselves down. Our energy is caught, held, and stagnant. The way forward is to dare to feel, to dare to face the emotions we hide from, to forgive others, and ourselves and finally, to have sweet gratitude for all that we have learned

People have found their way out of depression through physical activity, diet, Bach flower remedies and light. Vibrant activity, such as running or dancing, frees up the energy. Increasing omega-3 fatty acids in the diet (through fish oils, flax seed oil, Canola oil) has helped many people. Some people have been helped through energetic grounding because their energy was not flowing, not sufficiently integrated with their physical bodies to connect to the world around them, so they felt alienated and insufficient.

The Bach Flower Remedy Mustard helps when you feel gloomy for no apparent reason. Gentian works for despondency from a life set back or known situation.

Depression can be caused, or exacerbated, by lack of full spectrum light. Being out in the sun is a great help. Installing full frequency lighting in the rooms in which you spend time, also helps. Medical doctors have found success with full spectrum lighting that is programmed to fade in slowly like the dawn, imitating the light conditions of spring and summer, which helps to counteract the dimmer light of winter.

Lively colours can also help. Paint your walls amber, or wear red underwear and socks to bring more vibrant energy to your body.

Qigong energy tapping (tapping along all the meridians) can free up stagnant energy, clear blockages, and revitalize the energy fields.

Dark night of the soul

During transformation, we sometimes go through times of great darkness. We call these times 'dark nights of the soul,' after St. John of the Cross, who used this term to describe the utter despair he was experiencing at the severance of unity with God.

Some say that we can only emerge as true masters or healers after being through the dark abysses of the mind, so these times are not without their merit.

Dark nights of the soul often arise through life situations that challenge our sense of identify – our internal image of ourselves or sense of status we think we should have in the world.

Some of the darkest nights are around themes of surrendering the ego, the battles of dark and light forces within us, and our fears of giving up the ideas and possessions we cherish. We may never need to physically give anything up, but to move forward at certain times in our spiritual development, we have to come to a place where we can let all these things go. It sounds easy in print, but when faced with the vast expanse of the unknown ahead of us, we struggle with issues of identity and ego survival.

Dark times feel all the more awful when we have experienced the love, openness and lightness of being in oneness. The contrast is nothing short of excruciating. We find our way back to the light most easily by letting go of the ego-identity and aligning ourselves with our light and free inner nature.

Archetypal dreams and images

Images of battles between good and evil, images of life and death, male and female are common as spirit and shadow play together during transformation. Acknowledging both our free light and limited habits and fears, we gradually clear the impressions tucked away in memory and find resolution. The resolution process may take the form of vivid dreams or images that come in meditation.

Shamanic journeys often involve images of animal spirits or demonic beings in the underworld. The animal that appears is of significance. Guidance can be drawn from the animal totem.

Falling from openness
Often there is a sense that some very beautiful experience or awareness that was at one time experienced has now been lost. This is sometimes accompanied by a sense of being powerless to recreate this awareness, when it is seen that it is the very absence of individuality, ego and will that is the purity and expanse of this awareness. Through returning attention to the inner being, through regular meditation, higher awareness gradually becomes established as a constant reality.

Having experienced the profundities of spiritual dimensions, some find themselves experiencing a deep disinterest in ordinary life, which now appears bland, lifeless or purposeless. It is very common, and is even thought of by many as a 'spiritual' way of being. However, ultimately, this kind of split between consciousness and matter needs to be resolved - through meditation, and a more expanded understanding and insight - so that ordinary life is seen as the same as the spirit. In the meantime, it may be more comfortable for you to spend time with other people of a similar mindset than with those of more ordinary 'worldly' values. But unless you want to be isolated in a spiritual community 'away from the world' (is there such a place?!), it might be better to orient yourself towards seeing Consciousness (or God) in everyday life, resolving the split in your own inner world of seeing.

Another aspect of losing a cherished state of consciousness is making that state into a memory, which is then lived for, rather than being present, alive and open. This memory obviously gets in the way.

Virtually no one is permanently in an opened state. While lasting enlightenment is the goal of many spiritual practitioners, some people don't believe it's possible to stay there.

> *"Peak experience isn't something you can absorb continuously like a morphine drip. It's a peak: a pointed thing that pierces the clouds, a rarity, a wonder, a place from which you can view the world. It's an amazing place, but you can't stay there; there's nowhere to sit, and nowhere for your friends."*[21]

Once your free, loving, light inner nature is known to you, it's difficult accepting any other way of being. Yet, until all your shadows are purified, your times of blissful openness will probably alternate with times that are much less light. Most people who open to deeper states of awareness don't stay there first off. They slide, instantly or gradually, back into a more 'ordinary' human awareness.

You may well long for the light, even feel 'ripped off,' blaming any life circumstance that appears to have taken you from your inner knowing. You can regain quite a bit of light through spiritual practice – such as meditation, prayer, yoga, or time in Nature. Spiritual practices can take you to a place of inner serenity, centeredness, and bliss. Having established them as a natural way of being, having aligned your emotional, mental and physical life with your inner tranquillity, when grace next comes to you, you have a much better chance of remaining longer in the light.

Return to chapters 4 and 5 to find ways to best reconnect with spirit, and check out parts of the next chapter to clear the shadow that has come up and occluded your light. To reach your full potential, you need to keep your attention on light, your inner being, spirit, and the source of creation, while clearing all those facets of your psyche and emotions that in the past have not allowed you to live light – such as fear, limitation, insecurity and dogma.

Nothing means much
When our hearts are open and we feel connected to spirit-light inside, if the seriousness of life ceases to mean anything much to us, this feels liberating.

Without the spirit connection, when ideas and beliefs that used to mean something no longer do, life starts feeling bleak, meaningless and directionless. We live in an illusion of supposed meaning. Since all the meaning we have is an overlay, a creation of our minds, our essential reality does not have the meanings we attribute to it. Our thinking has created our sense of time; there is only the moment we are living in now. The personality we have constructed for ourselves is an overlay; it is not the true 'I'. Because they are illusory, overlays can fold or crumple at times.

When we feel hollow and empty, reflecting on the emptiness of our conceived reality, there are two options: One is to bolster our beliefs back into some semblance of meaning, and the other is to go for the light. When we are connected, the meaningless of our conceptual overlays is a great joy, liberation from the burden of our previous misperceptions. The key is an open heart – and perhaps a sense of humour!

We cannot truly and authentically move into our potential while remaining in the 'normal box ' – the trite social conception of normality. We have to step out. If we can step out and still play a game that at least looks on the surface somewhat like the game everyone else is playing, we'll be considered 'sane.' If we step outside the 'normal' behavioural borders, we could receive a diagnostic label. Receiving a label doesn't mean you are mentally ill, but it does mean that according to the observations of others, your behaviour falls into that category.

It also happens that during purification we can enter temporarily into dark holes in our minds that resemble psychoses. For example, while clearing a line of trauma that threads through your current life but originates in your past lives, in order to clear these past situations, you may find yourself living in those circumstances in your mind for a while. It will make no sense to people around you.

If you are in serious doubt as to your sanity, go to page 141.

Adapting to a more internal focus

Many spiritually oriented people are focused on internal processes and other dimensions of consciousness to the neglect of the day-to-day facets of their lives. It's understandable that sometimes so much is going on inside that it's difficult to concentrate on your work and daily responsibilities. If you want to put full attention on your process to the exclusion of everything else, try to find a retreat or ashram that is set up for this kind of inward orientation and personal processing.

If taking time off, or finding a retreat is not possible, be honest. Be direct with your friends and work colleagues, "I'm very absorbed in some personal matters right now, and I am probably going to be unable to give you much attention. My apologies. It's temporary, but I don't know how long it will go on for."

Try to be clear, yet diplomatic, in your communication to others, so that you don't mess them around. This means first being clear with yourself about what your priorities are, and what your goals and capacities are at this time. Being self-absorbed while you process something deeply might be acceptable to others for a while. Behaving conscientiously about the effects your withdrawal will have on others around you is likely to be more palatable, than your hoping no one notices, or expecting people to accommodate you.

You won't be deeply 'in process' all the time. Make a priority to use some of your good times to help out those who are helping you in your more difficult times.

Minimize your external responsibilities and commitments as much as you can. Take a part-time job if you need to work, or sort something out with your fellow workers. Trim down all appointments, leisure activities, and social events, so you are as free as possible to go with what you need to do. Hire home help, cooks, or babysitters if you can afford it. Re-prioritise your available spending money to maximally support your process so you can move through as easily and swiftly as possible. For example, if you are feeling quiet and sensitive, you may be less inclined to go out to movies and dinner. So the funds these activities would cost can be re-channelled into professional energy balancing, healing crystals and uplifting music CDs, as required.

Our lives are about becoming who we are in truth. We might as well make the shift now, and live the rest of our lives in the loving fulfilment this connection brings.

The ego struggles

Once spirit starts moving you into more expanded awareness and higher possibilities, it will continue. Spirit is way bigger than you are. You have two options: 1) to listen, to surrender, to open to the energy, and allow it to create the amazing person you could be, or 2) you can go kicking and screaming. It sounds like you have chosen the latter.

Spirit calls not just to those who are interested and willing, but also calls those who are not consciously aware of such calling. Spirit often beckons most loudly to those who are not living a life that is fully on-track with their inner nature, whose outer life no longer matches their soul purpose, or whose beliefs prevent them from living their core truth. The process of transformation is pretty similar for all, whether or not it is consciously engaged, and regardless of prior spiritual belief and practice, or lack thereof. You may be someone welcoming change, welcoming the potential to be all that you are. You may be eager to figure out how to maximize the ease and speed of transition into the new You that you sense is close by, waiting to blossom, emerge and shine. On the other hand, you may have considerable resistance to the changes that are happening to you, seemingly without your consent.

Our egos prevent us from moving on. They want us to remain where we are. What is this 'ego? It is the sense that creates 'me-mine', as separate from 'you-yours'. Out of the vast expanse of universal consciousness, the essential power of duality creates a vortex of energy that focuses around itself. It is like a whirlpool, which has formed in a large, previously undifferentiated ocean of water. This component of the water had been part of the ocean, but now is owned by the whirlpool. The whirlpool extends its ownership to all the leaves and twigs that fall into its concentric circles. "My Whirlpool! My twig! Me!" says the ego-whirlpool. Having become a separate entity, this whirlpool does everything it can to preserve its individuality. This separation or duality is the fundamental root of the fear of death.

From this sense of separation arises the sense of 'I' as individual, rather than universal. Our 'I' is the seat of our attention, where we rest within ourselves, the centre out of which our perceiving, feeling, and thinking radiates. What or who this 'I' is, depends on where our attention is primarily seated in the vast spectrum of our consciousness. We tend to say, "I am tall," identifying who we are with the shape of our body, rather than "I, as spirit, experience this moment through a tall physical body," indicating a deeper placing of the 'I' sense within us.

The 'I' sense is constant. When we were toddlers, we said, "I want… I am…" As we grew up, our ideas, interests and needs changed, yet we still refer to ourselves as the same, continuous, inner 'I'.

Love dissolves this sense of separateness. The opening of the heart is the beginning of the resolving of separation.

Transformational ingredients

There are three main ingredients at play in our transformation – our efforts; life circumstance; and grace.

Our own efforts are the aspect in which we feel we have the most say. We have a wide variety of choices. We choose how much value we place on our transformation, what priority and energy we give to our health, well-being, spiritual practice, therapy and healing. We can choose where we place our attention, whether we focus on the positive or negative in our lives. We choose our companions and our leisure activities. We choose whether to actually do the things that are beneficial for us, or just read about them.

Life Circumstance is a mixture of choice and life's wild cards. Life presents opportunities and challenges we didn't expect. We can pick, choose and plan a certain amount given our circumstances, yet, however well planned, life may not turn out as we expect. When life isn't the way we'd like, we can choose to be bitter and complain, or receive the life teachings, have gratitude, forgive and move on.

Grace is a totally wild card. Grace is the inexplicable hand of God that can open us up in a moment. It's outside science, outside reason, but it is a definite reality – as all who have been 'graced' will testify.

Since there is only so much we can do about life circumstance, and nothing we can do about Grace, we focus on the areas we can do most about – our values, beliefs, actions, attitudes, practice and awareness.

FAQ.

Q. I had this awesome experience of total, fearless love and light, and now I can't accept being 'ordinary'. I just want to be 'There.'
This is everyone's feeling who isn't afraid of vast openness. The experience fades because the 'gravity' of our conditions and beliefs draws us back into re-solidification. It's best not to be pre-occupied or hung up on these experiences, nor constantly seeking to re-experience them. Just be fully there with it, and then let it go. Desiring something puts you in a mindset of feeling like you don't have it. In this case, it is your essential core, your essence, You. The most useful place to put your attention is into preparing a balanced, strong, clear energy field and body, clearing old memories, dissolving habits and conditions, and settling your mind. When the love-light next opens, you will have built the capacity to retain the state for a longer time.

Q: I wasn't doing spiritual practice when this space of openness came. I lived in a state of love for a year or so, then got involved with this guy and it all faded. I have no idea how to get it back.
Observe yourself carefully. See what opens your heart and what closes it. The heart is a good barometer. Do and think those things that keep your heart open and you will start to bring the love back into your life.
Do you know about meditation? Meditation provides the quickest, most direct way of reconnecting to the open love space. This love is who you are. Find a teacher in your area if you need one.

Q: I don't seem to be moving forward. I've been where I am – kind of emotionally all over the place, oversensitive and out of balance for about two years. What now?
What kind of spiritual practice are you doing, and what kinds of help are you getting or looking for?

I stopped my mindfulness meditation practice when I read that spiritual practice should be discontinued if there are energy problems. I'm just going to work, and living my life, waiting for things to settle out and go back to normal.
Did your mindfulness meditation make things worse?

No, actually it gave me a kind of internal balance and perspective. I always felt good afterwards.

Mindfulness meditation is a balanced meditation when practiced correctly. If it helps you, continue it. Are you doing anything to help ground and balance your energy?

Grounding?
As your higher chakras open, you need to keep your base chakras equally strong to remain in balance. You could do with breathing into your lower spine and down through your feet into the earth, and doing earthy things like gardening. When this energy connection is well maintained, there is more inner centeredness, and experiences flow through you rather than accumulate in you, so you feel less sensitive.

Q: It started with some kind of kundalini energy, and ended up – well, everything has gone wrong. I'm just angry, frustrated, things aren't going the way I want. I want my life back.
Whose life do you think it is?
...I don't know.
What path do you follow?
I'm Catholic.
Did Jesus want to keep his life and have it run the way he wanted? Didn't Jesus said, "Thy will be done, Lord, not mine." What does this phrase mean to you? Contemplate it. Contemplate the relationship Jesus had with his Father in heaven. Doesn't a Christian seek to emulate Jesus? Surrender to God was a lot of what Jesus was teaching?

Q: I've been going through emotional hell for two or three years now. I'm doing my meditation, seeing endless therapists to help me through. I'm sick of it. I want it to finish.
You can ask it to stop. Cease your practice, return to an ordinary life.

I never asked for this difficulty!!
So you thought you could just have the light, not the purification that goes with it?

I don't want to stop here. I want to be free. I want to live my Buddha nature. I've tasted it. I know its there.

Then you need to accept the process. I sense you want to keep going, you're just in a shadowy place right now. The very second that you reconnect to your inner light, you'll feel amazing. Your trials will be instantly gone. It will all be so worth it, don't you think?

Yeah, well, I'm not always in the doldrums. I was fine last week.
One thing that helps is to fully be with the process – with the emotional hell, if that is what is happening. If you are really with an experience, you are also with the higher awareness that is observing. This awareness knows why you are clearing what you are clearing. The awareness is also imbued with blissfulness.

> Keep a diary. The wisdom of your open days will help guide you through the difficult days. The diary will also give you more perspective. When you are in any experience, light or dark, after a surprisingly short while it feels like you've been there forever. The diary will help you remember that you were actually fine just last week... and probably will be fine again very soon!

10

Spiritual Emergency

When a lot of energy is pouring through us, when we are so open we fear losing ourselves in infinity, when the mind feels like it is breaking apart or our emotions are full of strong reactions, it feels very intense. A transformational crisis of this kind is called spiritual emergency. They rarely happen. Skip to the next chapter if this doesn't apply to you.

If this is your condition right now, breathe, ground your energy, relax as much as you can, and trust the process. This is a time for love, trust, inner listening, and getting the right help.

At the time of crisis, it is hard to imagine that this is part of a larger transformation because it all feels so unmanageable. It may feel like some weird illness, going crazy, or hitting a wall in our psyche we can't get through. We may feel like we can't go another day like this because it is so intense.

Looking back as we emerge from a massive internal process, we feel enormous gratitude for all that has unfolded during that time, but in the moment, we may feel like we're about to die. Quite likely part of us is dying, but it isn't the physical body, it's the belief frameworks and control of the ego-mind that is being shifted that feels like dying. However it feels at the time, having made the shift we feel much better! During crisis, despite feeling that this intensity will go on forever, when clients in distress call in for an appointment, by the time the appointment comes around, they are usually in a very different place. This gives the impression that the intensity doesn't usually last. However, it may recur, giving the impression of being in an interminably long process.

Many people end up in crisis during their lives, some may wonder if their crisis is a "spiritual emergency" or not. If your inner wisdom/deeper awareness knows this is part of a bigger picture, if you are willing to use this time as an opportunity to grow, this is spiritual transformation – whether you had been engaged in spiritual practice or not. It may take many forms, many of which don't look that 'spiritual.'

You are in 'spiritual emergency' – a transformational crisis if:
- An influx of strong, high-frequency energy has flowed in, leaving you feeling swamped or as if under pressure from inside and you cannot assimilate the expanded awareness or energy you've opened to. The incoming energy amplifies previous imbalance. Your energy field may be out of kilter, bunched up, blocked, or creating pain.
- You are intensely afraid of what is happening within you, afraid of the openness, fearful of the energy, and afraid that you will lose your sense of self.
- Your higher chakras have become very open, and your lower chakras aren't strong enough to create sufficient stability for you to go about your life.
- The openness has stirred up past memories from your subconscious, creating inner turmoil, internal clearing and purification too quickly, and for you to handle it.
- You don't see the way you used to. The new perceptions to which you have opened don't fit with the ideas you previously held. You don't understand what you've opened to, or why others don't see this way.
- You feel like you're losing control, that you might go crazy, or that you are already crazy.
- You feel intensely depressed or want to finish your life
- You're worrying that there is something wrong physically because you are feeling strange pains and sensations.
- You've entered a dark hell realm in your mind or in consciousness and you can't find your way out.
- People around you think you're psychotic and want to take you to the hospital.

If under these circumstances you cannot function well enough to run your life, you need immediate help.

Tune in
Take time to sense what is happening. Put your mind aside, and sense what this is all about. Allow yourself to be guided to the people, places, books and situations that will bring the most healing and transformation for you.

Breathe.

Relax.

Cancel, delegate or postpone as many appointments, external pressure and duties as you responsibly can. Give yourself time for your process. If you had come down with the flu, no one would think anything of you taking to your bed for a few days, so why not treat this as a spiritual flu and do what you need to do to.

There is no replacement for your inner guidance. However, one of the definitions of spiritual emergency says that your inner resources are not sufficient during spiritual transformation, and outer help is needed.

This chapter assumes you have looked through the previous chapters, especially at sections on grounding and rebalancing. If after reading the relevant sections, and having done as much as you can to help yourself, you are still troubled; it would be good to seek help in the form of guidance, information, validation, support, medical expertise, energy work or functional assistance with your life.

The rest of the chapter is about the varieties of outer help available.

What kinds of help might be helpful?
- Talking to someone who has been through something similar, or at least someone who understands, empathizes and will not judge you.
- Having someone there for you because you don't want to go through this alone. This may mean having to sleep over at friends' or relatives' homes, or at least having someone on the end of the phone, preferably someone who can, in a pinch, be called at any time.
- If, try as you might, you have read the instructions on grounding, and your energy is still floating or not-integrated, you could probably do with a professional energy worker who is grounded and skilled in grounding others. This is a good first place to look for help, since energy imbalance, over sensitivity and busy-

mindedness may well balance out when you are more grounded/energetically connected to the earth.
- ❖ Understanding more about what is happening to you by putting all the changes in a context that you can understand. A spiritual counsellor could be of help.
- ❖ You may be overwhelmed by past memories surfacing, some of which you might have forgotten or buried deeply. You may need a skilled therapist to help you through. Therapists have their areas of specialty – sexual abuse, addiction, family dynamics, self-esteem, hypnosis, past life regression.
- ❖ Sometimes getting a sense of the bigger picture or receiving some deeper guidance is useful. Sometimes a reputable and skilled psychic or channeller can offer service.
- ❖ If you fear that you are going crazy or losing control, a spiritually open psychiatrist may help.
- ❖ If you feel depressed, despondent or in such darkness that you start to have suicidal thoughts, calling a help line or a friend is good.
- ❖ If the strange pains or sensations in your body are worrying, have a medical check-up.

What can you do?
If you have Internet access, check through the web sites. Google for 'spiritual emergence,' 'kundalini' or whatever key words fit your condition. Look for support groups, practitioners and services in your area. For example, in Canada, the Spiritual Emergence Service web site lists professionals in each province.

Some websites provide notice boards, e-mail groups, and other ways of getting in contact with people who will understand you.

Phone community centres, churches, help lines and support groups to see if you can find knowledgeable or open-minded counselling or support.

If you are in great distress, call emergency services.

Listening ear(s) – talking to someone who understands
Talking to someone who understands is a joy. For many people, it is a great relief to meet with other people who have had similar experiences. Talking to others can help link your new realms of consciousness to the physical world. You can glean information,

support, and a wider understanding about this new-to-you field of consciousness.

Nowadays, international phoning is so inexpensive, you can phone people who speak your language all over the world. Don't limit yourself to your hometown – pick up a phone card and search the net for contacts who are familiar with spiritual awakening.

When seeking listening ears, be clear about what your needs are, be it, "I need to tell my story, to be heard by someone who understands," "I need some feedback on what is happening," "I need loving support," or, "I need help!"

Lengthily worded problems take up a lot of conversation time, and can feel burdensome to the listener, so when you need help, keep your communication brief and clear. Put your needs into words rather than expecting the other person to trying to figure out what you are getting at. A communication like, "This weird thing is happening... and I feel all this stuff coming up... and I'm feeling kind of, well, I dunno, kind of strange..." doesn't give many clues about what you need. You would be more likely to get the help you are seeking saying, "I'm feeling troubled, over-sensitive and I could use some comfort and a quiet place to be for a while – can I stay at your place for a few days?" or "Could you take me to a doctor – I need to make sure that whatever this is isn't medical." If you can figure out what you need before contacting the person, it makes it easier for you to clearly explain your needs, and easier for your listener/helper to know what to offer.

Who is good to talk to?

Open minded, spiritually oriented family members and friends, open minded clergy, spiritual teachers, spiritual counsellors, yoga teachers with spiritual depth, open-minded, spiritually oriented professionals. Check out the websites in chapter 14 and see if there is a spiritual emergence network in your country, or area. The web is probably the best resource for finding people in your region. Some networks run support groups. Networks in countries or areas other than the one where you live, may list professionals or have contacts with sympathetic people near you. Some websites carry people's stories and include contact e-mail addresses so you can write to people who have had similar experiences. You could also talk to the person(s) who run your nearest spiritual book shop to find contacts of understanding people in your area. Use your intuitive nose in addition to recommendations from trusted sources. The integrity and depth of each practitioner varies greatly, so you have to check each one out as you go.

The best people to talk to are often those who have had personal experiences similar to yours, and some foundation in the anatomy of spiritual transformation, its wide reaching effects, kundalini and energy crisis. These people may not be easy to find!

Most meditators and yogis consider themselves spiritual and therefore knowing about spirit. However, people can meditate for years, have very deep insights in consciousness, and have developed wonderful healing and teaching gifts without knowing the hiccups of the transformation process. The ones who do know generally went through a process themselves, or know someone who did, but then, since this is the only experience they have had, they tend to fit all other experience into whatever they underwent.

This is not to say that you won't find excellent help, but be aware of this common limitation before you start out. Question anyone from whom you are seeking help and try to get a sense if the person really knows what they are dealing with in your case. Lend them this book if necessary so they can interlink their skills with this understanding.

You may have a few different needs and require help from a few different professions. If so, consider putting the professionals in touch with each other, so your treatment can be coordinated.

Where do you go for help?

A common first place to go for help is your family. Half of the participants responding to the PSE (Profound Spiritual Experience) questionnaire sought their family's help. A quarter found excellent help, but one in five found their families, 'unkind, not understanding,' and 7% were 'devastated' by their family's response.

Family members differ in their spiritual openness and ability to encompass new ideas. These are two different accounts written by PSE participants illustrate an ideal, and a less ideal, response to spiritual crisis.

> *my family has helped me by understanding that i cannot deal with intense emotional distress with those i am close to, and by recognizing that my experiences are real and by supporting me when i need help, without questions. recently*

my mother had me move back in with her until i felt stable and able, and she has not doubted the severity of what happened to me. [2]

My family were kind and helpful while it was thought to be a psychiatric problem. When it was called a spiritual awakening they became unkind, not understanding. [2]

If you sense your family may not understand you, or worse, might be freaked out, you have three main choices:
1. Go elsewhere for support.
2. Go to your family anyway and hope it works out.
or
3. Figure out what specific help you need that your family could provide (somewhere to stay, some nourishing food, familiar company). Present an explanation of your circumstances and needs that might best elicit the help you seek.

Two thirds of pilot study participants sought their friends' help, and nearly two thirds of these people found positive responses from their friends. However, again, there were 4% of friends listed as 'unkind, not understanding,' and 6% reporting 'devastating.' So not all good friends are necessarily going to understand where you're at, however long they've known you. Choose wisely.

In answer to the question, 'Who helped you?' a questionnaire participant wrote:

Friends who accept their darkness and their light, share the light and the dark truth of their journey, who own and share what they don't know as well as what they do know, who are their own best work, who fail graciously, who are generous and faithful, who attend to this moment, who allow room for what is arising to arise, who ultimately trust in the goodness of life and the human journey... [2]

Another participant wrote,

Advice from one friend and flatmate at the time who was very calm and matter of fact, he assured me I was not going mad, seemed unphased by my descriptions of the experience, indicating it was no big deal, not to make too much of it, that it's part of a bigger process and spiritually is 'just a beginning' of something, rather than an end point. I found this very reassuring, and felt understood. [2]

Of course, it would be wonderful if everyone around you, everyone you talked to, totally understood what was happening; and if they supported you in your process of unfolding, in full confidence that the outcome will be amazing. But then it would be a totally different world.

Hopefully you can find one or two new people who understand you, and don't think that there is anything wrong with you, if there isn't a soul in your world who understands you. When remembering how we were before our shifts in consciousness – how much more solid and tangible the world was, how much more important the social norms, standards and values were to you before, we can more easily understand where others are coming from. People can only fully relate to what they have directly experienced.

The most important thing is that you don't misunderstand yourself. Remain true to yourself, true to your spirit, and true to the process of transformation that is happening. You may not fit in with the people around you, but you are not alone. Thousands of others are feeling just the way you are right now. As Internet access continues to grow, spiritual emergence chat sites and web information is more and more available to put people in touch with each other all over the world.

As you read websites, you may notice people tend to write, or seek listening ears, in their times of trial rather than when they are merged in love-light. Don't be alarmed if you discover it is often the weirder, scarier stories that find their way on the pages, rather than the blissful-awe experiences. There are way more experiences of rapture and awe than converse. People who are blessed are usually content to live their blessedness – they don't need to write, or process, so these lovely experiences don't necessarily appear on the web.

Energy workers

If your energy/life force feels weird, unstable, ungrounded, out of balance or blocked, an energy worker could be helpful. A skilled energy worker can do wonders. When you work with a therapist of any kind, it is a joint operation.

> *When I got hooked up with the therapist he told me "You are going to learn how to manage the energy." He said also that it is necessary to clear the emotional blockages in the chakras to make a clear channel for the kundalini energy. When we did that, and worked through my emotional garbage, the horrendous symptoms I experienced vanished.*[2]

46% of the PSE participants sought energy workers. They were the most sought resource people used for help, after family and friends. Energy workers scored the highest rating from participants. 'Excellent' (65%). A further 24% scored 'mostly useful.'

In this study, only 1% reported 'devastating' results with energy workers. It's possible that this figure is lower than average. Accounts from people who received energy treatments that made them feel worse, are not uncommon from people who dealt with inexperienced energy workers. Some of these 'uncomfortable' treatments are Reiki treatments or other treatments that pour more energy in. If you are ill or exhausted, these kinds of treatments are wonderful. However, if you already have more energy than you can handle, Reiki treatments can feel anywhere between excruciating and a complete over-load. Best to avoid Reiki if your energy is already too open or strong.

Before booking a session, talk to the energy worker and check what kinds of methods he or she is using. Use your felt sense to check out: Is he/she grounded? Ask what skills the energy worker uses for grounding, and if he/she has previous experience with the sort of energy imbalance you are experiencing. Ask if he/she can help you. Check his/her answer with your 'intuitive nose.'

As a safety check, if you are in any doubt, you can do a kinesiology test before the treatment (which can be done by a friend beforehand or by the practitioner). Simply put, you hold your arm horizontally at shoulder height, and your friend or energy worker presses down on your arm to get a sense of how strongly your arm resists the push. Hold a vision or thought of the treatment to come, asking yourself if it is good to go ahead with the treatment, and again see how strongly your arm resists a push. Ask if you are ready for this treatment and if it will be beneficial. If your arm tests weaker on the second push, repeat both tests. If you receive the same results on repetition, your body is indicating that the treatment may not suit you, or you may not be ready for the treatment yet.

An advantage of this testing is that your active participation is needed, rather than you just lying passively on a table and expecting someone else to fix your life.

Spiritual Counseling

An increasing amount of information is available on web sites and in books, but it is not always obvious how to apply it to your individual situation and experiences. If you have no clue what is going on, or don't know where to start, a spiritual counsellor with personal experience of profound openings, kundalini and spiritual transformation might be able to help. Many spiritual teachers have not experienced spiritual crisis, nor have all spiritual counsellors. Years of spiritual practice do not indicate personal experience in the field. Many counsellors work in the framework of a religion (clergy and other religious counsellors). They can be helpful when you are a member of the religion and it works for you, otherwise you may feel you don't fit in their conceptual box. A counsellor with sufficient depth of awareness works with your words and understanding, instead of imposing his or her own.

Even kundalini yoga teachers don't know much about kundalini. Most of them have not experienced a powerful kundalini opening that radically changed their lives. The author has not come across a yoga teacher's training course that includes spiritual crisis, the after-effects of spiritual awakening, and basic care taking procedures.

Psychics

You may be experiencing astral entities, past lives, negative energies, communications from the dead, or from angels or spirit guides. If you need more information about what is happening, or are wondering if what you are experiencing is real, a good psychic might help.

One thing worth checking is where psychics read from – from your guardian, from your spirit guides, from their guide, from your auric field, or simply from your mind. Many psychics switch between true channelling, and speaking about what they personally believe. It can be difficult for the client to know what is what. While they can be very helpful as spokespeople for a world that is beyond our normal reality, their words can be very influential. "It must be so! The psychic told me!" The information they convey cannot be easily substantiated. If you have the means, you could always do a session with two different psychics, and see if their stories match up.

Psychics sound convincing. If they didn't speak with conviction, they wouldn't make a living. Is there really a fixed future which they can read, or are they providing a reading on one of an infinite number of possibilities to be decided by your choice? Science has never explored how the future works.

Entities

Entities are spirit forms which on occasion are attracted to, or attached to a person. They are not necessarily bad or malevolent, but they are a nuisance when they disturb your energy field, make your mind fuzzy or drain your energy. I don't have much experience in this field. Most of what I know I have heard from clients. If you think you have an entity (or a few!) attached to you, there are professionals who can help you clear them. These professionals tend to be psychic, and either do energy work, or work through prayer and affirmation. Most will contact the spirit and communicate your wish to be free from its presence; that it should move on.

> *About those pesky entities: I may have had entity attachments for several months or longer, up to 16 months ago. I'm still not sure. Sometime after I became aware of spirits, I thought I could talk to them, and they were all nice guys. I don't know if they suck energy, but they feel like a physical weight.*[2]

> *I am aware of the presence of spirits around me at times, but I am not usually friendly towards them. There is supposed to be some kind of a spiritual law according to people who write about these things, that your space is your own and other spirits have to leave if they are not wanted.. My impression is they still show up even if unwelcome but they have to leave eventually. I don't speak to them directly. I say*

that "No-one who is not to my highest good is allowed in my space", and I ask Archangel Michael to escort all unwanted visitors away. [2]

Like other subtle phenomena, there is no scientific validation for entities. If you talk about this kind of thing to people who have no place for them in their thinking, you may well be thought crazy. To clear these unwanted entities, what is generally recommended is that you come from a place of loving, centred acceptance (rather than being demanding, controlling or fearful). Some professionals in this field maintain these entities can be avoided by saying no firmly, not allowing them in. Apparently some entities are sexually seductive, or try to pose as a wise or loving presence at first.

Some people recommend not communicating with entities directly, even avoiding telling them to leave, because this engages with them. Instead ask spirit, God or your angels to clear you from any being who is not here for your higher good, and take the being to the light so it can be free.

Others advise contacting the entity with your thought, asking questions such as "Who are you, why are you attaching to me?" but without listening to the answers. To listen is to give it energy and hold it to you. Direct your attention to the light. Use great love – the entity also wants to go to the light, and your permission and guidance will help it. Think things like, "I give my permission for you to leave. You will be in a much more fun place. The light is waiting to receive you."

Are you crazy?

This is the question that bothers many people when they experience something out of the ordinary. In time, as unusual experiences become better documented and researched, many areas of life that bring up this question will be laid to rest – they'll be 'normal.'

> *"If the human race survives, future men will, I suspect, look back on our enlightened epoch as a veritable Age of Darkness... They will see that what was considered 'schizophrenic' was one of the forms in which, often through quite ordinary people, the light began to break into our all-too-closed minds."*
>
> R.D.Laing

When your experiences are intense and unusual, or you are in a dark hole in your mind, it's natural not to feel too good.

Fear of life, success, failure and utter humiliation. Feeling a conspiracy growing. My mind is mush, my spine is crushed and everyone (them) makes me mad. I'm hanging onto life by a thread.[2]

We can go through very intense experiences one day, and the next be comparatively 'normal.' It is important not to identify with the transient experiences. It's better to identify with our loving spirit essence, which is constant.

We live in continuums of experience rather than distinct categories, so sometimes there is a mixture of sublime light and what medicine calls mental illness at the same time. Every so-called 'normal' person has a certain percentage of mild mental illness. Socially, we call these quirks. We all have them. Profound spiritual experience amplifies any latent imbalance you have, and from time to time it can either look like, or temporarily cross the line, into illness of one kind or another. People in spiritual emergency can have parts of their psyche in such states of turbulence and change that they fit into one or more diagnostic categories for mental illness. Perhaps in time, we will discover that mental illness is the attempt of the psyche to transform itself into a better way of functioning. Right now, this kind of radical transformation gets a disease label, in the same way that transformation in the body is expressed through what we currently call illness. With love and time, illnesses of all kinds can improve.

If you were functioning fine before the transformational period, all things being equal, you will be back on your feet soon. You may feel to seek professional guidance, though, especially if you have a personal history, or family history of mental instability.

It is not always easy to evaluate yourself. What is described here are some basic ways of distinguishing between spiritual processing and 'losing the plot'; stepping too far from what the mainstream can tolerate as 'normal.' People and societies vary as to what behaviours and thinking they can accept. Acceptable behaviour is a cultural definition rather than anything fixed. Note well that even if you have 'lost the plot,' you can get 'your plot' back again. Nothing is permanent.

Only medical professionals are qualified to diagnose illness. However, if you are chewing on the thought that you may be crazy, these pointers may provide some clues or clarity.

- If you're spiritually open, you are in a reality which can be recognized by someone else who is open to that plane of consciousness. Whereas if you are living in your own little version of reality, you are the only one who relates to that reality. Of course, if you can't find anyone else who is spiritually open in the way you are, you may well feel like you are absolutely alone in your own world. While you might feel rather lonely, having experiences that are out of the ordinary do not in themselves indicate mental illness.
- If you're aware that others might think, or are thinking that you are strange or crazy, you obviously still have an awareness of the viewpoint of those around you. If you were totally lost in your own psyche, you would likely have lost this awareness.
- However weird your experience, you may have a sense that some transformation is taking place, that there is a higher purpose, a greater picture, a direction, (even if you cannot maintain this clarity all the time). This state of affairs differs from a situation where there is no sense of direction, no light at the end of the tunnel, no spiritual inspiration. Light will guide you through, if you trust it.
- If your actions are loving and life supportive, this is a good sign.
- You may be hearing voices from angels, ascended masters or guides, and you are aware that these are only heard by you, that they come from within you. This is different from thinking the voices are coming from the physical world around you and are physically 'real.'
- The information you receive from angels or inner masters is tangibly useful, positive, and helps you move through difficult times. It differs from receiving 'information' that leads you up blind alleys, leads you into trouble and adds to your confusion.
- If you are able to keep up a front, put on a social face, and more or less carry on, and you are managing your life more or less; it's is a good sign. Those who have 'lost the plot' are generally unable to keep up a front. They alienate others with strange behaviour and

thoughts, and are unable to interact smoothly with the world around them.
- Those in intense spiritual opening sometimes fear losing control, as if the power of this kundalini or light force flowing through them will cause them to 'go wild'. Those who have lost the plot are already out of control. Fearing losing control is different from having already lost control.
- Generally speaking, someone holding the vision that 'it is all God', is opened. Whereas the vision that 'I'm God and you are not,' although fairly common even among so-called 'spiritual' people, is obviously delusional, or at least ego-centric.
- When people are spiritually connected, there is a sense of intuitively knowing everything, an intrinsic depth of insight. This differs from your ego being convinced of its invincible all-knowingness, and the compulsion to tell everyone how they should be living, or how they should honour you as some kind of messiah. People are instinctively adverse to 'know-it-alls'. They may feel you should have a psychiatric check up if you're too over-the-top. If your openness, awareness and insight are pure and true, you will see the light of your openness in all beings and all life around you. You will respect others' lifestyles, beliefs and practices rather than assuming that what you believe is necessarily better.
- An opened person tends to feel 'lit'; whereas one who has lost the plot tends to appear entrenched in fixed ideas, or dark spaces of consciousness without any reference to experiencing light.
- You may be able to distinguish between inner and outer realities, even though your experiences (say, a past life flashback) may be strange and intense. This differs from someone who cannot make this distinction, and has 'as-if' stepped entirely into the past life situation and is living 'there' in his or her head.
- Interestingly, those who are 'open,' including those who are in institutions due to an opening, can distinguish between those who are just plain crazy and those who are open. One opened person can recognize another.[22]
- Inappropriate behaviour with no regard for morals and ethics differs from being endearingly 'off-the-wall,' eccentrically inspired, and following your truth.

If after reading this list, you have a sense that you are probably doing OK, great. If not, don't be afraid to find some guidance or help. Particularly if you are feeling uncomfortable, suicidal, or destructive, or when you have fallen into a dark hole in your mind that you cannot get out of on your own. Don't stagnate in these kinds of conditions. Some good help at the right time can save you a great deal of anguish.

If you feel fine about being a bit eccentric or 'off the wall,' and no one is bothered by you, you could let things be for a while and see how it goes. Many people go through weird patches. The chances are no one around you has really noticed how you're feeling; perhaps because they are too busy dealing with their own inner (eccentric!) world to notice yours.

If you are managing to look somewhat normal to the outside world, it means you have enough power of observation and objectivity to play the social game. Who knows how many people around you are going through all kinds of inner turmoil and are putting on a good face? This is the way life is socially conducted.

If you can keep your outer world on a fairly even keel, your inner world has time to gradually sort itself out. There is nothing wrong with going through a more turbulent or unsettled time. These things happen. Society could do with encompassing a wider range of possibilities.

If you get a sense that you are probably not fine, and you need help, where do you go for help? For medical help, go to your doctor, to emergency at your nearest hospital, or track down a good, intuitive psychiatrist, preferably one who is spiritually open or at least broad minded and empathic. If you are feeling suicidal, many regions have telephone help lines that will provide immediate assistance.

Medical help

If you are feeling very troubled, depressed, suicidal, or unable to manage your life, an empathic medical doctor or psychiatrist can help you. Sometimes a small amount of medication can help tide you through a difficult time.

What can you expect from traditionally trained health care professionals? Likely you will first be given a series of medical tests to make sure that what you are experiencing is not a biochemical or hormonal imbalance. They will likely test for thyroid, B_{12}, sugar levels, liver and kidney function, and diabetes. If they find, say, a thyroid imbalance, they will first take steps to correct this imbalance. Even if there is a measurable biochemical imbalance, this may be only part of the picture – there may also be, say, energy phenomena that are purely kundalini related, but kundalini is not part of medical training. Unless the professional you are seeing has some first hand experience or has done some reading, the best he or she will be able to do is to translate kundalini into medical terms.

After the medical, they will listen to you, ask questions, and categorize your condition according to a statistical diagnostic system called the DSM-IV. Since 1994, a new section has been included in the DSM-IV that authenticates religious and spiritual problems as a legitimate focus of medical attention. The section is called V62.89. So far the new category hasn't made much difference. Most medical doctors have little information about the effect of strong kundalini energy, mystical experiences or spiritual emergence. However, the inclusion of this category in the DSM IV recognizes spiritual emergence as a legitimate focus for medical doctors. Medical doctors need to justify their time with a patient by treating an illness. An illness has to be reported on their forms in order for them to treat you. So if some awful sounding medical label arrives on your form, don't worry; it doesn't mean you have this condition, it means it is the nearest 'filing box' the DSM IV offers.

An increasing number of medical doctors are taking courses in alternative medicine as part of their training or interest, so in the future we might see traditional medicine include more intuitive approaches. In time, what we currently call mental illness may be understood to be the psyche's attempt to transform itself into a higher level of functioning. At which point all conditions, including physical illness, will be seen in transformational terms.

For example schizophrenia is thought by some[23] to be a disintegration of the previous mental structures to make way for new organization. It's like when you tidy your closet, sometimes you have to pull everything out of the closet so you can sort it and put it back in a sensible order. If someone comes into your room when you're in the middle of tidying your closet and throws a fit saying, "Oh my God, what a terrible mess in your room!" what are you going to do? You could stuff everything back in the closet quickly so that its outer appearance looks all right. However the re-organization process has already started. You're mid-way through. Stuffing everything back in the closet and closing the door on it might, at best, give a temporary look of tidiness to a bystander, but is not helpful in the long term.

> *There were signs that my life was careening out of control. Moments of anxiety and confusion started to become my reality. It climaxed into a constant state of intense paranoia and fear. The first psychologist I went to see diagnosed me as simply 'immature'. That was it! He wrote me a prescription...I suppose one to help me grow up?*

What the labels mean:

Currently, few doctors are trained in intuitive approaches, so their diagnostic system is what they use. The diagnoses they make sound very serious, but in their mild forms are commonly found in 'normal' personalities. We are all mildly psychotic, we just call it 'character' or eccentricity.

The kinds of labels someone in profound spiritual transformation might receive include:

- Hallucination (seeing something that isn't measurably there)
- Delusion (when you are convinced that something is other than it actually is)
- Dissociative episode (spacing out, not being fully integrated or grounded)
- Schizophrenic break (breakdown in relation between thoughts, feelings and actions)
- Schizoid Personality Disorder (emotionally restrained, disinterested in socializing or intimacy)
- Depersonalisation experience, exhibiting tendencies that are inconsistent with your usual personality.
- Hypnogogic state (altered state of consciousness)
- Delirium (not comprehending your surroundings well)
- Manic episode (euphoria)
- Psychotic episode (disintegration of mental functioning – not making sense, not cohesive)
- Ego regression (returning to a childlike way of thinking or behaving)
- Partial seizures (abrupt energy conditions)

If you receive one of these labels, it is because the way you look and behave puts whatever the health professional has understood about you in a particular category. It's not about the real You, but about your current symptoms. It doesn't mean you are mentally ill. It doesn't mean that your current condition will be permanent. It means that right now your condition most resembles the set of diagnostic criteria your medical doctor has been trained to see. There are only so many diagnostic boxes. The medical doctor must fit your experiences into one or a few of these boxes in order to treat you.

A few physicians and psychiatrists, through their own meditation, personal growth and awareness, have knowledge and experience of spiritual transformation. It is worth looking for one. However, in general, don't be surprised that your spiritual experiences lie outside their science. Don't expect anything different, or take it too personally. Their training doesn't include meditation, prayer or the anatomy of consciousness.

Even a doctor who does have some spiritual awareness will likely go through standard medical procedures before providing any intuitive comments. The reason being that they are supposed to go through the procedures. They would be criticized for doing otherwise, even if the procedures were counterintuitive. They are supposed to be scientific in their work. You will get the most intuitive side of your physician if you help him or her feel comfortable and safe with you.

For some reason, talking about spiritual states is touchy, whoever you are talking to. The medical profession is no exception.

> *I realized, and this is still the case today, that when one speaks of spirituality, the person hearing us feels attacked if that person is not in touch with their spiritual side. They must unconsciously feel guilty. So they are defensive. Instead of hearing me out, they focus on themselves!*

Medication

Giving medication is standard medical procedure. The medication ranges from tranquillisers to anti-psychotic drugs. In the pilot study, some participants found the drugs helpful, some rated them as 'OK,' some found them not useful, or 'didn't feel good,' or 'detrimental.' So it's a mixed bag how people respond to drugs.

When energy is unmanageably high, a small dose of the right medication can take the edge off the intensity.

Medication was excellent when the experience went out of my comfort zone of being capable of managing it, however it blocks the process rather than allowing healing. Homeopathy meant I did not need to consider medication. It saved me from being hospitalized and, sometimes, saved my life.[2]

The use of medication is not necessary – most people emerge from their spiritual transformation without using drugs. Psychiatrist Dr. Stanislav Grof is concerned that sometimes during spiritual transformation, people can neither return to what they were before, nor transform through the experience since the medication 'freezes' them in their process.[24]

What are the alternatives? Certain herbs, vitamins and nutrition can help. An experienced naturopath might help you. Energy work, grounding activities, breathing, walking in nature, and giving the process a little time can also help.

Dr. Grof has demonstrated that even chronic schizophrenics can be healed if unconscious material is allowed fully into awareness, rather than suppressed.[25]

Dr. John Weir Perry had established a special resident facility in San Francisco, California, in the 1970s to provide a safe retreat for people in spiritual emergency and certain people diagnosed with schizophrenia, (a common diagnosis for people in spiritual emergency). The facility was staffed by people who were empathic. The staff possessed certain personal qualities: sensitivity, deep understanding, and personal experience of altered states of consciousness, warmth, honesty, and genuine caring. They agreed to a non-sickness view of spiritual opening. Diabasis worked.

No matter how disturbed clients were when they arrived, under these understanding and empathic conditions, turbulence settled within a short while. Dr. Perry found that after about 40 days in a supportive environment, people would spontaneously get better, and that this wellness rarely relapsed afterwards. He concluded that part of the healing process was a dismantling of the mind, followed by putting the mind back together in a more organized fashion. Since many of these patients had been diagnosed with schizophrenia, one could conclude that schizophrenia can be cured and may not necessarily be a life-long condition as some medical professionals suppose.

Perry found that what was needed for treatment was a 'deep relation with another individual who empathizes and encourages, but does not interfere.' Success at Diabasis was far greater than at institutions using standard psychiatric methods and medication.

Many people have been helped by the medical profession, but not all have been. This is the personal experience of Dr Edward Whitney, M.D.

> *Medical education does not prepare psychiatrists to deal with spirituality in human experience. ... It saddens me to report that physicians were the main obstacle that I had to overcome on my quest for a hope-filled view of the world.*
>
> *It is a very serious matter when a physician mistakes a healing process for a pathological one. The intention of the doctors was positive, but their expression was most destructive. The head of psychiatry at the hospital told me that I was in denial if I insisted that I had been having a spiritual crisis. No, he said, this is a medical disorder like asthma or diabetes. When I finally understood that he meant what he said, I was devastated, and was feeling suicidal within hours. I could not argue with his self assured expert manner.* [26]

No matter how qualified a professional is, it doesn't mean he or she knows anything definitive. Thousands of people have been categorically told, by medical professionals of good standing, that they will never walk/see/live without medication again, and showed otherwise. If true for measurable, physical ailments, how much more true of the psyche that changes like the wind?

It's a very deep teaching that we should never be persuaded to leave our inner truth, dignity and soul direction. If you end up seeking medical help, remember that spirit lies outside the measurable, and therefore outside scientific medicine. Don't lose faith in spirit because science doesn't believe in it!

Institutions

Even if you receive an illness label during your medical diagnosis, you will not necessarily be admitted to hospital. One of people's greatest fears is that they will be locked up in some crazy ward. In countries where hospitals are private, a filled bed is good business. These days, in countries with free medical coverage, hospital beds are in short supply. So if you're remotely OK, and you don't want to stay in hospital, unless you are a real danger to yourself or a nuisance to other people, you are unlikely to be encouraged to stay when you don't want to. The exception is if you indicate in any way that you are feeling suicidal. This is an immediate ticket in. Medical doctors are trained to ask questions like, "Are you having suicidal thoughts?" The job of physicians is to preserve life. You will immediately be placed under close surveillance if you are feeling suicidal.

In most countries, you likely won't be 'put' in hospital if you are not considered to be doing harm to others or yourself, but you can be offered the opportunity for admission. If you are in great distress, a few days being looked after might be a great comfort.

My clients have reported that there are few services available, other than a bed and regular meals, yet hospital staff have assured me that spiritual counsellors, art therapy and all kinds of services are available. For example, many ministers visit hospitals offering spiritual counselling. Even if there are no spiritually open doctors on the ward, there may be spiritually open nurses or social workers who can understand you. Perhaps it's a matter of asking for them. Find out what is available.

The biggest downsides of being in hospital include being forcibly medicated. It can be very uncomfortable if you are sensitive to chemicals. Another downside is that energy fields are never cleared inside a hospital, so a lot of negative, discordant and diseased energy builds up, making it more difficult to find inner stability and health. It is wise to use an energy shield and other techniques for your personal protection (see page 86). However, when you can't manage on your own, at least you will be fed, have some basic care, and have a place to sleep.

> *Ultimately, if they had a spiritual counsellor with personal experience at the hospital or that came in once a week to speak with the patients and evaluate which ones were having spiritual experiences, and place these people in a special ward or section, with relaxing music, nicer staff, teachings of some kind, focused on meditation, getting out of the mind and getting into feeling the heart, teaching patients*

that each experience is valued and not discount it, access to spiritual books, etc, this would be much better! [2]

Ask for what you need. You might just be able to get it.

What helped me most?

To share the wisdom of those who have gone before you, these anonymous quotes from the PSE questionnaires are in answer to the question:
What advice has been most useful to you?

Remembering to listen to my heart and my breath and to keep with that advice

Breathe! Relax......Trust.....Let go attempts to control....read this or that (I have always been an avid reader).....Ask inside, because all the answers are there....ask and you shall receive....follow your own heart's urging.

Keeping a journal of all the weird things that happen to me, but I haven't been very disciplined at it

Find a practice which works for YOU: a 'path with a heart'; follow it; NEVER GIVE UP

Surrender to the Divine Mother. Let the Divine Mother Re-raise me.

Listen to my own body...go within

I did not receive any advice that was useful.

The internal advice was the most help.

There is no black and white, only grey

It's okay to be cookie and crazy sometimes

To listen and be open to your inner voice and to keep an open heart to all possibilities.

To not be fearful of the unknown.

Talking with others about my experience and feelings

To continue to work within the white light and to continue to serve others within that light

To love myself, to play, to grow plants, to have a pet

Darkness is the light,

We are where we are supposed to be,

still the inner voice

Keep Breathing

Most everyone has these experiences

Stay Grounded.

Can you still get up in the morning and feed the children?

Self Help

Non-Violent Communication

Have patience - talk with others - trust myself - when there is light there is also darkness

 Yoga study

Deep shadow (spiritual/spiritual) work; various energetic and therapeutic processes- too numerous to mention even if i remembered them all, which I don't! chiropractic adjustments; understanding nutrition; nature, nature, nature! and flower essences

Learning to learn again. Learning to love again

A 40 day meditation helped unlock and release old memories and emotions

Take time and be still and allow spirit to assist you.

Watch the edges of events and be aware of the whole scene and not jump straight into it.

Accept your experiences, don't try to control them, they are bigger than you

Accepting my experiences, no matter how out of the ordinary they may be

Meditation.

I can't remember specific advice, but I now believe that we are always serving, just in choosing to be on earth, even the entities that make different choices. This gives me the power to fully believe in myself as I have always believed in others and to 'get on with my life'.

Learning yoga to stretch and relieve stress. Massages also good for the same reason, ... but not using any sort of energy work as this only made it worse

40 day practice - then 90 then 120 then 365 then 1,000 - the cornerstone of spiritual work!

Relaxation techniques of any and every variety, essential and ongoing. Biofeedback, progressive relaxation, autogenics, yoga, self-hypnosis

Cold showers.

Food guidance

Saying prayers specifically designed to address the subject of "forgiveness". Prayers regarding "healing" were a strong healing tool as well, however, secondary to those focusing on forgiveness

The most useful has been the feeling of acceptance from my wife and my own courage to persevere

Receiving help in discovering my life purpose 'gave me permission' to take on greater challenges than I ever dreamed about before.

Empathy

Books e.g. Conversations with God series, Richard Bach, various channelled books

Regular Tai Chi practice – daily

To allow feelings to take their course, as they are only temporary manifestations of energy to trust my inner sense of what's right to go without understanding what and why to treat the body well, energy work, body work, strong spiritual person who would comprehend what was going on

The discipline of regular practice plus a support group

Under no circumstances should we interact with negative mind. There is no negativity in God

Who helped?

Jesus and the angels and my best friends

Discussion with other pilgrims

Spiritual mentors

The inner guidance of the Ascended Masters

The teachings of the masters-gurus from all over the world

My best connections were with people who absolutely loved the experience and glowed when they shared their story. We were absolutely amazed and we laughed a lot.

11

Standing on our Tails

Why does the mind habitually deny or resist the Now? Because it cannot function and remain in control without time, which is past and future, so it perceives the timeless Now as threatening. Time and mind are in fact inseparable.

Eckhart Tolle

With all of the best intentions in the world, if we are standing on our tails, we won't go far.
This chapter examines the ways we hide from our power and light, sidestep transformation, and oh so subtly avoid achieving our full potential. Even when we diligently practice, the ego-mind is cleverly steering life so that it remains in the driver's seat. Many practitioners are, unbeknown to themselves, bound by the very practice that is supposed to liberate them, or are hiding from Truth through their practice.

Part of us is reaching for light, another part is clinging to dark – the dark being the familiar, which includes our suffering. By naming the ways that prevent us from moving to our potential, we can become more conscious of these subtle patterns. What we are conscious of does not rule us in the same way. When you read about one of these patterns and think, hmmm, I think I'm doing this, don't gloss over it by reading further on right away. Take a few moments to fully perceive exactly how, where and why you use this pattern. Conceive of another way... rewrite the script.

What most enables transformation?

Trust, surrender, love, giving, centeredness, inner listening, simplicity, ease, and happiness most enable transformation.

Identification with our spirit essence, rather than our body-type, thinking, possessions, qualifications, etc. Our accoutrements are transient and changeable. Our spirit is constant.

What resists transformation, and why?

In a nut shell...

...fear.

Fear of death, fear of life, fear of being different, fear of losing control, fear of change, fear of feeling, fear of going crazy, fear of stepping into the unknown, fear of losing what you have, fear of your own power and light, fear of abusing your power should it open.

Fear is also the basis of control, desire, and insecurity.

So how do we stand on our tails? Some common ways.

We want to change, but:

We want to stay in control. What a fairy tale! Who do we think is running your show – 'you' or 'You'?

We don't want to disturb our daily routine. Oh, I'm sorry spirit, I can't be attuned with you right now because I need to do the laundry, then go shopping for some new jeans, and play with my dog, in time to meet my friends at the movie theatre...

Preoccupied with serving/pleasing others. We can't love ourselves directly, so we get busy serving others in the hope they will love us.

Holding back. Perhaps you're afraid of the power you will open to in case you misuse or abuse it.

We want to change but we have a fixed idea of how we want this change to look, so we block all the changes that don't look like our idea.

We're overly bound to practicalities. We'll make time for meditation, healing and fun, when all the practical things are done. Only trouble is, the 'to-do' list is longer than our waking hours, so our life purpose remains on the back burner our entire lives. We may admire others for following their dreams, but we don't allow ourselves to do the same. Why?

Lack of confidence in our vision. We see with clear insight, but we have too little confidence to live by our perceptions.

Identification with habits. We say, "I'm just like this. I've always been this way," even when your spirit calls you to something else.

Fear of criticism We are full of opinions about other people, many of them less than positive, yet for some reason we feel terribly unhinged by the idea that someone may have a critical thought about us. Reaching the place where we do not live for approval or fear criticism, we can start to Live.

Avoiding stillness: If you are afraid of the unknown, afraid of the vastness of expanded consciousness, you may get busy by filling your mind with activity, chatting to yourself incessantly to avoid the unknown. It's OK – but if expanded consciousness is what you want, you'll be waiting a while.

One version of avoidance is to go to lots of groups, classes, talks and workshops. No doubt you'll learn a great deal, but you may be way too busy to unwind, to Be, to touch the essence. You may even be escaping into spiritual-flavoured activity, much as a workaholic does. You wouldn't do that, would you?

Procrastinating: Putting the day when you will start 'living in the moment' sometime in the future, conveniently keeps you just where your ego-mind would like you to be. Like a diet that is going to start tomorrow, you content yourself with your good intention, and remain just where you are. Hey you! If you are not Awake in this moment, what other moment is there to awaken in? There is only this one!

Being 'cool': The easy-going types look like they've got it made – no effort, no sweat, take it easy, every day is a nice day. It's OK, but maybe there's a difference between appearing to feel good, getting Real, and being fully Awake.

Being 'religious' You can avoid awareness by being a very dedicated religious or spiritual practitioner. You can fill your days with the form of practice that never reaches the deep, open places within you, but satisfies your mind that you are doing all the right things.

Spiritual practice: You can be so busy practicing techniques for your enlightenment, that your striving itself consolidates the very 'I' sense, you are trying to dissolve. You are trying too hard.

Philosophical havens: Most paths promise that you will achieve liberation through their means. The very promise itself creates a spiritual hidey-hole – a haven cushioned with ideology and the sweet assurance that since you have found the best/highest path, liberation will surely be yours. The master will see to everything – have no concern. Just do this, believe that, eat this, wear that, and all will unfold.

Social climbing: Here and there are people who have 'been here, done that'. Whatever you discover, they already know. They like to be seen to be with the right people, and drop names of internationally known spiritual speakers/teachers – can we social climb our way to self-actualisation?

The ego's desire is to remain not only in existence, but also in control. The ego thinks social climbing is cool.

Knowing As soon as we think we know something, we cease to deeply inquire about it. We sleep. It's much easier to go on believing in what we already believe, than to question the assumed, to step out of the box of our thinking, and move on. We seem to like being on automatic.

Fear of death You might be unconsciously avoiding letting yourself go deeply into consciousness because its vast, timeless infinity somehow feels like death. Perhaps the release into light we experience when our bodies pass away (die) is the nearest experience we have known to the deep release into universal consciousness.

(If this is one of your fears, be assured; even if ego does temporarily dissolve, it is remarkably competent at reforming itself again afterwards. Try to dissolve it forever! There would be more Buddhas around if our egos weren't so very resilient. Our minds are similarly resilient, and will be there after deep transcendent experiences, waiting to immediately re-boot and resume their chatter.)

Fear of being abnormal

We are all so very afraid of being 'abnormal!' No one is normal, but everyone is afraid to not be normal! The fear is: "What if by becoming free I become different?" There is no Mr. And Mrs. Normal on this planet, yet we somehow still bound by this myth, still afraid of being 'not normal.'

The nearest we get to normality is a 'Mr. Able-to-project-fairly-normally-to-the-point-of-not-being-very-noticeably-abnormal.'
However, if you sit with this fellow and let him ramble about himself for a while, you will be sure to find all kinds of quirks, and so-called 'abnormalities,' – including spiritual insights and mystical experiences.

One of the quirkiest things about people today is their feeling that anything supernatural, supra conscious or Godly is abnormal. Fears of being different, abnormal, mystical or godly comprise some of our biggest fears.

Other versions of this fear include avoiding our empowered light-love inner being because we are afraid that we will change, and people won't like us if we're different. Many of us carry deep-rooted past life memories of the Inquisitions, witch burnings, and ostracizing of heretics. Our memories have scarred our subconscious, which imprint the importance of looking 'normal.'

It is this prevailing attitude idealizing a smooth, controlled, scientific, 'normal' life, which creates the context in for many of the problems due to spiritual transformation and awakening. The fear of abnormality makes us unnatural, unresponsive to our real needs and life direction. One of the reasons we are afraid of higher realms of consciousness or of anything supernatural or 'unknown' is simply a fear of being different, as if… what? As if we will be ostracized, thrown out of our society… the Inquisition will get us…

Name the fears. Put them in the past where they belong.

Our spontaneity, wonder, exploration and discovery are constantly sacrificed for the mundane pre-ordained, structured known. Awareness of timeless, dimensionless space and its joy and freedom have been traded for social conventionality. It is an unfortunate trade, generally made at such a young age, we were not even aware of it. Put another way, internal security which rests on inner connectedness and trust has been traded for the tenuous security of parental and societal approval - and we wonder why we feel insecure!

Do we dare stand true to your perceptions or will be block our way forward because we are we afraid of what Mr. Normal is going to think about us?

Fear of insanity

Taken one step further, fear of being abnormal turns into fear of being thought crazy, or even more intense, fear of actually being crazy. Since these fears create a major brake on our radical transformation, they are worth perusing.

Our ideas about who is sane or not, seem largely based on a person's ability to act and think in socially conventional ways.

Since our current religion is science, this framework is firmly founded on time, space, causality and the sense of individuality. According to this thinking, any glimpse of other dimensions must, logically, lie outside the realm of the sane.

Once the trade for conventionality has been made, and we adopt the limited patterns of behaviour and thinking of those around us, we are considered sane. Despite the fact that in our society, this sanity rests on a belief in a reality that excludes the Real. As some radical thinkers have pointed out, to be well adjusted to a sick society is perhaps the characteristic of serious mental illness. The so-called 'sane' are the ones who are actually out of their minds - or, to be precise, 'in' their minds. As R. D. Laing wrote:

> Our sanity is not 'true' sanity. Their madness is not 'true' madness. The madness of our patients is an artefact of the destruction wreaked on them by us, and by them on themselves. Let no one suppose that we meet any more 'true' madness than that we are truly sane. ...

Real sanity can never rest on faulty and transient identification with a changing body and mind. Real sanity is an open, illumined being, unconditioned, responsive, intelligent and free. Laing goes on to say,

> True sanity entails in one way or another the dissolution of the normal ego, that false self competently adjusted to our

alienated social reality: The emergence of the 'inner' archetypal mediator of divine power, and through this death a rebirth, and the eventual re-establishment of a new kind of ego-functioning, the ego now being the servant of the Divine, no longer its betrayer.

What, if anything, needs to transform, and why?

To reach your highest potential, to be free, to be maximally open, loving and responsive, essentially you need only transform those lifestyles, patterns and preferences that actually limit you or somehow block you from your direct inner knowing, your life direction, and your connection with spirit.

You may be shy or introverted, but maybe it suits you and suits the way you live and practice your spirituality. You don't have to be bright and outgoing to know your light and inner freedom. On the other hand, if your shyness constantly prevents you from going out, meeting people and doing things you would love to do, or if you feel blocked, suppressed and held in by your shyness, the transformation of your shyness will immediately pave the way to more freedom.

If your body handles your drinking coffee just fine, and you notice no adverse effects, you're in a different position from the person who gets wired, has stomach acidity, and can't settle into meditation after even one cup. No doubt it is generally healthier not to drink coffee, but maybe drinking coffee doesn't present an immediate limitation to your freedom and awareness. Your inner perception will tell you, if you listen, if or when your coffee drinking needs to change.

Maybe in reading this you will find excuses for life habits that get in your way, by saying to yourself, "In my case it's ok that I live in this unhealthy/limited way. It's not really a problem, I'm fine."

You choose what you look at and what you ignore. No doubt you will turn your attention to what needs attending in time – hopefully before life backs you up against a wall with a health condition or relationship crisis!

Contradictions with religious or spiritual beliefs

We may need to look more objectively at some of our spiritual myths. We've been sold the promise of enlightenment without being told what kind of efforts might be required. Spiritual paths show us the luminous faces of enlightened masters, but not the internal rubbing that they went through to become so luminous, which leaves the impression we can all instantly step into this wonderful state of being without any internal clean up or life change. One satori moment, and poof! we're fully enlightened. The truth is most of us need major washing and ironing before we're fit for full-on Light. When we idealistically expect a smooth path, we can end up thinking something is wrong with us because challenges have arisen. The disparity with our idealism then adds a whole layer of extra unnecessary confusion, doubt and resistance to our process.

It's like a TV ad for soap powder in which we are shown the bright white clothes obtained after washing with Suzie's new stain removing detergent, but we don't see Suzie repeatedly rubbing the clothes to get the stains out. In the ad, the detergent makes things clean automatically, like magic.

We see people practicing daily meditation, yoga, prayer, chanting and rituals – which are kinds of internal laundering. Laundering is a good and necessary process, but we get surprises. Sometimes a delicate item needs stitching up afterwards. Stretchy pants may be out of shape, a white T-shirt has picked up blue patches from those new socks, underwear elastic has unravelled. Internal transformation is much the same – there may be unexpected hiccups along the way.

Some teachings claim that their path will protect us from challenges – at least, will protect anyone who is *really* devoted and *really* practicing – implying that if we go through a major internal process, it is because we are not practicing correctly. Part of this idealism has no doubt come about because spiritual teachers, by the time they are teaching, have invariably long moved through their personal hurdles, and are speaking from a transcended or detached place that knows no problems. Who knows, perhaps these spiritual teachers believe that it is not good for their business to explain that unravelling on some deep levels might occur? Unfortunately these kinds of teachings often focus on enlightenment, but gloss over the personal purification, internal clearing and alignment that are invariably needed to attain enlightenment.

In contrast, many shamanic teachers maintain that true sages or healers only emerge after passing through the eye of the storm, having visited the shadows, and having dared to step outside the ordinary into the unknown.

Internal contradictions

We switch between the wish to be united, melted, open and surrendered, and the wish to strive towards goals, make something of our lives. Fundamentally, we are switching between the wish to simply Be and the wish to become – to become someone or something. We switch between love and fear.

The heart of each person longs for union. It's the primary reason people seek love, sex, intense experiences and spirituality. Part of each person yearns to merge in deep, blessed, long-lasting union with God or a lover. At the same time, another part of that same person strives toward further individuation, more perfect control over life or self-betterment.

For the spiritual seeker, these contradictory forces are an anomaly. The seeker wishes total union with God, yet clings to individual existence. Seekers pick up beautiful philosophies of oneness and divinity, yet continue to choose to be comfortably embedded in the habits and thinking that keep them separate. They profess to be surrendered to God, yet continue to want their lives to go according to their plans. They invariably believe that they can give up the ego and still live according to their preference. They do not realize that ego is created from preference – the preference to remain an existing somebody or something, being primary.

True resolution does not happen through finding or creating a philosophy that encompasses contradiction – although it's a good second best – nor does it come through trying to abandon all thinking due to the inadequacy of the intellect to understand. True resolution comes through the direct melting of separation. Contradiction ceases because you realize that nothing is really happening in the way the intellect conceives it. There is nowhere to go because you are Here.

Honest self-observation

We would all like to see ourselves as kind, loving, generous, compassionate, fearless, receptive, good-humoured and wise people, but are we? It takes a brave and honest mind to notice when and why we hold back on generosity, when and why we get pinched by someone else's success, when and why our love is conditional, when and why we ignore another's cry for help.

There need be no judgment. There need be no sense that jealousy, fear, or resentment should not be happening. We observe simply to know ourselves. From this well-turned soil can sprout the flower of true freedom, for what we can clearly see can no longer bind us. We are most bound by those characteristics we desperately want to pretend we don't have. If you want to know what these characteristics are, notice the behavior for which you most criticize others.

When there is a mismatch between internal self-image and our actual performance in live situations, many people prefer to escape into a self-elating, heroic fantasy world rather than honestly seeing things as they are. Fantasy provides a great way for the ego to maintain its false sense of self, and to continue living obliviously.

Some spiritual paths use idealism to encourage followers to achieve certain standards or ideals. While offering an easy-to-follow path, modeling on an ideal is fertile ground for all kinds of pretence.

Our smiling personality-masks barely cover our pretence. If you must pretend to the social world around you, then at least don't pretend to yourself. You cannot be free while you try to see yourself in a way that you actually are not. You whole life will be caught in a series of coverings, each one trying to smooth over, or account for the previous covering. In honesty, there is nothing to hide, nothing to defend against. You are as you are. In this beautiful, open, inclusive acceptance of all that you are, spirit can flow through you freely.

There are so many subtle ego mechanisms at play. If you watch carefully, you see the little tendencies - wanting to be the knowledgeable one, holding back, needing to be needed, one-upmanship, wanting attention. None of them are a big deal in themselves, but added together they create a net that binds you to human ways of thinking and behaving, rather than to the freedom of your spirit. Nothing needs to be changed; astute observation is the key. It is in the flickering background of our barely conscious thinking that subtle motivations insidiously influence our every thought and action.

Our intellects are powerful influences in our lives. They are quick to pick up information and quick to imitate. As such, intellects are both a great tool and a great source of delusion. For example, intellects can imitate the impressions created during a spiritual opening or deep insight, recreating these impressions, such as remembering how the experience looked, and now believing the image is the experience.

Intellects can also hear information about higher states of consciousness and assume they know these states, because they understand the words. An intellect is also good at filtering the impressions received from the world, so that it only sees what it wants to see. It can take the facts and twists or reshapes them, so that they seem more comfortable. It can bolster its self-image, or destroy our confidence through excessive focus on negative thoughts, whether about construed or real problems. When we base our sense of ourselves or the world around us on our thoughts and beliefs, we will live on a roller coaster of ideas that change with every read or heard word.

When we identify with our inner being as who we really are, rather than the body-mind-personality, it is easier to notice and acknowledge our less shiny sides. We can more readily sense when jealousy, anger or frustration is arising, or that we feel competitive, fearful, needy or resentful. We can be the one with courage who can take a humorous, candid look at what actually is.

Where are we going?

We tend to get what we put our attention. If you are practicing meditation in order to gain happiness, you tend to get it. Ditto tranquility, transcendental bliss, equanimity, and escaping the world.

What qualities do you want? Envision them!

Then quit standing on your tail.

12

Re-aligning our Lives

We've explored the inside picture of the spiritually awakened person, the range of energies, experiences, effects, sensations, inner purification and resistance to growth. Let's now explore bringing our outer world – how we live, eat, relate, love, give and work – into alignment with our new awareness. When we change inside, we need to upgrade our life to match this new awareness. It helps to complete the transformation process.

When our external, day-to-day life matches our inner awareness, it feels good. We have chosen work that is inspiring. and rewarding;

the people we have chosen to be around us understand us and celebrate our steps forward; we feel on track, joyful, vibrant, and going what we took birth to do

Sue doesn't feel like this. Her mind is pre-occupied with financial concerns. She is always busy. Numerous people for numerous reasons seem to need her time and energy. Her house and garden take hours to maintain – a never-ending 'to-do' list. She loves food, so much that her remaining time is culinary pleasures, though

focused on making tasty she feels fat. The time Sue longs to spend in meditation and quietly in nature doesn't ever seem to happen at Home. She meditates in classes and workshops, and walks in woodland during retreats. These nurturing facets of her life are like disconnected islands. The creative and explorative areas close to her soul purpose are not even in her life picture.

Constantly multitasking, constantly stressed, Sue always feels run down and often exhausted. She feels like the ground beneath her feet is not solid, and could crack and give way at any moment, because her life had no roots and no real purpose.

Sue's address book is full of phone numbers she no longer wants to call. She wants to be with people who are more like-minded, but she hasn't made available the time and energy to start reaching out to find them. Left to her own devices, she'd eat raw, organic food, but she continues to cook for family and friends the meals they enjoy. It's practical to eat with them, but then she worries about weight gain. The career direction she chose years back no longer means anything to her. She feels she has no option but to continue working in a well-paid job that bores her, so she can meet the payments on her spacious house and garden that then takes much of her spare time to maintain. She is happy in nature. In meditation she connects to a space of love and oneness that nurtures her spirit. She senses she is totally vast and free inside, and feels inspired to bring more love and peace into the world.

In short, Sue's life is not aligned with spirit.

Do you recognize any of these elements in your life?

Bringing our day-to-day life into alignment with our inner awareness is no small work, yet without it, we are not congruent, integrated and living in harmony with our inner nature. It is particularly important to re-align our lives after coming through profound spiritual transformation. We are different afterwards. Our lives need to reflect this difference.

When our lifestyle, values and actions align with our life direction, our vibrational rate and universal spirit, we feel uplifted, energized, and enthusiastic about what we are doing.

Situations, actions, thoughts and orientations, which deplete our energy, scatter our attention, and erode our self confidence are not just uncomfortable; they slow us down, and can even significantly block our transformation.

Each instance of incongruence is somewhat energy draining and distracting. We need our energy to transform, to laugh, to do what we took birth for. It is easier to live consciously when we have good energy levels, so observing what depletes us can be very useful.

How aligned are we?

Take a moment right to tune into your every-day life as it is right now. Some of the main areas include: work/career, relationships, friends, leisure activities, diet, lifestyle, and life direction. Ask yourself: Does your lover resonate with your current awareness, values and lifestyle? Does the way you earn money reflect your true gifts and calling to serve humanity? Do you continue activities that you used to enjoy, but are not fun for you the way you are right now? Does your heart call you to live closer to Nature, or to live amongst people rather than alone, but you continue to live the way you used to?   Rather than stoically continuing on our usual track, in our usual patterns, it is refreshing to explore the ways we live our lives, and fine-tune our lifestyle to fit more closely with our awareness. Transformation is an ongoing 24-hour process. It is reflected in our every thought and action, our dreams, as well as in our times of quietness or spiritual practice.

We know what makes us feel vibrant and alive, and what makes us feel dull, bored and lifeless. Drawing a line down the middle of a piece of paper, we can put the activities and situations that drain us, that scatter our thinking or energy, or make us feel grey on the left side. We can write the activities that uplift us and increase our health and vitality on the right side. Is it possible that we could engage only in the activities on the right side of the page? What would happen if so?

Perhaps the page with two columns is too simplistic. We might prefer to list our activities/situations and rate them from, say, - 4 (dreary, depleting) to +4 (inspiring, uplifting) with 0 being 'no particular effect.' Maybe we engaged in an activity at a particular time, so we use the rating for the after-taste of the activity or situation. How are we left feeling attending a particular event, being with a particular individual? What are our energy levels like? What is our state of consciousness afterwards?

If you'd like to take a moment to explore your life, first put in the chart all the activities and situations you choose: friends, lover(s), social and leisure activities, spiritual practice, reading, surfing the internet, movie watching.

Activity	-4	-2	0	+2	+4
Career / work / money earning	x				
Lover				x	
Sport / leisure activities		x			
TV / movie watching	x				
Video games / surfing the net		x			
Friend - Jean					x
Friend - Kim			x		

Notice how you feel after an activity, or after spending time with a friend or group of friends. Do you feel uplifted, energized, creative and inspired, or drained, exhausted, with a jumbling mind?

We are the masters, the creators of our lives. We have many choices available to us; yet we often habituate in familiar patterns of behaviour, rather than consciously choosing what we do. After an awakening or a time of inner transformation, it is especially important that we observe our lives, and re-choose when necessary.

Our minds are affected by the way our companions think and feel. Our emotional field is charged, lifted, angered, opened and contracted by our responses to those around us. Our energy levels and the quality of our energy fields, is affected by the energy levels of those with whom we spend time. Our intent, our values, and our priorities are reflected in these actions and choices.

The first step is to pay attention, noticing our energy levels and state of consciousness in each activity or situation.

In order to tangibly align our outer life with our awareness, we next need to prioritise our values. For example, is it more important to please our friends and family or to be happy ourselves?

In instances where our lives don't feel aligned with our deeper selves, our next task is to lovingly make the changes we need while maintaining great respect to both our needs and the people around us.

Changes in diet or eating patterns

If our internal vibrational frequency changes, it's a good idea to bring the kind of food we eat into balance with this inner change. We may find some challenges in doing this.

❖ We are creatures of habit – we may need to break our previous habits before we can freely choose what is right for us now.

- We eat with family or friends, so it's an effort to do something different.
- We use food to keep ourselves at a vibratory rate that is familiar. After a high-vibrational meal that is different to what we are accustomed, say, of fresh picked organic salad and sprouts, something in us may yearn for a chocolate brownie or chips afterwards. We are used to how we feel after eating familiar foods, and we don't recognize the way we feel after the salad. If we stave off our eating habits sufficiently, we can become accustomed to a high vibration.

Switching to a vegetarian diet

Many people switch to a vegetarian diet after a shift in consciousness. For some people, it is because they feel energetically heavy after eating meat, for others, it's due to increasing sensitivity to animal welfare and environmental issues. Switching to a vegetarian diet is a quick solution to the ills associated with meat production - animals being penned up, force-fed, filled with antibiotics and growth hormones, and killed in fear and pain. All of this is taken into our bodies when we eat meat.

There are more environmentally sustainable, healthy options. Protein can be obtained from combining grains, beans, legumes, nuts and seeds, and from soy products such as tofu, tempe and soy milk.

Switching back to meat eating

In some cases, people have been vegetarian for years only to find that they are now feeling too spacey and floaty, and consider returning to eating meat as a grounding option. It is probably healthier to work on energetic grounding than to rely on food to ground you, but certainly meat is a heavier food, which will tie you more to the earth. Consuming organic, field grazed animals that are sacredly killed, sidesteps some of the grimmer aspects of meat production.

Onion and garlic are grounding foods. In the east, onions and garlic are thought to close the higher spiritual channels and create more 'rajas' or active energy in the body which can be useful if you feel overly open. Grounding foods also include dense, salty foods like olives, miso, bean burgers and nut roast.

Friendships

When our vibratory rate, values and interests change, we may find that some of our friends no longer resonate with us.

Our options are:
1. Keep things as they are (and stoically suffer.)
2. Keep things as they are, and strengthen your inner core, surrounding energy fields, inner connection, and grounding to the extent that you can remain in these situations, without compromising your openness or spiritual direction.
3. Transform the energy of your friend by inspiring him or her to read, think, travel, take time off, meditate, be in nature or whatever works to raise the vibratory rate or openness of your friend. (In so doing you help the planet as a whole.)
4. Develop new ways of relating to your previous friends. For example, rather than meeting in a coffee house or bar, meet for a country walk. Direct the conversation towards your topics of interest. Let your friend know you cherish the connection, but at this time you need...
5. Cease to spend time with your friend (either by explaining what is happening, or by quietly becoming busy elsewhere.)

Hurdles:

1. Friends may be troubled by your distance, and may not understand the change.
2. Depending on where you live and available opportunities, you may or may not be able to find like-minded company. This situation leaves you with the choice between being in uncomfortable company, or being on your own; choosing between a rock and a hard place!

Not fitting in - with friends

When we wake up to more expanded and beautiful possibilities, it's hard to imagine that everyone you know wouldn't want the same love and light. It's a shock to find that mainstream people find it disconcerting when people think differently from the way they do. Theirs is the right way – they are the social majority. Since their identity is embedded in their beliefs, they will quickly feel threatened by views other than the ones they hold. The easiest response is to criticize anyone who is outside the paradigm.

Criticism can be painful when coming from a good friend, but try not to take it too personally – human nature is like this. Thinking in a different way from those around you may leave you feeling like an alien. If you are loving, authentic, and true to your spirit, in the long run you may win the respect of those who find you to be 'different'. But it is also possible that you will come to realize that these people no longer deserve your respect. There is no point in remaining in company that does not appreciate you.

I don't belong here!

Not fitting in - with your family

We are deeply connected to our families – emotionally, energetically, and sometimes even financially. We can change our friends, but we cannot just drop our family connections, and find a new family that we connect with as organically as our own. If we become so 'different' that our families reject us, it is painful. In time, if we can remain open and loving, our family members will likely adapt and develop new ways of relating to us, and we to them.

If you feel like rejecting your family, take care how you do this. Many people need some time away from their families in order to shake off life-long, ingrained ways of being and relating. Some people need time away from their past to discover their new selves. It can be done lovingly, or hurtfully by criticizing your family's way of being and overtly arguing, and rejecting them.

In a certain way, rejecting our families is like rejecting part of our own DNA, rejecting our emotional roots, so it is not the best option.

Not fitting in socially

We are social animals. We are brought up to harmonize with those around us. As we become more true to ourselves and more in tune with spirit, our beliefs and actions may become different from, or even at variance with, the prevailing ideas around us. Our choices are to:
- ❖ Figure that freedom is an inner reality not an outer one, and try to fit in as best we can to keep the peace.
- ❖ Adopt the appearance of fitting in, and quietly do and think as we feel.

❖ Stand like a lion in what we believe and take whatever flack goes with it (which might turn out to be none, but might be considerable).
❖ Try to draw other people to our values and way of being.

Being different may be considered a sign of genius or a sign of madness. How do we know which way it'll swing? One factor is whether our way of being works in this physical world. Another is the confidence with which we stand in our truth. Perhaps the most important factor is how open our hearts are. People will accept those who they feel love and accept them, those that emanate warmth and caring. If we're going to step outside the norm, having an open heart when we step out will greatly help.

Not fitting in with your spiritual group

Think about it – who would devote themselves to a path or teacher, if it were not the very best choice they could find? If we could find a better teacher or teaching, we would naturally gravitate there. So it's not surprising that most groups claim to be on the best or quickest path, or the *only* true path.

When we awaken, we directly experience inner truth. We start to see with our own eyes. We may now have little or no need for an intermediary, priest or teacher, because we have a direct connection to spirit within ourselves. This new connection, in itself, challenges followers. It is also challenging for us because some aspects of our group or religion, may have to do with people giving their power away.

After an awakening, we change. Group activities can look exceptionally imbued with light and inner meaning, but they may also look rather silly.

Most groups have clearly defined the ways that those on the path are supposed to follow. If we perceive or behave differently from the these ways, from the point of view of the other followers, our way has to be less good, because the path/teacher has clearly been chosen as the best. Depending on the open-mindedness of our group, our 'different-ness' could be judged as: 'wrong,' 'off the path,' 'gone astray' or even 'gone to the devil.'

So often it happens that as we open up to amazing new perceptions, abilities and creativity, lit in love and light, purifying, clearing our old limitations, we find the most spiritual people we know can't relate to us. How disconcerting! In time we come to see that the repetition of rituals, practices and techniques, however diligently done, is not the same as having one's vision open, or going through major internal clearing.

When we are part of a spiritual or religious group, particularly when we are disciples of a charismatic leader, we need to be very clear about our values and priorities. Group members are a bit like siblings – there is a pecking order, a way of doing things, a way of holding back someone who is considered to be getting 'too big for their boots', or moving too far out of line (ahead?). It's a matter of, "You can't be like that; you're supposed to be like us."

It is easier for spiritual teachers, masters and gurus to remove 'alternative' thinkers from the flock, than to allow them to rock the nice devotional boats. Spiritual leaders are supposed to be needless, but they are usually emotionally and financially dependant on the devotion they receive. These needs will never be outwardly stated as such. Spiritual philosophy is used in such a way that the guru and the group is considered to be perfect, your differences are imperfect.

Most groups, in order to maintain their faith and self-esteem, feel they have to denounce a group member who is no longer as devoted to the group ideals. A common tactic is to focus in on an area where you are less strong, and use that to validate their disdain or rejection. It takes strength of mind and clarity to stand in your awareness, otherwise they will convince you of your imperfection, which kind-of proves that you need their teaching to get better.

If your direction is genuinely towards love and light, and you are rejected for being the way you are, your group is not living the unity consciousness and love that they say they are. There are no genuine spiritual excuses for such rejection, however well phrased or scriptural, and however far up the group hierarchy the philosophy comes from. Becoming more loving, and close to spirit and your inner knowing is what spiritual teaching is about. There is no single way of behaving, believing or being that is the only 'true' expression of spirit.

When we don't fit in with our spiritual or religious group, our choices are to:

❖ Focus on the positive benefits of the teaching / path, and try to ignore the rest.
❖ Adopt the appearance of fitting in, and quietly do and think as we feel.
❖ Speak our wisdom, name the ignorance we see, and handle the flack.
❖ Encourage other group members to perceive and live more authentically.

Leaving a group often feels like being in disgrace, especially leaving one that you have been in for many years. It may entail leaving your emotional and spiritual support, a large chunk of your social life, and your closest friends. In many groups you are either 'in' (totally devoted) or you are 'out' (rejected by the group). It has the same emotional impact as a divorce. You are leaving a group marriage. You might fear that you are forfeiting a golden opportunity, that you will lose your light if you leave the path, that you will no longer progress, that you will lose your chance of going to heaven or achieving enlightenment. Leaving a spiritual group is not a small thing.

Yet staying in a group that does not value the transformation that is happening to you is not healthy in the long run. Have courage – if you cannot value your own perceptions, what can you trust?

Feeling alone

While well-meaning and kind, many people simply cannot relate to any consciousness other than the one they are used to.

You may well feel like an alien, the only weird one, who sees your way in a world that is totally different from you. You may well feel more alone in company than on your own. You may

feel just as alone with so-called 'spiritual' people who know all the spiritual words, have learned a philosophy verbatim, but aren't living the openness they are talking about.

It may feel particularly excruciating after a mystical experience, retreat, or profound shift in consciousness. You yearn to have even one person *hear* you and really *grok* what you are saying, to be there with you in that place. It's like being in a world where people's physical bodies stop at the neck and you alone have a head. No one else seems to perceive as you do right now. In time you'll likely find more people who see and feel as you do.

> *The majority participants, who filled in the PSE questionnaire wished they had more friends who understood them.*

How to meet like-minded people

❖ Most cities have an alternative magazine advertising upcoming workshops, trainings and classes. You can also go to your local health food store and check out the notice board for workshops or classes that are in your area of interest. Make a point of exchanging phone numbers with anyone you feel good with, in the classes or groups you attend.

❖ Join a local meditation/discussion/spiritual study group. To find these groups, look in your local alternative magazine, or do an Internet search with your hometown + some keywords representing your interest. Many spiritual groups hold satsang, (satsang is a term meaning 'in the company of truth') usually with no charge or on a donation basis.

❖ Keep your eyes open for awake, growing people. Use your intuitive nose to sense who they are. Scan crowds. When you arrive at social gatherings, rather than make a beeline for the people you already know, or for a pretty face, look around with your inner eye and sense who there is most open and light. Be bold – chances are a spiritually oriented person will be just as happy as you are, to have a conversation about something more meaningful than the usual trivial chitchat.

The work ethic - live to work (rather than work to live)

Mainstream society believes life is about survival through constant production and material acquisition. To live in the joy of the present moment without regard to future security is unthinkably irresponsible to a mainstream mind. Time in meditation is a waste of precious moments that could have been used to accomplish the endless tasks that need to be done; taking quiet time is being 'lazy.' In the absence of productivity or profit, according to this way of thinking, spiritual practice has no worth.

A university student spending considerable years and thousands of dollars tucked away in libraries while studying law or medicine is deemed honourable. Spending the same amount of time becoming spiritually wise or an adept healer has not yet earned the same reputation as a career option. We all agree that the world needs more aware, wise and loving people, yet our world doesn't value the time taken to unfold this awareness.

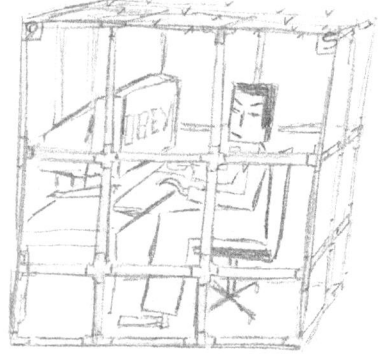

While millions choose to align with traditional material values, working 9:00 to 5:00 o'clock (often feeling dissatisfied), thousands choose to follow their spirit. Following any direction that is different from the mainstream, requires trust. Each person who emerges from a period of spiritual preparation, who can be seen by other, more material minded people, to be helping the world in tangible ways, helps legitimise the spiritual life choice.

In primitive and traditional cultures, there is still a place for spiritual elders, wise ones and healers in the community. This place has been lost in the west.

The work ethic is a foundation stone of western culture; it will not easily shift. If you do not have the courage to fully stand for what you are doing with your life, an option that might be next best is to present what you are doing in terms that are closer to the values respected by those around you. For example, rather than saying that you want to deepen your spiritual awareness by spending a year at a yoga and meditation retreat, this information could presented as a career plan. Since the principles of meditation and yoga form the basis of many stress management programs, you could say, "I am applying to attend a one year stress management course at an institute abroad." The principle thing for 'mainstream' people seems to be that you look like you are going somewhere and doing something with your life. It is just unfortunate that knowing who you are in truth doesn't seem to be high on many people's list of gainful life directions.

Health and well-being
For some reason, many of the activities considered fashionable, fun or cool, are unhealthy. Social circles differ as to which kind of un-health they gravitate towards. Some popular choices are: drinking alcohol, absorbing hours of TV, watching violent movies, hanging out in fast-food restaurants, playing aggressive video or computer games, visiting pornographic websites, over-eating, smoking cigarettes and taking recreational drugs.

In this mind-frame, enjoying health food and watching a sage's discourse on video is 'boring.' Only wet blankets stay at home quietly on a Friday evening, meditating to clear the week's work out of their minds rather than going to a party. Other people don't understand. "Hey, come on man, have some fun!"

It takes courage to stand up to our peers, to drink a juice in the midst of beer drinkers because that is what suits us. It takes integrity to stand true to our awareness that one of the things we most like to do in our spare time is to be still.

Non-genuine 'cool' is copying social norms and keeping up a cool image, whereas genuine cool is akin to spiritual centeredness and autonomy. To the extent that we are really centred, standing firmly with our felt-sense, intuition, physical needs and life direction, we re-define what cool is.

Changing your work direction
Many people these days are doing work that their heart and soul are just not inspired and thrilled by, especially the 9:00 – 5:00 office workers.

> ***24% of PSE participants needed a new career direction***
> ***after their spiritual awakening.***

When we transform in our awareness and lose interest in our current work, what then?

Three possible options are:
- ❖ To redefine your job in ways that makes it more meaningful for you, or more in tune with your spiritual practice.
- ❖ To consider taking a new career direction, acquiring new training or confidence in some of the training you already have.
- ❖ Taking the plunge by leaving your job and trying something new.

Society has not yet given sufficient value to healing and intuitive work to support institutions providing hands-on healing work and spiritual teaching, in the way that hospitals and academic education institutions are supported. If societal values shift, there could conceivably be good employment prospects in many intuitive areas. In the meantime, intuitive practitioners who need more financial support than their intuitive work can provide, are typically remaining in work that is not resonant with their awareness until such time as their client base grows, or opportunities present themselves, so they can move into an area of work which is closer to their hearts.

If you have not yet clarified an alternative life direction

These questions may be useful:
- ❖ Instead of thinking, "How can I make money?" the starting place is to ask yourself, "What service would I most like to give the world/humankind?"
- ❖ If you had a million dollars in the bank, and no longer needed to work for money, what would you do with your time? If there is any doubt about what your inner calling is, imagine winning the lottery (really imagine it – it's fun!). Imagine what you would most like to spend the rest of your life doing. What gift(s) would you choose to bring to others?

(You might think that hanging out on a sunny beach would be wonderful. Yet, when you really consider beach lounging for the rest of your life, while still seeking inspiration, and a deep and wonderful sense of meaning, you may well discover much more interesting occupations than sunbathing.)

- ❖ What did you come here (take birth) for? Your spirit or soul has a life purpose, a reason for incarnating. When you align your life with this purpose, even if you encounter challenges, it feels right.

Redefining our work

We may decide not to change our job, but instead change our orientation to it. We can go to work with the intention of remaining relaxed, and fully aware all day, sitting without slumping, taking full, nourishing breaths. We invite spirit to work through us, to breath through us. We learn to live in the moment, without fear or judgment, and just do what needs to be done without resistance. This orientation immediately transforms our working life into spiritual life. As a bonus, we leave work with a whole lot more energy!

Taking the plunge

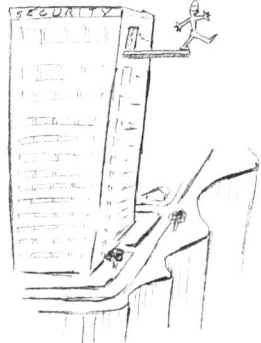

Sometimes we just have to take a chance, and just go for what we want. We may leave our nice secure, job, retrain in a new field, or set up business doing something we are passionate about. We head out into the unknown, and hope it all works out. It's like stepping off a cliff blindfolded. We just trust. It's not so different from any other life choice. A businessman will risk borrowing vast sums of money to set up an enterprise. Sometimes it fails; sometimes it does well.

Today's Religions

After touching openness and incredible love, we may wonder why the world isn't more compassionate, why humanity is continuing in its current direction when it could be so much more caring, respectful of the environment, and intuitive. Part of the reason is that there are two prevalent 'religions' in operation: the science-religion and the money-religion. Much faith is put in these religions. Many people believe we cannot survive without them, yet many spiritually open people feel at odds with these powerful institutions that rule so many aspects of our lives. Because these religions are so pervasive it's better to understand them and learn to work with them, rather than to be in opposition to them, or be disillusioned by them. We do not need to align ourselves with their values, but we do need to accept that most people have done so. To reject them, is to make ourselves unnecessarily weak.

There is no point in denying ourselves money because the overall money-system is not operating on optimally aware principles.

It is useful to see these institutions for what they are, and see the extent to which their values form the fabric of our own thinking and values, even as we reach for a higher truth.

Science

The fundamental principle of science is that anything that cannot be tangibly measured does not exist. We should not be surprised or disappointed to learn that in this 'religion', the intellectual plane takes precedence over all others. Science is an intellectual field.

According to this view, anyone who sees energies or possibilities outside the current science-based empirical standards is seeing immeasurable things that do not exist.

The science monks train in monasteries called universities. The high priests are the PhDs and post doctorates who establish methodology for scientific research and our medical system.

Rather than being one of the many possible ways of knowing, science has become **the** way of knowing. Luckily, on the cutting edge of science, quantum physicists are thinking their way out of previous confines, and are moving towards the same conclusion that the sages through the ages have – that there is one being. Quantum physicists recognize that the world is not made of "objects" that exist "out there", that there is no future or past, and hints that some greater energy or consciousness is moving us through this life. Because they are scientists, they have some credibility in the 'science religion'.

For eternally and always there is only now, one and the same now; the present is the only thing that has no end.

Erwin Schroedinger

Something unknown is doing, we don't know what.

Sir Arthur Eddington

If quantum physics replaces Newtonian physics as our science base, science will harmonize more with intuitive awareness.

Money

Making money, increasing profit, buying larger houses and faster cars, trading on the stock market, owning luxury consumer items and buying security in the form of insurance and pension, are all part of the 'money religion.' Some devotees of the money religion believe that those who have more money are more spiritually deserving.

The intellect also rules this church. Regardless of character, honesty, state of mind or any other intrinsic value, a person tends to be more highly valued in this society, if they have money. The priests are the MBAs, the cardinals are the bank owners.

We can ask ourselves, 'to what extent are we run by the money god?' Are we staying in a dull job to secure a pension, rather than following our inspiration? Did we trade our life direction for security? Do we buy clothes and CDs, and then tell ourselves that we can't afford a massage or energy treatment when we need one?

Every perceptive person in society realizes that the material values on which most people focus are shallow, and do not bring any lasting, or even temporary, fulfilment. Yet for some reason we can rarely put our finger on, we disregard these perceptions and carry on as if there is no other choice. Even people who uphold monetary values see all kinds of drawbacks in our financial system, but we have not yet evolved a better vision.

There will always be compromises, but it is much more possible to live close to your ideals than most people ever actualise. Each single person who dares to live attuned to his or her body, mind and spirit helps pave the way for others to do the same. Someone must set the example. As Marianne Williamson wrote, quoted by Nelson Mandela in his Inaugural Speech,[27]

> *And as we let our light shine,*
> *we unconsciously give other people*
> *permission to do the same.*
> *As we are liberated from our own fear,*
> *our presence automatically liberates others.*

Aligning our lives with our inner awareness rarely happens overnight. Every single facet of our lives is included in our transformation, from our career to our personal life habits and much more. We need to observe ourselves with great honesty to become in alignment.

Remaining true to yourself
Millions of people around the world are waking up, becoming more conscious, and wishing for more peace, love, compassion and giving in our world. However, the value-priorities of the majority of people centre on immediate creature comforts, and financial security.

Criticizing life
When we feel connected to spirit, when our hearts are open, accepting life as it is, comes easily. We keenly observe life and the situations around us, yet have little criticism or judgment. Things are as they are.

When our hearts are less open, we might find ourselves feeling critical or even cynical about the world around us. Our heightened sensitivity picks up on all kinds of idiocies. We think we know how things should be. The rest of the world looks 'out to lunch.' We want to separate ourselves from the nonsense 'out there.'

We might be absolutely, perfectly correct about all that we see. The world probably is just as 'out to lunch' as it looks. If we can laugh at it all, that's great. However, when we feel dark, saturnine and despondent about the many ills of the world, and fixing the world seems to be an endless task, opening our heart more brings immediate relief. Criticism comes from a place of contraction and separation. When the heart is open we can see things keenly without feeling jaded or grey. Our most fundamental choice is to remain with love, or not.

Your ideal
Having reached deep into your being and discovered your true nature and soul purpose, you can then take some time to create a clear image of how your life could look. Draw it, write about it – get tangible about your dreams. What kind of work, what kind of friends and relationships, activities, lifestyle, and home would you like? Then bring your dreams into the present and establish them as already happening. (Putting dreams in the future creates a time separation. The only time you can manifest your dreams is in the moment you are in.) Dream high, dream beautifully, and dare to manifest your dreams.

13

Reaping the Fruits

Having come through extraordinary experiences or tumultuous times, the intensity of internal purification, energy adjustments and over-sensitivity gradually slows, and our boats sail from turbulent waters into a calm, expansive ocean. We emerge to find ourselves in a new place, often with new gifts: creativity, empathic abilities, insight, healing skills and access to intuitive information.

We first need to recognize these gifts. If we are not already familiar with the seemingly miraculous possibilities that exist outside our usual physical reality, it helps to name the skills, and validate them. It helps to know that other people also have these skills.

We then need to learn how to use these gifts with love, balance and integrity. We need to learn to work with spirit, and to serve the higher good so that we increasingly become carriers of light, knowledge, peace and healing.

In time we may harness our new skills sufficiently to earn a living with them. There is nothing more satisfying than being able to help people by doing something we enjoy, thereby keeping us in our spirit-flow. It's a bonus to be paid for it, and wonderful to be paid sufficiently that we can dedicate our lives to our work.

The kinds of gifts that may come our way:
Spiritual transformation brings us into close alignment with our spirit nature, our one essence. For some people this transformation opens higher chakras allowing more love, light and sensitivity. These are the 'bottom up' transformers who start off grounded and well integrated in the physical world. For others, their transformation may be more about opening and strengthening lower chakras, being able to

manifest their inspiration, healing and creativity in this physical plane. These are the 'bottom down' transformers. There are also people whose transformation includes opening both higher and lower chakras. Love, compassion, self-acceptance and inner peace are common fruits of this process.

Intuitive skills may also open up. These abilities, often called extrasensory perception or ESP for short, are literally senses that exist beyond the five ordinary senses. Most people experience intuitive perception now and then, but few develop intuitive channels that are constant and reliable. Extrasensory skills include telepathy, clairaudience, clairvoyance, medical clairvoyance, channelling from guides and other non-incarnated beings, prophetic insight, and seeing auras (energy fields).

ESP sounds cool. It is cool. When these channels of perception open, we first need to become familiar with them, and second, learn how to use them safely, wisely and with integrity.

Let's take a closer at look at some of these extrasensory skills.

Telepathy means to know what others are thinking, and to communicate by other means than through the normal five senses, from mind to mind. Knowing what people are thinking isn't all roses. Behind the nice social masks lurk all kinds of emotions - including judgments and criticism, perhaps even unspoken criticism about you. You sense it all. It is not always comfortable.

> *She was smiling, and speaking nicely, but that wasn't what was really happening. She is full of ideas about me. She thinks I'm stupid. It's a smile of pity that her face wears!* [1]

> *As my teacher presented me with my certificate, she gave a little whoop and did a little dance. She was trying to convince me she was celebrating, but I read her (I couldn't help it) and I could tell quite clearly that she felt contempt for me, and thought I did not deserve the honour. I felt quite insulted! Still it's useful to know that this person is not in my corner.* [2]

Clairaudience: Able to hear things at a distance, or things that are inaudible to the human ear.

Clairvoyance: Able to see at a distance. Police have used clairvoyants to psychically see where a missing person is. Clairvoyants can also see astral forms and energy fields.

Medical clairvoyance: Able to directly see/intuit a sick person's internal organs and know not only what type of disease they have, but what underlying beliefs or life-style imbalance is causing it. Medical doctors have used medical clairvoyants to help with their work (e.g. Caroline Myss).

You may have an occasional insight, or may have an ability that becomes consistently available to you. Either way, these kinds of perceptions open you outside the usual physical senses. Although little talked about, psychic perception happens quite regularly to people living very ordinary lives.

> *I'd gone with my partner to the movie theatre. We found good seats and sat down. Soon after a woman plumped down in front of us. I leaned over to my partner and said, "I'm sorry, I can't look through her energy field for the whole movie – she's too uncomfortable to sit near." We moved back a few rows. As people filed in to the theatre, they would go to sit where we had sat, then instinctively move away and sit elsewhere. Finally a woman marched in and took a seat behind the first woman. I was almost amused to notice she had a similarly discordant energy*[1].

If you ask around, most people say they can't see energy fields. Moments like this show that very ordinary folk, arriving in a cinema for an ordinary film, are intuitively aware of energy
fields, although they may not be intellectually conscious of them.

Channelling from guides and other non-incarnated beings
Channellers are able to access information from sources other than their minds, and the usual hearing-reading-watching physical methods. These sources include angels, spirit guides, and spiritual masters. Some write down their information, others speak it, often in a voice that sounds different from their usual voice.

Prophecy is the ability to accurately see events that are yet to come. When we have prophetic insights, we may feel sure they will come to pass. We could feel the need to tell others our prophecy with great certainty. Yet the future isn't fixed – it is forever changing as we change. We can never say anything is certain, we can only say that we sense a fair probability. Our certainty tends to create a particular reality, for better or worse, since our lives' events are created fundamentally from our beliefs.

Why are you have these new perceptual skills?
- ❖ You are accessing more planes of consciousness than you did before (i.e. your inner radio now has more channels available on it)
- ❖ Your mind is ceasing to screen out the perceptions you have always had but perhaps didn't give yourself permission to use.
- ❖ You now acknowledge your perceptions, you give value to them.

Great possibilities!
You will know so much more than you did before. You may have a flash of insight when wondering why your friend is late, catching an intuitive glimpse of the massive traffic jam that she is stuck in. No worry – she will be here soon. You may be able to intuitively pick up that another friend is sad and needs you to call.

However, be cautious – it is easy to confuse intuitive perception with your thinking or imagination. If you think you are having psychic perceptions, keep note of the perception and check it. For example, check your flash of your friend in the traffic jam when she arrives to see how accurate your perceptions are. Your other friend might be sad, but did he actually need or want you to call?

Integrity and good judgment
When we see something at a distance that others don't see, what do we do then? Say something? Stay quiet? With all abilities comes the responsibility to use the ability wisely.

Gifts are powers which can be well-used or misused, depending on your intent, clarity and empathic caring. With every power or gift comes the responsibility to use the gift wisely. You may have serious choices to make – do you warn someone of the impending accident you see? Do you speak about the dark clouds in the aura warning of cancer? Will you misuse the information you gain telepathically to gain personal advantage?
- ❖ Having abilities that not everyone has can make the ego feel special and 'spiritually superior'. Rest assured that everyone except you will find your 'special-ness' distasteful.

❖ Mystical addiction – everything in life becomes something 'special' and 'esoteric' that you 'just knew' about. Every synchronicity, every gesture, everything that happens to you, creates whole stories full of meanings, wrapping you up in mystical cobwebs. Your mind becomes so caught up in itself, it no longer rests in the peace and simplicity of inner truth.

FAQ

Am I imagining this, or is it for real?

If you're wondering if you are really seeing something real or if you are just imagining it, get reality checks. Be scientific. Find ways of checking your perceptions. Ask people. Get feedback. Observe.

> *I saw this dark thick grey patch around Stan's neck. I thought 'he has cancer'. My friends repeatedly assured me that he had tests and his previous cancer had cleared up. Well then, I didn't know what it was. I found it painful to even look at.*
>
> *I was sorry when Stan got his next medical test, but relieved to get a reality check on what I'd seen. It's weird to feel like I'm imagining something when I feel it so strongly. Stan is doing chemotherapy now.*[2]

People say and project one thing, and feel something else. Which do you go on? What do you respond to?

Unless someone is directly asks for your special perceptions, or the circumstances clearly indicate to you that your reflection or reading is required, it is generally best to relate and respond in the way everyone else is – to the tangible, stated and obvious. Though you see the underlying reality, you respond to the surface reality, in the usual social manner. You notice everything, but gently keep your telepathic observations to yourself. Do you have the maturity to do this?

I told my friend that I was telepathic. She said, "Go on, prove it! What am I thinking?" I didn't know, nor did I know what to say.

First, what was your motive in telling her this?

Secondly, why did you state, "I am telepathic" (a constant, always available ability) rather than, "It sometimes happens that I know what people are thinking."? If you watch, you'll see that people are thinking hundreds of things, but only certain things from certain people are available to your mind to know. So then the question is: what kinds of information are you attuned to, and what is to be done with this information?

The little-self personality is quick to claim these abilities, and to use them for its own benefit. Telepathic abilities come through us. They don't belong to us. The ego steps in afterwards and says, "Wow I did that!" It would be more accurate for the ego to say, "Wow! That only happened because I got out of the way!" The ego is 'wow-ing' in both cases, but at least the second statement is more accurate.

If these kinds of skills are misused, they may fade away – which is probably a good thing. A great deal of integrity, maturity and responsibility is needed to use spiritual insight and skills for the good of everyone.

Learning to work with intuitive gifts

Healing

Intuitive skills come to us directly from spirit. We may not have a full understanding of what's happening. We may not have the confidence we would have had if we'd been through a formal training, and been given the nod of approval from an instructor that we were ready to use these skills.

Healing others is a basic human instinct and talent. Everyone can heal. The more open our hearts, the more we feel moved to help people in need. The more you use your healing skill, the stronger it becomes. There are a few basic principles that will make using this gift most effective and comfortable for you.

- ❖ Before starting any healing work, ground yourself. Stand. Let your weight drop into your feet. Run your energy into the earth beneath you. Connect to your body, your feelings, and your hands. Take your time. Don't start until you have grounded. Why? If you are not sufficiently grounded, you may pick up whatever you are trying to heal.
- ❖ Align yourself with love. Ask that all you do be in the service of the greater good. We actually have to put aside our wish – or need – for someone to get better. We need to be detached and centred enough, to allow spirit to work.
- ❖ Open to the life current that moves through you. It is this energy that will be doing the healing. You are the catalyst, the transformer, the

conduit the energy comes through. The more your ideas, preferences and individual sense can step out of the way, the more this energy can do its work.

❖ If you are not absolutely clear about what is needed and what the underlying issues are, just lay your hands on the person to be healed and allow the love-life-force-light to channel through you. Laying on hands can be tremendously effective, as all Reiki practitioners can testify. Don't pretend you know more than you do, or start moving energy around, without having a clear experiential sense of what energies you are moving or why you are moving them. Some people believe that it is good to move energy upward, whereas in actuality it is sometimes more balancing to move energy downward. If you are being very clearly and directly guided from a spirit guide or guides, and have learned, through feedback from your clients, that this guidance is to be trusted, follow it.

❖ If your eyes are clear enough, or your hands sensitive enough, to directly sense what needs healing or rebalancing, your method of healing can be varied and tailored to the person's needs. You can use visualization, crystals, sound, your intent, acupressure points and many other means to facilitate the healing process. Just don't use your personal energy, don't become invested in 'trying to make it happen.' The healing is between the person and spirit. You are only a catalyst in the process.

❖ At the end of the healing, step outside the aura of the person you are working on. Return their energies to them. Return your energies to yourself. Ground yourself, and flow into the earth any energy that doesn't belong to you.

❖ If a healing happened, it happened because the 'little-individual-you' stepped out of the way, not because *you* did it. The life force or spirit – the deeper You – is the healer.

❖ Remain simple, and your healing abilities can continue. If you feel all clever about it, your ego will cloud your inner sky, toning down or even stopping your healing ability.

Millions of human hands are currently awakening. Our power of intent combined with visualization is being harnessed for healing. Everyone has an inherent healing ability. Everyone has a life force pouring through his/her hands. We are collectively waking up to this potential power.

Healers used to be virtually unheard of. Now there are thousands of professional healers working in our communities. There are tens of thousands of people receiving healing treatments, reading about healing skills and their outcomes, and training to learn the skills.

People are discovering the uses of magnetism, coloured light, various oils and aromas, crystals, sound and silence for healing. Reiki healers and teachers are now present all over the world teaching their easy-to-master techniques to hundreds of thousands. Herbal medicines are quietly finding their way back into medicine cabinets.

If this healing potential is opening in you, wonderful! If you get a sense that you can heal, go with it. Try, see what happens, and note what results you obtain. The more we use our hands, the more the energy opens through them.

Healing and psychic abilities occur partly because the ego-mind is sufficiently out of the way to allow the change.

> *"How do we learn how to heal?"* I asked my teacher. *"We get out of the way so our hands can do what they already know how to do."*

That same ego can then afterwards step back into the picture, claiming the changes as its own, using the newly opened energies and skills for its own power, aggrandizement and opportunity. This is the beginning of what is called by some, 'black magic' – the use of spiritual skill and energy for personal gain. Black magic is about satisfying desires, wanting power, wanting what others have, and goes as far as finding ways to hurt or banish those who aren't in accord. Rather than drawing from the wellspring of life, black magicians look to the material world and other people to satisfy them.

In order to be a 'white magician', you must draw your energy from the source of being, and dedicate the use of this energy for the good of all beings. You wish to help align each person with *their* soul purpose (not yours!). The primary principle is love. White magic is about expanding consciousness, healing, bringing love and light on the earth for all to enjoy. Even a worthy sounding ambition is a 'personal ambition' when it is not aligned with spirit light and an intent for the good of the whole – 'grey magic!'

Everyone can heal. We don't need to take courses and workshops, but they can help to open our hands, and increase the sensitivity of our perception. Completing a course also helps to give us confidence –

the teacher has validated our ability to do this kind of work. Our society is very qualification oriented, so often people feel more 'qualified' to do something when they have completed a course. Courses also help open our eyes to new ways of perceiving things, introduce a wider range of human experience, and often help to integrate the skill into our current social context. Courses help us to just get going and do what we were born to do.

Other benefits of spiritual transformation
When we know who we are in truth, we realize that who we are in truth cannot die. We no longer fear death in the way we used to. We say, "I took birth" – implying that 'I' was in existence prior to birth. We directly sense that the 'I' we were when we took birth is unchanged throughout our lives, and will be there when this physical body returns to the earth. The body we inhabit may change, but our essential nature lives on.

After a deep spiritual awakening or revelation, we no longer need to say "I 'believe' in God" – we **Know** God. We have experienced God for ourselves, even if briefly. We can never wander too far from this truth once we have glimpsed it. We can never entirely go back to seeing the way we used to do.

We may well find we are able to read and understand spiritual books from all traditions. We now perceive the common essence, and we can adjust to the words and expressions each tradition uses. We no longer think there is only one way. If we were dogmatic before, we are gradually able to see beyond the dogmatism, increasingly accepting all paths and practices. We realize that what everyone needs, regardless of their creed or colour, is more love and oneness.

Coming through profound spiritual transformation, we often find we have much more trust in Life, more ability to flow with Spirit, and a greater tendency to let things be as they are, without having to exert control as much. Great inner peace and relaxation comes with this, for ourselves and for those around us.

As people emerge from profound personal transformation, values of love and well-being often replace previous money and status values. Those who have been on the earn-spend-consume treadmill relax considerably. Religious and spiritual people who have led simple lives and stayed away from the monetary rat-race may experience that money is also God, and cease to reject money.

When we have suffered, when we have had our lives or ideas turned inside out through spiritual transformation, we have much more compassion for others. We usually have more concern for humanity as a whole, since we are no longer as pre-occupied with our individual selves. We have more time and energy available to help the health of the environment.

Transformed minds are less black and white. The maturity is there to encompass both the positive and negative aspects of people or situations simultaneously – i.e. seeing both sides of the coin becomes natural.

Profound spiritual experiences open us up to much deeper insights into the nature of the mind, and the nature of human beings. Life becomes a beautiful flow of reflections and revelations.

Addictive habits often heal since the emotions, that alcohol and other substances were used to damp down or avoid, have been cleared. Deep inner peace, self love and the ability to transcend life problems can be found through meditation.

When past unresolved emotional issues resurface in the wake of a powerful experience we have a chance to clear it. In the process we become lighter, freer and more adaptable. We become less likely to get upset about life or take life too seriously.

If you have a sense that our physical bodies and illnesses are not as solid and fixed as they once appeared to be, you're right. We're all discovering that when we change our thought, our energy field changes. As the energy field changes, our physical bodies change. We are newly empowered.

Since our health is very closely linked to our well-being, we are quickly discovering powerful keys to much greater happiness.

Four fundamental stages for complete transformation.
- **Tuning in to spirit** – through profound experiences or through meditation, love, being in nature, listening to teachings, contemplation, participating in spiritual groups, taking time to just 'be' or whatever works to best connect you to Spirit.
- **Strengthening and deepening this inner connection.** Cultivating your inner awareness until it becomes continuous in your life, something that you stand for, and have the courage to live.
- **Align your day-to-day life with your soul purpose** – creating the lifestyle, diet, leisure activities, relationships, emotional desires, and

career direction that best support, express and resonate with your inner truth and life direction.
- **Allow your gifts and unique abilities to flower.** The gifts could be healing, teaching, conscious parenting, gardening, creating art or music, or whatever service unfolds through you.

Not everyone takes birth to do a lot of service. Many souls come to heal, to clear their karmic slate, or to explore human nature. It is a huge task just to heal oneself, so if this is completed in a lifetime it is wonderful.

Some people go through a lot during their transformation. Is it all worthwhile in the end? Do people go through powerful transformation and at the other end look back and think, "Boy, that was a waste of time and energy!"

Taking a look at the participants in the PSE study, we see that some people simply had no difficulty with their experiences. For them it was a breeze. They thought the whole process was totally positive.

Perhaps the most interesting responses came from people who had been through an enormously difficult time. Some had been hospitalized, been on medication, and were unable to work for a time. How did these people feel about their transformational experience? Did they wish it had never happened or are they all the better for it? Not a single person felt less happy, less free, less creative, less intuitive, less compassionate, less able to serve humanity, less dedicated to spiritual practice, or less aligned with their life purpose. Only a tiny percentage (1-2%) indicated that they did not feel **more** happy, compassionate etc.

More than ¾ of the people who responded to this section indicated a firm 'yes' in each category. 86 – 88% of people felt happier, freer, more intuitive, more compassionate. The lowest scoring were 'feeling more creative' and 'able to serve humanity' which received a firm yes from 76% and 71% respectively.

Clients whom I've counselled in the middle of their transformational crisis give some interesting responses to questions like, "Would you prefer to return to the way you used to be?" Despite their anguish, they have all responded very similarly, "Oh no, I couldn't possibly go back. I want all this to happen. I want to move on through. I just wish it wasn't so @#$* difficult!"

Many spiritual traditions say that a true teacher, healer or shaman is only created after he or she has been through the eye of the storm. We have to hit bottom, go right into the shadow, and emerge again to be authentic. Extraordinary things are possible after this process.

> "Our greatest blessings come to us by way of madness, provided the madness is given us by divine gift."
> Plato (Phaedrus)

In a nutshell, it's all about getting the mind out of the driver's seat and putting spirit in its place. When spirit starts running our lives, things go very differently. We all kind of know this, but the ego doesn't surrender easily.

History provides us with many wonderful examples of people who allowed spirit to be their inspiration and guiding light. William W. had a drinking problem that was so severe both he and his doctor figured he had very little chance of recovery. Lying in his hospital bed, this extraordinary experience happened.

> *Lying there in conflict, I dropped into black depression. Momentarily my prideful obstinacy was crushed. I cried out, "Now I'm ready to do anything. " ...Expecting naught, I made this frantic appeal: "If there be a God, will he show himself!" The result was instant, electric, beyond description. The place lit up, blinding white. I knew only ecstasy and seemed on a mountain. A great wind blew, enveloping and permeating me. It was not of air, but of spirit. Blazing, came the tremendous thought, "You are a free man!" Then ecstasy subsided. Still on the bed, I was now in another world of consciousness which was suffused by a Presence. One with the Universe, a great peace stole over me and I thought," So this is the God of the preachers; this is the Great Reality." But reason returned, my modern education took over. Obviously I had gone crazy. I became terribly frightened.*

General service of Alcoholics Anonymous, 1995

As a result of this profound experience, Alcoholics Anonymous was founded, a group that has helped over 2 million people worldwide.

Uri Geller, who demonstrated performances of paranormal ability, psychokinesis, dowsing and telepathy, wrote:

> I believe my own powers were switched on when I was four years old. I was playing alone in the garden when I saw a strange light in the air above me. I watched it, fascinated. A beam of light suddenly focused on the spot between my eyes, I was knocked over and I must have been unconscious for a long time, for it was getting dark when I opened my eyes. Strange things started to happen to metal objects around me after that. I remember sitting at the dinner table eating soup one time – the spoon bent in my hand and splashed the soup on to my clothes. I believe that the light in the garden was from a higher intelligence, but I also think that everyone can switch on powers like mine, simply with self belief."[28]

William Blake's believed that his poems came to him from sources other than himself. His poem <u>Jerusalem</u> came to him entirely through an inner voice.

> 12 or sometimes 20 or 30 lines at a time, without Premeditation and even against my Will; the time it has taken in writing was thus rendered Non Existent, and an immense Poem Exists which seems to be the Labour of a long life, all produced without Labour or Study

> "I am under the direction of messengers from heaven, daily and nightly."

> "I dare not pretend to be any other than the secretary, the authors are in eternity."[29]

Martin Luther King, Jr. was often threatened with death during his time as leader of the Civil Rights Movement. An inner voice he felt to be the voice of God kept him going. He wrote,

> God has been profoundly real to me in recent years. In the midst of outer dangers I have felt an inner calm. In the midst of lonely days and dreary nights I have heard an inner voice saying, "Lo, I will be with you." [30]

People from all walks of life are experiencing radical shifts in consciousness. Most we don't hear about. From time to time, someone who is in the limelight undergoes a shift such as an MP who recently had a near death experience, lost her fear of death, and felt a spiritual call to resign from politics. Newspaper items like this appear in local, and sometimes national papers, from time to time. Who knows what the general population make of them.

Written on a PSE questionnaire was this comment:

> *Just to love myself the way I am, then love of all people will come. It works to be who I am, not someone I'm not. I now have great self worth.*
>
> *People – this is my opinion – are so important I give my last ounce of breath to help them*

The final words from one of the interviewees in my documentary "Spiritual Emergence" are:

> *If I were to do one thing with this experience, it would be to help others. Being alone is the hardest part.*

This is a sentiment shared by many who have been through the eye of the storm during spiritual emergence. Certainly a wonderful new gift people gain through their transformation is the ability to deeply empathize and offer support for others going through their transformation. We look forward to a more compassionate world based on love, sharing and spiritual principles. It will probably take a lot more people completing radical spiritual transformation to create this loving world.

People in our lives are gradually waking up right now. One thing we can all do for each other is to validate the spiritual awakening and the transformational process people are going through. It is deeply rewarding to be able to support another being on his or her path.

Humanity is the sum of all the consciousness on the planet. Our consciousness makes a difference. One gift to ourselves, and everyone around us, is to live the highest resonance, and let our love shine.

14

Visions and Resources

We live in a pragmatic, profit oriented era. Perhaps it will not always be like this. We could envision a time when love and compassion are valued more than intellectual knowledge and material wealth. Our entire society would be different.

What would it take to make this change? It requires each one of us to make this shift within ourselves until a critical mass is reached when this orientation becomes the norm. This is why your transformation is so important. A loving, harmonious way of being is more nourishing and pleasing; money is a poor substitute for inner peace, love, and connection with nature.

Such a society would be much more empathically attuned to its members, more able to sense when people need time to be still or support. Mystical states and revelations about life and the universe will be part of life, welcomed rather than thought strange. This shift is helped by all of us who have become aware of these states of consciousness standing in our awareness, and accepting them.

Native communities value their members who go through intense spiritual transformation and emerge as shamanic healers and seers. Imagine how it could be if our society also recognised and validated spiritual transformation as a useful process. With greater validation, society as a whole would be giving more value to their evolution, rather than valuing accumulating wealth. This validation would also encourage sharing their internal experiences, and would give people more space and allowance to go through their respective processes.

Previously, people could spend time in a monastery during their spiritual transformation. Today there is nowhere to go. What if there were houses in the country where people could stay for a while in the midst of Deep transformation. What if there were places that welcome their more spiritually attuned services afterwards.

Perhaps in time spiritual health will be regarded as part of health in general. In addition to traditional medicine, health care facilities could offer kundalini clinic times and support groups lead by spiritual counsellors trained to help people through spiritual emergency. Spiritual transformation could be a specialised study within both medicine and spirituality. Clients could be referred to spiritually open medical doctors for specific help.

The current illness model, which regards out of the ordinary states of consciousness or behaviour as pathological, could be replaced by an encouragement to see all the phenomena we now call illness as part of a transformative process, and connection with spirit as an essential part of healing.

For times when spiritual transformation is intense or confusing, let us envision departments in Transformation Centres staffed by emotionally attuned therapists trained to help people deal with emotional issues underlying physical and mental illness. Other departments staffed with energy workers would help ground and rebalance energy, helping the emotional therapists by clearing emotions from the client's energy fields. We could envision health care professionals and spiritual teachers working together to help people through transformation – the divide between science and spirituality having melted.

The pragmatist may roll his or her eyes, wondering how all this is going to be paid for, not imagining that this is likely a less costly route than our current ways, such as declaring people 'ill,' hospitalising them at enormous expense, and administering long term programs of expensive medication. Country retreats staffed by spiritually empathic people offering support and information could well be more cost effective than numerous lost or ineffective work days which result when people are juggling powerful inner processes with earning a living. Retreats are also cheaper than our current hospitals. To the extent that people come through their mental or physical illnesses, there will be more people returning to the work force with new skills, and fewer people on long-term disability.

For humanity to evolve into its full potential, we need to recognize the signs of spiritual transformation, support the process, and value the outcome.

Resources

Our very best resource is our inner wisdom. Our wisdom can be enhanced, or clouded, by what we read. We use the same inner wisdom – call it gut sense, intuitive nose or feeling to assess how true or how relevant what we read is to our current needs.

We learn a great deal from each other, and there is an increasingly wide range of books and web sites dedicated to spiritual emergence and spiritual transformation. We listen and read with the same discernment.

The Internet is a fabulous resource, if slightly unreliable in that anyone can post anything at whim. Key words like 'mystical experience,' 'chakras,' or 'spiritual emergence' reveal lists of web sites, many of which will contain interesting and anecdotal articles.

The web can also be used to track down your local spiritual emergence support network.

Canada www.spiritualemergence.net
Spiritual Emergence Service – Canada (SES).
E-mail ses@spiritualemergence.net

U.S.A. www.cpsh.org/
Spiritual Emergence Network – USA (SEN). Call (415) 648 2610 for information or referral to registered professional therapists who understand psycho-spiritual crises. sen@ciis.org
See also www.kundalininet.org - the Kundalini Research Network dedicated to stimulating cross-cultural research and education related to kundalini and other spiritually transformative experiences.

England www.SpiritualCrisisNetwork.org.uk

Australia www.nor.com.au/community/spiritualemergence/
E-mail senaus@nor.com.au, 53 McKenzie Rd, Eltham NSW 2480 AUSTRALIA

Germany www.senev.de

Scandinavia www.kundalini.se/eng

Belgium www.tetra-asbl.be

Czech Republic http://www.diabasis.cz

http://www.eurotas.org/members.shtml
Transpersonal Psychology associations in twenty countries. Transpersonal psychologists study altered states of consciousness and other spiritual aspects.

An excellent resource for caretakers is David Lukoff's site http://www.spiritualcompetency.com/ which offers extensive information, resources and free courses on spirituality and mental health issues and could be a useful source of information for someone who is trying to help you.

David Lukoff is President of the Association for Transpersonal Psychology, USA, and co-author of the diagnostic manual DSM-IV which has recently included category 'Religious or Spiritual Problem.'

http://www.elcollie.com/st/st.html
Shared Transformations newsletter gives personal stories of spiritual emergencies, visions, awakenings, and their effects, along with practical resource information.

http://hmt.com/kundalini/index1.html
Kundalini resource site founded by a community of people working together on the Internet to raise public awareness of kundalini, and to help those who are experiencing a kundalini awakening better understand what is happening.

http://www.kundalini-gateway.org/
Kundalini list (800 subscribers worldwide) and info.

http://www.realization.org/page/topics/kundalini.htm
Various references and people's stories about Kundalini:

http://www.kundalini-gateway.org/links01.html
Major list of websites dealing with Kundalini

http://www.atpweb.org/
THE ASSOCIATION FOR TRANSPERSONAL PSYCHOLOGY. Professional association for transpersonal psychologists. ATP publishes *The Journal of Transpersonal Psychology,* and sponsors yearly conferences, which play a leading role in transpersonal psychology education.

http://www.ecomall.com/gopikrishna/livingwith.htm
Gopi Krishna wrote extensively and lucidly about his kundalini experiences.

Supportive resources

If the anatomy of transformation, chakras and energy fields interests you, Barbara Anne Brennan's classic "Hands of Light" is a lucid and well-illustrated book showing the energy of the chakras and the energy fields surrounding the body.Brennan, Barbara Anne, <u>Hands of Light</u>, New York: Bantam books, 1988.

We are better off seeing through our spiritual illusions:

Caplan, Mariana, <u>Halfway up the Mountain: The Error of Premature Claims to Enlightenment</u>, Prescott, AZ: Hohm Press, 1999.

Myss, Carolyn, <u>Spiritual Madness: The Necessity of Meeting God in Darkness</u> - 2 cassettes

Vaughan, Frances, <u>Shadows of the Sacred: Seeing through Spiritual Illusions,</u> Quest Books, 1996.

The purification and alignment needed on the path is well discussed by Jack Kornfield in <u>After the Ecstasy Now the Laundry: How the heart grows wise on the spiritual path</u>, New York: Bantam books, 2000.

For more on mystical experiences, kundalini and spiritual awakening:

Krishna, Gopi, <u>Kundalini – The Evolutionary Energy in Man,</u> Boulder, CO: Shambhala, 1967, 1970.

Mookerjee, Ajit, <u>Kundalini: The Arousal of the Inner Energy,</u> Rochester, VT: Destiny Books, 1991.

Mumford, Dr. John, <u>A Chakra & Kundalini Workbook: Psychospiritual Techniques for Health, Rejuvenation, Psychic Powers and Spiritual Realization</u>, St. Paul, MN: Llewellyn Publications, 1994.

Ram Dass, <u>Journey of Awakening</u>, New York: New Age Bantam Books 1990.

Sannella, Lee, <u>The Kundalini Experience,</u> Lower Lake, CA: Integral Publishing, 1987.

Selby, John, <u>Kundalini Awakening: A Gentle Guide to Chakra Activation and Spiritual Growth,</u> New York: Bantam, 1992.

Small, Jacquelyn, <u>Awakening in Time</u>, New York: Bantam Books, 1991.

Tart, Charles, <u>States of Consciousness</u>, New York: Dutton, 1975.

White, John, editor, <u>Kundalini: Evolution and Enlightenment</u>, New York: Paragon House, 1990.

For caretakers of those in spiritual crisis:

Bragdon, Emma, The Call of Spiritual Emergency – From Personal Crisis to Personal Transformation., San Francisco: Harper and Row, 1990.

Bragdon, Emma. A Sourcebook for Helping People in Spiritual Emergency, San Francisco: Harper and Row, 1990.

Greenwell, Bonnie, Energies of Transformation: A Guide to the Kundalini Process, Cupertino, California: Shakti River Press, 1990.

Grof, Christina and Stanislav Grof, The Stormy Search for the Self, Los Angeles: Tarcher, 1990.

Grof, Stanislav and Christina Grof, editors., Spiritual Emergency, When Personal Transformation Becomes a Crisis, With contributions from: R.D Laing, Roberto Assagioli, John Weir Perry, Ram Dass, Lee Sannella, Jack Kornfield, Paul Rebillot, Holgar Kalweit, Anne Armstrong, Keith Thompson and others. Los Angeles: Tarcher and Perigree, 1993.

Grof, Stanislav, M.D., Beyond The Brain : Birth, Death And Transcendence In Psychotherapy, Albany: State University of New York Press, 1985.

Harris, Barbara, Spiritual Awakenings : A Guidebook for Experiencers and Those Who Care About Them,
Baltimore, MD: Stage 3 Books, 1993.

Hazel, Courteney, Divine Intervention, Hillsboro, Oregon: Beyond Words Publishing Inc., 1999.

Irving, Darrel, Serpent of Fire: A Modern View of Kundalini, York Beach, ME: Samuel Weiser Inc., 1995.

James, William, Varieties of Religious Experience, New York: Collier, 1968.

Personal narrations:

Adler, Janet, Arching Backwards: The mystical initiation of a contemporary woman, Inner Traditions International, 1995.

Krishna, Gopi, Living with Kundalini, Rev. by Leslie Shepard. Boulder, CO: Shambhala, 1993.

Tweedie, Irina, Daughter of Fire, A diary of a spiritual training with a Sufi master, Golden Sufi centre 1986.

When misdiagnosed by health professionals:
Nightingale, Kaia, Spiritual Emergency, Documentary DVD, 2006.

> A 40 minute documentary validating unusual experiences during spiritual emergence, alerting health professionals to the signs. Documentary includes interviews with 3 medical doctors and 6 clients, plus graphic illustrations of common mystical and transformative experiences. It is available at www.kaia.ca

Distinguishing spirituality and madness
Gersten, Dennis, M.D. Are You Getting Enlightened or Losing Your Mind? Three Rivers Press/Harmony Books/division of Random House, 1997.

Elam, Jennifer, Dancing with God Through the Storm: Mysticism and Mental Illness, Way Opens Press, 2002.

John Lilly, The Centre of the Cyclone, New York: Marion Boyars Pub, 1973.

Perry, John Weir, The Far Side of Madness, Upper Saddle River, NJ: Prentice-Hall, 1974.

Perry, John Weir, Trials of the Visionary Mind, New York: State University of New York Press 1999.

Sannella, Lee, , Kundalini – Psychosis or Transcendence?, San Francisco: H.S. Dakin, 1976.

Szasz, Thomas Stephen, The Myth of Mental Illness: Foundations of a Theory of Personal Conflict, New York: Hoeber-Harper, 1961.

Near Death Experience
Harris, Barbara and Leonard C. Bascom, Full Circle: The Near-Death Experience and Beyond, New York: Pocket Books, Simon and Schuster, 1990.

Kason, Yvonne, Farther Shores: Exploring how near-death, Kundalini and mystical experiences can transform ordinary lives, revised edition, Toronto: Harper & Collins, 2000.

Morse, Melvin with Paul Perry, Transformed by the Light: The Powerful Effect of Near-Death Experiences on People's Lives, New York: Villard Books, 1992.

Whitfield, Barbara Harris, <u>Spiritual Awakenings: Insights of the Near-Death Experience and Other Doorways to Our Soul,</u> Deerfield Beach, Florida: Health Communications, Inc., 1995.

Academic and scientific perspectives:

Assagioli, R., <u>Psychosynthesis – A Manual of Principles and Techniques,</u> London: Harper Collins, 1965.

Clarke, Isabel (ed.), <u>Psychosis and Spirituality: Exploring the new frontier</u>, With contributions from : Peter Chadwick; Gordon Claridge; Chris Clarke; Isabel Clarke; Etobicoke, ON: John Wiley & Sons Canada, 2001.

Grof, Stanislav, M.D. <u>The Adventure of Self-Discovery: Dimensions of Consciousness and New Perspectives in Psychotherapy and Inner Exploration,</u> Albany: State University of New York Press, 1988.

Grof, Stanislav, M.D. <u>Realms Of The Human Unconscious : Observations From LSD Research</u>, New York: E.P.Dutton, 1976.

Laing, R.D., <u>The Divided Self,</u> New York: Pantheon, 1962.

Laing, R.D., <u>The Politics of Experience</u>, New York: Ballantine Books, 1968.

Maslow, Abraham H., <u>Religions, Values, and Peak Experiences,</u> New York: Viking Penguin, 1970.

Perry, John Weir, <u>Trials of the Visionary Mind: Spiritual Emergency and the Renewal Process</u>, Albany: State University of New York Press, 1999.

Wilber, Ken, Jack Engler and Daniel Brown, <u>Transformations of Consciousness: Conventional and Contemplative Perspectives on Development</u>, Boston, MA: Shambhala Publications, 1986.

Index

advice, 159
alien encounters, 28, 34
Angel, 27
angel guides, 27
Astral, 5, 8, 27
Auras, 32
autonomous, 18, 39, 69
Bach Remedies, 102
Blaming, 57, 59, 91
bliss, 19, 39, 40, 47, 53, 91, 129, 173
Buttons', 10
career, 13, 20, 21, 69, 176, 177, 186, 187, 188, 191, 203
Causal, 5
celestial sounds, 27
Chakra, 8, 211
changing moods, 65, 119
Channelling, 28, 195
Chronic fatigue, 20, 117
Clairvoyant, 27
Cloth wraps, 68
Coloured light, 26
compassion, 4, 5, 8, 9, 15, 28, 38, 46, 192, 194, 202
Confusion, 21
Consciousness, 2, 37, 128, 211, 214
contemplation, 113
continuum, 4
Crawling sensations, 78
Crawling skin, 26
crazy, xi, 19, 32, 42, 55, 137, 138, 140, 148, 150, 151, 158, 159, 164, 168, 204
creative, 9, 13, 18, 56, 58, 65, 176, 178, 203

Crown, 9
Crystals, 68, 103
Dark night of the soul, 127
depression, 19, 53, 126, 204
Depression, 20, 126
Despondency, 125
Diet, 20, 64
discomfort, 21, 58, 59, 81, 86, 88, 93, 108, 113
Distortions in time, 86
dizzy, 20, 124
downward shifts, 3
ego, 12, 31, 32, 37, 38, 42, 50, 53, 55, 56, 58, 77, 104, 124, 127, 128, 131, 132, 137, 151, 163, 165, 166, 168, 171, 172, 196, 198, 199, 200, 204
Emotional, 5, 8, 92, 113
energy fields, xiv, 4, 30, 38, 41, 44, 53, 62, 92, 115, 125, 127, 158, 178, 180, 194, 195
Energy pouring in, 26, 30, 84
energy psychology, 10
Energy sensations, 26, 73
Energy swings, 83
ESP, 194
evolution, 19, 91
fasting, 16, 118
fears, 10, 11, 33, 49, 101, 120, 127, 158, 166, 167, 168
fibromyalgia, 20, 78
Fitting in, 68
food, xv, 3, 59, 62, 69, 70, 76, 80, 94, 98, 102, 103, 118, 119, 123, 124, 143, 175, 176, 178, 179, 185, 187

gifts, x, xii, 19, 57, 111, 142, 177, 193, 198, 203
guides, 4, 27, 43, 119, 146, 150, 194, 195, 199
headaches, xiv, 20, 21, 73, 76, 77, 84, 117
healing, xvi, 8, 18, 28, 57, 59, 84, 91, 104, 111, 122, 131, 133, 139, 142, 156, 157, 161, 165, 188, 193, 194, 198, 199, 200, 203
Healing ability, 28
Health, 187
Hearing voices, 27
Heart, 9
help, 142
Humming, 109
insanity, 168
integration, 17, 18, 20, 44, 87, 90, 92, 119
intense energies, 21, 43
intuitive, xiii, 3, 4, 18, 19, 29, 34, 38, 57, 58, 69, 76, 82, 83, 99, 141, 145, 152, 153, 154, 155, 185, 188, 189, 190, 193, 194, 196, 198, 203
Kriyas, 20, 26, 77
kundalini, i, xii, xiv, xviii, xx, 28, 29, 44, 47, 63, 74, 78, 79, 80, 81, 82, 84, 86, 90, 119, 122, 134, 140, 142, 145, 146, 151, 153, 209, 210
Left-right side imbalance, 83
Life-force, 5, 8
lifestyle, 13, 18, 19, 20, 21, 70, 76, 87, 176, 177, 192, 202
Listening ear, 140
losing control, 19, 138, 140, 151, 164

Love, 5, 8, 9, 54, 132, 194
lucid dreams, 33
mantra, 109
meat eating, 179
Medical help, 152
meditation, xiv, xv, xvi, xviii, 4, 7, 8, 13, 16, 23, 24, 29, 32, 33, 38, 40, 43, 66, 69, 74, 83, 85, 91, 93, 94, 108, 110, 115, 122, 128, 129, 134, 135, 155, 158, 160, 165, 169, 170, 173, 175, 176, 185, 186, 202
Mental, 5, 8, 58, 213
mentally busy, 107
misunderstood, 20, 51
multiple chemical sensitivity, 20
Mystical, 23, 25, 48, 50, 197
NDE, 33, 34
Near death experience, 27
Negative psychic, 20, 27
New skills, 21
No interest, 20
normal consciousness, 1
nurturing, 64
Others' reactions, 59
Out of body experience, 27
Pandora's box, 19, 93
Paranormal experiences, 4
paranormal phenomena, 21
Past life, 27
Physical, 5, 8, 26, 58, 64, 88, 116, 117
positive thinking, 11
Pranayama, 39, 109, 115
prayer, 16, 38, 78, 100, 129, 147, 155, 170
Protective crystals, 68

psychic invasion, 20
Purification, 18
qigong, xvii, 4, 16, 38, 53, 86, 115
reactions, 18, 45, 47, 48, 49, 50, 56, 57, 59, 60, 109, 137
Relationships, 21
resurfacing memories, 19
Revelations, 27, 35
Root, 9
Sacral, 9
Sahasrara energy, 30
self-centred, 11
Self-condemnation, 50
sensitive, xvi, 18, 61, 62, 65, 70, 71, 73, 79, 80, 124, 131, 134, 141, 158, 199
sex, 94, 119, 121, 122, 171
shadows, 18, 19, 88, 89, 91, 92, 129, 170
Shifting Consciousness, 1
Singing, 109
Sleep, 119
Sleep teachings, 28
sleeping patterns, 119
Solar plexus, 9
spectrum, 2, 7, 31, 118, 126, 132
Spiritual Emergency, xxi, 212, 214, 218
Spiritual practice, 16, 166
Spiritual transformation, 87, 193
States of consciousness, 1
strange pains, 21, 73, 74, 138, 140

subtle planes, 6
suicidal, 20, 140, 152, 157, 158
Telepathy, 26, 194
The multi-layer approach, 58
Third eye, 9
transcendence, 19, 106
Transformation, i, 15, 16, 17, 23, 47, 61, 73, 87, 90, 107, 108, 110, 116, 119, 123, 137, 163, 175, 177, 193, 207, 212, 218
transformational crisis, 138, 203
trauma, xvi, 45, 99, 100, 113, 130
UFO, 28, 34, 35
Undiagnosable, 20
Unity consciousness, 9, 25
upward shift, 3
upward spiral, 12
vegan, 16, 118
vegetarian diet, 179
vibrational frequency, 2, 3, 64, 94, 178
vibratory level, 9
vibratory rate, 2
Visualization, 65, 103
Waking up, 119
Weird energy, 79
White light, 26
wonder, x, 12, 19, 32, 45, 46, 78, 111, 122, 128, 137, 167, 189
yoga, xi, xvi, xx, 4, 16, 23, 26, 38, 39, 43, 77, 86, 90, 119, 129, 141, 146, 161, 170, 186

FOOTNOTES

1 Author's experience
2 Anonymous PSE participant in response to the Profound Spiritual Experience questionnaire
3 Gopi Krishna: http://www.ecomall.com/gopikrishna/livingwith.htm
4 PSE participants were largely from Canada, some from USA, UK, Europe, Australia and New Zealand drawn from workshop participants and willing clients, either through direct contact or from the electronic distribution of the questionnaire to friends and colleagues.
5 James Mauro, *Bright lights, big mystery*. Psychology Today, July 1992.
6 Etzel Carden et al, Varieties of Anomalous Experience p. 268, 2000.
7 Whitley Strieber, Communion, HarperCollins Canada, revised Feb 1988.
8 George Gallup, Adventures in Immortality, New York: McGraw-Hill, 1982, p.76.
9 P.M.H. Atwater, Is there a Hell? INDS 10, No. 3 (Spring) 1982, p 150.
10 Philip St. Romain, Kundalini Energy and Christian Spirituality, Crossroad, 1996
11 Palyne "PJ" Gaenir, an excerpt from Bewilderness, (a case-study), 1995
http://www.firedocs.com/remoteviewing/pjarchives/pj_Chakras.cfm, www.bewilderness.com
12 Stanislav Grof, M.D., and Christina Grof, "Kundalini: Classical and Clinical page 106 in Spiritual Emergency: When Personal Transformation Becomes a Crisis, Jeremy P. Tarcher, Inc. LA, CA, 1989, p 106
13 http://www.ecomall.com/gopikrishna/livingwith.htm
14 Client report
15 Client training as a healer
16 Affirmations written by Louis Radakir
17 National Population Health Survey (NPHS), Statscan, Canada, 1998/99
18 Statistics Canada Community Health Survey www.statcan.ca
19 K.P. White, M. Speechley, M. Harth, T. Ostbye The London fibromyalgia epidemiology study: the prevalence of fibromyalgia syndrome in London, Ontario. *Journal of Rheumatology,* 1999, 26(7):15700-1576.

[20] http://www.mefmaction.net/Patients/Disability/IllnessCost/tabid/157/Default.aspx

[21] Cary Tennis, author and advice columnist Extract from *Since You Asked*, on www.Salon.com.

[22] Lee Sannella, M.D., Kundalini Experience, Integral Publishing: Lower Lake, CA, 1992.

[23] Dr. John Perry, Jungian psychiatrist who founded an experimental residential facility called Diabasis, in San Francisco, California, during the 1970s

[24] Stanislav Grof, M.D., and Christina Grof, Spiritual Emergency: When Personal Transformation Becomes a Crisis, Jeremy P. Tarcher, Inc. LA, CA, 1989

[25] Stanislav Grof, M.D., Realms Of The Human Unconscious : Observations From LSD Research, E.P.Dutton: New York, NY, 1976.

[26] Edward Whitney, M.D., Personal Accounts: Mania as Spiritual Emergency
http://www.psychservices.psychiatryonline.org/cgi/content/full/49/12/1547

[27] Nelson Mandela Inaugural speech, South African Statesman, First democratically elected State President of South Africa, 1994

[28] http://www.roger-moore.com/uri-geller.htm

[29] Teri Degler, The Fiery Muse: Creativity and the Spiritual Quest,- Random House of Canada, 1996

[30] Alex Ayes, The Wisdom of Martin Luther King Jr., NewYork: Meridian, 1993, p.95

www.ingramcontent.com/pod-product-compliance
Lightning Source LLC
Chambersburg PA
CBHW061254110426
42742CB00012BA/1907